Difficult Situations in Business Coaching

Heidi Möller · Jannik Zimmermann

Difficult Situations in Business Coaching

Practical Examples, Perspectives and Possibilities for Action

Springer

Heidi Möller
Institut für Psychologie
Universität Kassel
Kassel, Germany

Jannik Zimmermann
Institut für Psychologie
Universität Kassel
Kassel, Germany

ISBN 978-3-658-35086-4 ISBN 978-3-658-35087-1 (eBook)
https://doi.org/10.1007/978-3-658-35087-1

This book is a translation of the original German edition "Schwierige Situationen im Business-Coaching" by Möller, Heidi and Zimmermann, Jannik, published by Springer Fachmedien Wiesbaden GmbH in 2020. The translation was done with the help of artificial intelligence (machine translation by the service DeepL.com). A subsequent human revision was done primarily in terms of content, so that the book will read stylistically differently from a conventional translation. Springer Nature works continuously to further the development of tools for the production of books and on the related technologies to support the authors.

This Springer imprint is published by the registered company Springer Fachmedien Wiesbaden GmbH part of Springer Nature.
The registered company address is: Abraham-Lincoln-Str. 46, 65189 Wiesbaden, Germany

Preface

Why This Book?

Another book about coaching ...! The publication landscape is not exactly poor in publications on the topic of business coaching. If we follow Scherf (2010), we find on the one hand consulting concepts "brimming with unambiguity" (cf. Scherf, 2010, p. 11; translated) and on the other hand a clear lack of consulting research. Coaching research continues to develop briskly, but is mainly to be found in English-language journals, to which the practicing experts have no access and which they often also find uninspiring and uninstructive. The gap between experience-based practice knowledge and theory-based guidance research has often been described (cf. Kotte et al., 2015; Möller et al., 2014; Scholl et al., 2018). However, we can by no means describe the gap as closed.

What Is Our Intention? What Do We Do Differently?

Viewed uncharitably, in many coaching publications we find case vignettes that could be considered "heroic tales." "The authors of the contributions are not concerned with scientific reflection, but with marketing their own person or company" (Scherf, 2010, p. 12; translated). The challenges, the doubts, the difficulties, and the failures are rarely made a topic. Similar phenomena can be described for coaching congresses, and when attending these we often ask ourselves: Is this about the struggle for knowledge, about critical professional scrutiny or are we participating in a promotional event that we had not signed up for?

If coaches use their publications and public appearances for marketing purposes, showing the underbelly—at least that is the assumption we do not ascribe to—would be missing the point. In most articles, the processes run like clockwork. No freelance coach writes about difficulties in getting enough clients, about fears that coachees might drop out or that they might not do justice to the emergent phenomena in coaching conversations. As one colleague aptly said, "Nowhere is there as much lying as in the consulting industry!"

But how will the expert community help the working world to be more error-tolerant, honest and humane if we do not start with ourselves? In intervision groups and in the supervision of coaches it seems to succeed, there troubles and questions can be addressed. Against the background of a trusting relationship with a supervisor (cf. Müller et al., 2020), one confronts pressing concerns.

The starting point of our reflection was that the discussion of difficult situations in coaching can also take place publicly. How can learning together and the further development of the coaching community succeed if not through courageous confrontation with challenges—be they located in ourselves or in the coachees or in our interaction? We think that by refraining from "impression management" and showing ourselves in our uncertainty and in the struggle for the right path for our clients, we come to a broadening of perspective.

With our book, we want to dispel the idea that revealing your difficulties is bad for your image, your profession, and your wallet. We would like to thank all our research partners for taking the risk and appearing in coaching situations that they experienced as difficult.

Our investigation started with an online study: Difficult situations in (individual) coaching, in which more than 70 coaches have now participated. The comprehensiveness of the descriptions we asked for, the richness of detail in the accounts and the courage of the colleagues surprised and delighted us. The evaluations of the study can be found in the first chapter, for which Silja Kotte is co-responsible. We would like to take this opportunity to thank her once again for her contribution and her valuable input.

The clustering developed from the mixed methods study establishes the further structure of the book. This second, qualitative study shows the results of nine group discussions with experienced coaches in German-speaking countries. Upon request, the colleagues agreed enthusiastically and sacrificed a great deal of time and concentration to transcribe the transcribed results of the group discussions. A heartfelt thank you to all those involved! We all found the group discussions enriching and horizon-opening. The whole is more than the sum of the parts, this was our experience together. The discussions as a "joint community" opened our minds and gave us all a lot of pleasure.

We would like to pass this experience on to our readers. You too will probably be reminded of your own questions when reading the practical examples. The reading alone will set your own hypotheses in motion. You will find your own answers to the question of how the *difficult* situations you experienced came about (diagnostic perspective). You will also have ideas about what you would do in such a situation (intervention perspective). You will be surprised what thoughts experienced coaches, prominent and less-prominent representatives of this profession have on the case vignettes. Some will be similar to their assumptions and hopefully many will be quite different, new, and enriching.

The practical examples of difficult situations in this book are very closely based on what the coaching community has provided us with in terms of content. Where it was necessary to ensure maximum anonymity, we have changed a little. Certainly, we were missing a lot of information at one point or another: but we could not ask for it and had to be content with the information given in the group discussions. Often the gender of the reporting coach or coaches was also not apparent. So, for this book, we decided to roll the dice when assigning gender in the text. If we did not know whether the coach and/or coachee were female or male, we varied the language arbitrarily. The same was true when referring to other groups of people and professions, such as employees, board members, or CEOs. This may seem strange at first, but in our experience, it is more reader-friendly than always referring to the coach as male.

In Conclusion

With the selected difficult situations, we also hope to reach further continuing candidates in coaching training. The questions at the beginning when entering a new profession are numerous. To use these vignettes also for the didactics of coaching seems advisable to us. We hope that watching the experienced coaches at work and, as it were, peering into their brains, will inspire and enrich you all!

We hope you enjoy reading this.

Kassel, Germany
November 2021

Heidi Möller
Jannik Zimmermann

Directory

Carla Albrecht[1] Dr.
Thomas Bachmann[2] PD Dr.
Ulrich Beumer[3] Dr.
Claudia Beutter[4]
Uwe Böning[5] Dr.

---

[1] Dipl.-Psych., Managing Director of M19 Manufaktur für Organisationsberatung; psychodynamic-systemic organizational consultant and coach in the for-profit and non-profit sector, systemic couple and family therapist; main areas of activity: Organizational culture development, promotion of female leaders and dealing with stress in different areas of life.

[2] Dipl.-Psych.; founding member and partner of artop GmbH, consulting, training and research institute at the Humboldt University of Berlin; studied industrial and organizational psychology, clinical psychology and computer science; research assistant at the Chair of Methodology and Statistics. Assistant at the Chair of Methodology and Statistics, 1997 PhD in Cognitive Psychology, 2019 Habilitation on systems theory and Gestalt therapy, among others. Since 1993 consultant, trainer and coach (DBVC, ICF, IOBC), since 2001 trainer and teaching trainer for coaches and consultants.

[3] Dipl.-Päd., coach and supervisor (DGSv) with numerous psychoanalytical and psychodynamic continuing training courses. Since 1987 active as coach, supervisor, trainer and management consultant. Partner and managing director of inscape gGmbH, an advanced training and consulting institute for organizational consulting, coaching and training based in Cologne; guest researcher at the Sigmund Freud Institute in Frankfurt a. M., working areas: Coaching research with a focus on psychoanalysis and society; member of the International Society for the Psychoanalytic Study of Organizations (ISPSO).

[4] Lic. phil. psychologist; lecturer and consultant at the Institute of Applied Psychology (IAP) of the Zurich University of Applied Sciences (ZHAW); coach, supervisor and organizational consultant BSO; Master in Consulting & Coaching for Change. Main areas of work: Organizational development and change consulting. Contact: claudia.beutter@zhaw.ch

[5] Dipl.-Psych. and Clinical Psychologist (DGVT); Managing Partner of BÖNING-CONSULT® GmbH; Senior Business Coach (DBVC; IOBC) and Management Consultant. Co-initiator and co-founder of the DBVC; author and lecturer at various universities (Fontainebleau, Osnabrück, Freiburg, Mannheim, Frankfurt); management consultant and business coach at top management/

Isabell Braumandl[6]
Claudia Bredt[7]
Agnes Büchele[8] Dr.
Peter Döring[9]
Klaus Eidenschink[10]k
Beate Fietze[11] Dr.
Edeltrud Freitag-Becker[12]

---

executive level in DAX companies and large medium-sized businesses. Main topics: Leadership, collaboration, conflict and stress management. Considered one of the pioneers of business coaching in Germany.

[6]Dipl.-Psych., Dipl.-Ök., sports psychologist; owner/manager of the Coaching- & Beratungs-Centrum Regensburg; lecturer and instructor at the University of Salzburg (e.g. career and project coaching) and at various other institutions (e.g. SMBS Salzburg Management Business School, OTH Regensburg, SRH Hochschule Berlin). Contact: www.cobece.de

[7]Organizational consultant (M.A.), supervisor (DGSv); teaching in adult education and teacher training; project development on self-efficacy in organizations; lecturer in the master's program COS at the University of Kassel; teaching supervisor at the International Psychoanalytic University Berlin and the University of Kassel.

[8]Psychotherapist, supervisor, coach; director of the Centre for Applied Psychology, Women's and Gender Studies, Cologne; studied psychology, philosophy, education and sports science in Innsbruck, doctorate in psychology. Lecturer and teaching supervisor at the University of Kassel. Focus of consulting: gender-sensitivity. Contact: www.buechele-beratung.de

[9]Dipl.-Psych., psychoanalyst (DGPT, DPG), group teaching analyst (D3G), supervisor and organizational consultant. Psychoanalyst and consultant in private practice; Chairman of the Lou Andreas-Salomé Instituts für Psychoanalyse und Psychotherapie Göttingen. Main focus: Organizational and team development, leadership development and individual counselling, mentalization-based psychotherapy. Contact: www.peter-doering.de

[10]Studied theology, philosophy and psychology; organizational consultant, coach trainer, executive coach, supervisor, keynote speaker, publicist; director of a psychotherapeutic institute, founder and director of HEPHAISTOS, Coaching Center Munich for training and continuing education for trainers and consultants; background of his consulting style is many years of training and experience in humanistic and depth-psychological psychotherapy methods, system theory, group dynamics, systemic consulting, organizational and leadership psychology as well as conflict research.

[11]Dipl.-Soz., Dipl.-Psych., doctorate at the Berlin Graduate School of Social Sciences of the Humboldt University Berlin; research and teaching at various universities, 2013-2016 research officer of the German Society for Supervision e.V.; among others, Sci. Advisory Board of *Roundtable Coaching e.V.* and co-editor of the journal *Organisationsberatung, Supervision, Coaching*. Since 2003 self-employed consultant and coach; 2007–2008 human resources manager of a ministry of the state of Brandenburg; since 2016 consultant at artop GmbH, consulting, training and research institute at Humboldt University Berlin. Contact: www.artop.de/team/dr-beate-fietze/

[12]Consultant for organizational development, supervisor (DGSv), coach and trainer, instructor and teaching supervisor in advanced training in supervision; shareholder of the inscape-group; has been active as a consultant in various organizations and sectors for many years.

Brigitte Fritschle[13]
Regina Gibhardt[14]
Thomas Giernalczyk[15] Prof. Dr.
Ursula Hermann[16] Dr.
Eva Jonas[17] Prof. Dr.
Andreas Knierim[18] Dr.
Wolfgang Knopf[19] Dr.
Silja Kotte[20] Prof. Dr.

---

[13]Managing Partner of BÖNING-CONSULT® GmbH; business coach, management and organizational consultant; co-author of reference books and other media contributions; leader of change projects: Reorganization, Process Optimization, Post-merger Integration, Complementary Consulting; passionate career changer. Press and public relations until 1985. Motto: Alone always works, together works better. For the sake of design.

[14]Several coaching training courses and over 20 years of experience in systemic family constellations; has accompanied companies in their growth and change processes for three decades; before becoming self-employed, worked as a manager in a medium-sized company; expert at the interface between organization and people; own coaching practice in Kassel. Contact: info@regina-gibhardt.de, www.regina-gibhardt.de

[15]Dr. phil., managing partner of M19-Manufaktur für Organisationsberatung GmbH; psychoanalyst and honorary professor for psychological interventions and therapy at the Faculty of Human Sciences of the Bundeswehr University in Munich. Co-founder of the Instituts für Psychodynamische Organisationsberatung München (IPOM). Main areas of work: Cultural development, change facilitation and coaching.

[16]Self-employed supervisor, coach (ÖVS), management consultant, teaching supervisor; lecturer at the University of Applied Sciences St. Pölten (Department of Social Work), the Bielefeld University (Master's course in Supervision and Counselling) and responsible for the content of the course in Supervision and Coaching at the Fachhochschule Vorarlberg/Schloss Hofen. Contact: supervision@ursula-hermann.at, www.ursula-hermann.at

[17]Dipl.-Psych., Dipl.-Volksw.; Head of the Department of Social Psychology at the Department of Psychology, University of Salzburg; Head of postgraduate courses, Coach/Supervisor ÖVS, Salzburg.

[18]Studied economics; has been active in process consulting for over 20 years; specializes in individual coaching for female entrepreneurs and managers with a practice in Kassel; accompanies owners, managing directors, dual heads and takeovers in family businesses in their professional and personal growth; comes from a family business herself, dedicates herself to systemic contexts, coaching writing and creative developments in the studio in the Inner Workshop. Contact: dr.andreas@knierim.coach, www.knierim.coach, www.coachingschreiben.de, www.innerewerkstatt.de

[19]Dr. phil., supervisor and coach (ÖVS), teaching supervisor, management trainer, adult educator, and group dynamics specialist; director of the university course in supervision and coaching at the University of Vienna—SuCo (together with Kornelia Steinhardt); lecturer in supervision training at the University of Zagreb and Triangel Institute Berlin.

[20]Dipl.-Psych., Coach/Supervisor (DGSv); Professor of Business Psychology at the Hochschule für Medien, Kommunikation und Wirtschaft in Frankfurt a.M.; several years of experience as an employed consultant and as a strategic personnel developer. Doctorate on leadership development and habilitation project on coaching at the University of Kassel. Main areas of research and teaching:

Sebastian Kunert[21] Dr.
Sandrina Lellinger[22]
Tom Levold[23]
Eric Lippmann[24] Prof. Dr.
Mathias Lohmer[25] Dr.
Magret Lüdemann[26]
Achim Mollbach[27] Dr.

---

coaching, supervision, leadership, personnel development, group and team processes. Freelance consulting and training in the for-profit and non-profit sectors. Scientific direction of the M. Sc. Supervision and Coaching at the Vorarlberg University of Applied Sciences/Schloss Hofen.

[21] Dipl.-Psych., systemic consultant, gestalt psychological coach, certified trainer and former university of applied sciences professor; focus in coaching practice is on managers and executives with primarily role-related issues. Research interests in organization, culture, change management, leadership and failure. In addition to coaching, advises companies and public authorities in complex change processes, supports team development processes and moderates a wide variety of (large group) formats.

[22] Educational Science (M.A.), Systemic Coach, Systemic Organizational Consultant and Supervisor at artop GmbH, Consulting, Training and Research Institute at the Humboldt University of Berlin; studied Educational Science with a focus on research and development in organizations, Educational Science with a focus on adult education, as well as Psychology and Philosophy. Many years of experience in the management of social organizations; currently in training as a Gestalt therapist.

[23] Social scientist and publicist, teaching therapist, teaching supervisor and teaching coach (SG); after many years of working in youth welfare, active since 1989 in his own practice as coach, supervisor and couples therapist in Cologne; numerous publications on systemic theory and practice; teaching activities in Germany and abroad. Co-editor of Kontext, editor of systemagazin—online journal for systemic theory and practice.

[24] Psychologist, sociologist and publicist; further training in couple/family therapy, supervision, coaching and organizational development. Head of the Center for Leadership, Coaching & Change Management at the Institute of Applied Psychology (IAP) at the ZHAW, Zurich University of Applied Sciences. Main areas of activity: Co-direction of the MAS Coaching, Supervision & Organizational Consulting at the IAP, leadership development and coaching. Publications on leadership, coaching, intervision and identity, among others.

[25] Dipl.-Psych., psychoanalyst (DPV/IPA), organizational consultant, coach and supervisor; co-founder of IPOM (Institut für psychodynamische Organisationsberatung München) and M19-Manufaktur für Organisationsberatung. Lecturer at the IPU-Berlin and the University of Kassel.

[26] Dipl. Soz.; independent consultant for supervision, coaching and organizational consulting in Hamburg; teaching supervisor and senior coach in continuing education.

[27] Studied psychology and economics/organizational studies; management consultant and coach for companies in various industries; advises on organizational and corporate development and change management; offers individual and team coaching for executives and management teams; accompanies succession processes, especially in family businesses. Lecturer in the training of coaches and consultants.

Klaus Obermeyer[28]
Joachim Sauer[29] Ao. Univ. Prof. i. R. Dr.
Sandra Julia Schiemann[30] Dr.
Kornelia Steinhardt[31] Dr.
Peter Uffelmann[32]
Robert Wegener[33] Dr.
Eugen Würz[34]

---

[28] Psych. psychotherapist, supervisor and coach (DGSv), mediator (BMWA); freelance supervisor, coach and mediator in Hamburg; co-director of the Triangle Institute for Supervision, Coaching and Mediation Berlin, Hamburg.

[29] 1970–2008 at the Department of Psychology of the University of Salzburg (Dept. of Social and Organizational Psychology), 1987-2012 Head of the University Course for Supervision/Coaching. Main research interests: Intelligence research, educational research, effectiveness of psychotherapy & supervision, burn-out, suicide prevention. Currently working: Clinical & health psychologist, person-centered psychotherapist (ÖGWG), supervisor/coach (ÖVS) in private practice, teaching supervisor for psychotherapy & supervision/coaching, member of the Institute for Supervision and Organizational Development in Vienna.

[30] Dr. rer. nat.; Postdoc of the Department of Social Psychology at the University of Salzburg with research in the field of coaching and training (here also Harvard Medical School Affiliate). Also co-responsible for coaching and mentoring training and active as a coach. Certified career coach (University of Salzburg), certified trainer for social skills (LMU Munich), certified mentor (LMU Center for Leadership & People Management), certificate for business start-up (LMU Munich) and certified yoga teacher (yoga teacher training, Munich).

[31] Coach and supervisor (ÖVS), organizational consultant, psychoanalyst (WPV), group analyst (ÖAGG) and teaching supervisor; head of the university course in supervision and coaching at the University of Vienna; was a research associate at the Institut für Bildungswissenschaft at the University of Vienna; network partner of the advisory group naschmarkt (Vienna), member of the Institute for Supervision and Organizational Development (Vienna). Contact: kornelia.steinhardt@univie.ac.at

[32] Systemic-integrative coach; Managing Director of Competto Consulting Network GmbH in Greifenberg; Senior Business Consultant at bcs-people GmbH in Dreieich; expert for development and change processes in the design of powerful relationship architectures at the interface of digitalization, leadership and collaboration.

[33] Co-director of the Coaching Studies FHNW, lecturer for coaching in the MAS Coaching and director of various CAS courses. Since 2010 head of the International Coaching Congress "Coaching meets Research". Focus topics (among others): Analysis and control of significant moments in coaching. Since 2020 co-editor of the journal *Coaching Theorie und Praxis*; publication of various publications as initiator and co-editor, e.g., "Meaningful Moments in Coaching", "Coaching Practice Fields" and "Coaching and Society." Currently researching future scenarios in coaching (together with Prof. Dr. Carsten Schermuly) and the use of psychological tests in coaching. Since 2010 business coach in own practice with focus on individual and team coaching and coaching supervision.

[34] Mag., Msc., mediator, coach, supervisor (ÖVS) and organizational consultant, trainer in adult education, personnel matters at *Rettet das Kind Salzburg gGmbH.* Main fields of work: Multipliers in youth work, mental area of competitive sports, coaching, supervision in the social pedagogical and social area, multiplier work with people with disabilities.

Contents

1 Difficult Situations in Job-Related Individual Coaching from the Perspective of the Coaches: An Empirical Examination 1
1.1 Case Study 1
1.2 Introduction 2
1.3 Difficult Situations in Coaching and Therapy Research 3
1.4 Kassel Study on Difficult Situations in Coaching from the Perspective of Coaches 4
1.4.1 Issues and Methodology 4
1.4.2 Results 6
1.4.3 Discussion 11
1.5 Conclusion and Outlook 12
References 12

2 Behavior of the Coachees 17
2.1 Practical Example 1 17
2.2 Practical Example 2 23
2.3 Practical Example 3 29
2.4 Practical Example 4 34
2.5 Practical Example 5 38
2.6 Practical Example 6 43
2.7 Practical Example 7 49
2.8 Practical Example 8 53
2.9 Practical Example 9 57
2.10 Practical Example 10 59
2.11 Practical Example 11 63
2.12 Practical Example 12 67
References 70

3 Challenges with Psychological Problems of the Coachees . . . 75
3.1 Practical Example 13 . . . 75
3.2 Practical Example 14 . . . 79
References . . . 83

4 Expectations of the Coachees Towards the Coaches . . . 85
4.1 Practical Example 15 . . . 85
4.2 Practical Example 16 . . . 93
4.3 Practical Example 17 . . . 98
4.4 Practical Example 18 . . . 101
4.5 Practical Example 19 . . . 106
References . . . 111

5 Demanding Working or Living Conditions of the Coachees . . . 113
5.1 Practical Example 20 . . . 113
References . . . 117

6 Own Delimitation of the Coaches . . . 119
6.1 Practical Example 21 . . . 119
6.2 Practical Example 22 . . . 126
6.3 Practical Example 23 . . . 129
6.4 Practical Example 24 . . . 134
6.5 Practical Example 25 . . . 140
References . . . 145

7 Influence of and from the Commissioning Organization . . . 149
7.1 Practical Example 26 . . . 149
7.2 Practical Example 27 . . . 153
7.3 Practical Example 28 . . . 156
7.4 Practical Example 29 . . . 158
7.5 Practical Example 30 . . . 162
7.6 Practical Example 31 . . . 166
References . . . 172

8 Concluding Remarks . . . 175
References . . . 178

Further Reading . . . 181

1 Difficult Situations in Job-Related Individual Coaching from the Perspective of the Coaches: An Empirical Examination

1.1 Case Study

I knew the coachee from a previous collaboration about a decade ago. At that time she worked in a care facility and was in a middle-management role, which she suffered from. As a team leader, she was responsible for her own team and was under intense pressure from her management: to work more efficiently with patients. She was also struggling with increasing physical discomfort in her neck area. The earlier coaching course enabled her to develop more understanding of her own position and to better manage her position. She also learned to better appreciate her own performance and developed plans to build a new career perspective. This new career perspective should be beneficial for her health.

Now she sought me out again to be coached. The coachee had been on long-term sick leave some time ago and had subsequently become unemployed. According to her own statement, she was aiming for early retirement. Although she had qualified for another job, she was unable to pursue it for health reasons. In our current coaching session, I experienced her problem as extremely complex. The coachee's illness was accompanied by severe physical and psychological problems. In addition, she was struggling with her own unemployment and the associated social and personal devaluation of her own person.

For me as a coach it was difficult to work with the coachee not in a progress-oriented way, but to be primarily oriented towards accepting the life situation and maintaining self-respect. I realized how success and progress-oriented I am myself—the coaching confronted me with my own demands on myself and my own limitations.

H. Möller, J. Zimmermann, *Difficult Situations in Business Coaching*,
https://doi.org/10.1007/978-3-658-35087-1_1

1.2 Introduction

This case study comes from a coach who was interviewed by us about difficult situations in coaching. We wanted to learn more about what *exactly* are the situations[1] that coaches experience as *difficult* in their professional practice and how they handle them.

It is known from situation research (cf. Rauthmann et al., 2014; Sherman et al., 2013) that intersubjective perceptions, descriptions, and evaluations of one and the same situation are often similar. Nevertheless, intersubjective differences may well occur. Here, the process underlying situation perception plays a crucial role. Put simply and referring to our case study, the coach cognitively processes the different stimuli he encounters in the coaching situation in different ways. Individual aspects (for example, his own personality aspects) also have an influence here. The information processing results in his or her own idea of the real situation, composed of the perceived characteristics, i.e. the interpretations of situation-related stimuli (cf. Funder, 2016; Rauthmann et al., 2015).

The cognitive evaluations that are central to the transactional stress model (cf. Lazarus & Folkman, 1984, 1987) can explain how exactly the judgment becomes *difficult* during information processing[2]: The situation is apparently important to the coach and makes heavy demands on his resources, possibly exceeding them. Thus, we assume: A situation is experienced as difficult whenever it is personally relevant, exceeds one's repertoire of action strategies, and/or overloads or makes heavy demands on personal resources.[3] The judgement *difficult* in turn triggers coping strategies, which are aimed in particular at overcoming the demands and consequences of the situation and restoring individual well-being.

The case study reflects only one of many conceivable *difficult* situations that can occur in the coaching process and to which it is necessary to react as a coach. It is precisely these *difficult* situations that are the focus of this book. In what follows, we will briefly review what is already known in coaching and psychotherapy research about such challenges and difficulties. We will then present the Kassel study on difficult situations from the perspective of coaches and go into more detail on its findings.

---

[1] A situation is not so much an entity that is clearly and objectively delimited in terms of time or content in each individual case, but rather a coherent factual situation due to which someone takes action.

[2] Primary appraisal and secondary appraisal.

[3] Intrapersonal (e.g., mutual respect), individual (e.g., openness), but also external resources (e.g., room to maneuver in the situation).

1.3 Difficult Situations in Coaching and Therapy Research

Even though a line of research on more-problematic aspects of work-related coaching (e.g., on negative effects of coaching, cf. Schermuly, 2018a) is now emerging, difficult situations have received little attention in coaching research to date. An exception to this is the annual ESMT Coaching Colloquium, which offers a platform where past difficult situations and one's own handling can be presented and discussed. For more information and contributions to past colloquia, see Korotov et al. (2012) and Korotov and Bernhardt (2018).

Nevertheless, coaching research in the past has dealt with at least some issues that have a certain intersection with the topic of difficult situations. More precisely, these issues sometimes include individual situations or types of situations that can be experienced as difficult by coaches. In particular, these include:

- critical (or significant) moments[4] (see Day et al., 2008; d Haan & Nieß, 2014; Milner et al., 2013; Wegener, 2019);
- ethical situations, especially dilemmas (see Diochon & Nizet, 2015; Duff & Passmore, 2010; Turner & Passmore, 2018);
- emotional situations (cf. Cox & Bachkirova, 2007).

Somewhat more attention is paid to difficult situations in psychotherapy research. Therapists are also regularly confronted with difficult situations in their professional practice. Some, albeit few, research studies address these situations in more detail (a review is provided by Odyniec et al., 2016). To date, little is known about the precise impact of difficult situations on the course of therapy and on the parties involved. However, existing evidence on ruptures in the therapeutic alliance (cf. Safran et al., 2014) at least suggests that this influence may well be negative should the difficult situations not be resolved appropriately. These findings lead us to assume that in coaching, too, difficult situations that are not resolved appropriately[5] have a detrimental effect on the process and the results.

More knowledge exists about the different types of difficult situations that can arise for therapists during the therapeutic process. Individual attempts exist to adequately map these types using categorizations (see Davis et al., 1987; Henkel et al., 2019; Plutchik et al., 1994; Smith et al., 2007). Existing experiments reveal a wide range of situations that are experienced as difficult. In some cases, these situations are closely related to the patients'

[4]Exciting, tense, and significant moments, but also moments of cluelessness and key moments (cf. Day et al., 2008); these are also interpreted as turning points and indications of change (cf. d Haan & Nieß, 2018), they also contain different situations that are not experienced as difficult, in addition to potentially difficult situations.

[5]Given the triadic nature of work-based coaching (cf. Bozer & Jones, 2018), we assume that "well-resolved" means considering the interests of all stakeholders involved in the coaching engagement (i.e., coach, coachee, organization).

mental disorders (e.g., a patient's existing psychosis); in other cases, they are completely disconnected from the disorders (e.g., a therapist's sense of incompetence). The existing categorizations also indicate that what is *difficult* about the situations can come from different sources; thus, difficult situations during the therapeutic process are not so much the *exclusive* result of a competence deficit or difficult patients.

This becomes clear, for example, in the three types of difficulty proposed by Schröder and Davis (2004): The first type is temporary and dependent on the therapist: The therapist lacks competence, knowledge, or experience. The second type is stable and also dependent on the therapist: Personality traits and existing patterns in the therapist's interaction and response explain why the situation is experienced as difficult. The third type is situational and not conditioned by the therapist: The context or the patient's characteristics make the situation difficult. Because a difficult situation is often complex, it often involves more than one of the three types of difficulty, according to Schröder and Davis (2004).

Attempts to categorize difficult situations are in part accompanied by a consideration of how therapists responded to each situation (see Henkel et al., 2019; Smith et al., 2007). Researchers identified different ways of responding based on real case descriptions. The range of identified coping strategies extends from *seeking out third parties for supportive reflection*, to *insisting on already established rules,* to *denying what happened*. Preliminary findings (cf. Henkel et al., 2019; Smith et al., 2007) indicate existing tendencies of therapists to react similarly to specific difficult situations.

A practice-oriented view of difficult situations during psychotherapy is provided by the following authors in particular: Fliegel and von Schlippe (2005), Noyon and Heidenreich (2020),[6] and Jacob et al. (2009). The works contain collections with examples of difficult situations and offer suggestions for dealing with them.

1.4 Kassel Study on Difficult Situations in Coaching from the Perspective of Coaches

1.4.1 Issues and Methodology

With the study presented in the following, we would like to contribute to the topic of *difficult situations* receiving greater attention in coaching research as well (cf. Zimmermann, 2019). Through a more detailed investigation and a deeper understanding of these situations, they could become more manageable for those involved in coaching.

The aim of our study was to gain more detailed insights into the range of different situations that coaches experience as *difficult.* In addition, we wanted to learn more about

[6] This book contains explicit situations and explanations that are also relevant for other consulting formats (including coaching).

how *exactly* coaches experience the situational characteristics of a difficult situation, how they deal with such a situation, and what consequences the difficult situation may have for the coaching process. Therefore, we focused on the following research questions:

- What situations do coaches experience as difficult in the coaching process?
- How do coaches deal with these situations?
- What is the outcome of the coaching process after the difficult situations?

We conducted an online survey with professional coaches about their experiences working with individuals. The survey included open and closed task formats; one survey could capture up to three difficult situations. The questions used referred in the first part to detailed explanations of a self-described difficult situation, in the second part to descriptions of one's own handling of this same situation, and in the third part to one's own socio-demographic data and professional background. We used two open-ended questions for our three research questions, which were adapted from already used questions (cf. Henkel et al., 2019) from the clinical context. To collect situational characteristics,[7] we used the S8-I scale (cf. Rauthmann & Sherman, 2016)—a short form of DIAMONDS[8] (see more detail in Sect. 1.4.2.2).

In this study, it was important for us to approximately represent the coaching market in Germany in terms of its socio-demographic characteristics (in particular age, experience as a coach, and share of coaching activity in total working hours) and thus to investigate *typical* experiences in coaching practice. Therefore, we recruited participants for the online survey via various German-speaking coaching associations and our own coaching network.

Since business coaching in practice must be related to the world of work (cf. Böning, 2005; Möller, 2016), we only considered survey results for this study that were related to situations *from work-related* coaching. In order to be included in the study, a situation experienced as difficult thus had to fulfill the following criteria:

- the reported situation has been experienced by a coach him- or herself (not invented or handed down from third parties);
- the reported situation happened in a coaching session that was job-related;
- the reported situation occurred in a single setting.

To analyze the first part of the online survey, the open responses, we carried out a qualitative content analysis (cf. Mayring, 2014; Schreier, 2014); this made it possible to reduce the text material to its essentials and to analyze it in a systematic and intersubjectively comprehensible way. In the analysis of the concrete difficult situations, we proceeded

[7] In a situation, physically measurable and/or objectively quantifiable stimuli ("cues") are present and salient (e.g., the coachee is present). When an individual processes and interprets these stimuli, the perceived characteristics of the situation are formed. They provide information about how a situation is experienced (e.g., the coach experiences a high level of involvement) or what the situation is about (e.g., the coach sees himself in the position of having to become active).

[8] Taxonomy of perceived situational features.

inductively (cf. Mayring, 2014); we summarized the relevant contents of the material on the basis of categories derived from the material itself. In the analysis of the handling and outcome of difficult situations, we have largely proceeded deductively (cf. Mayring, 2014); we have summarized the relevant content on the basis of theory-guided categories. At a lower level, these theory-guided categories were substantiated by inductively formed categories. This procedure allowed us to take into account previous research findings (cf. Day et al., 2008; Schermuly, 2018b) and, in the case of *Families of Coping* (cf. Skinner et al., 2003), also to adapt them to the application domain, dealing with difficult situations.

Our sample includes 66 coaches who described a total of 96 difficult situations. The coaches were between 38 and 70 years old and 65% female. On average, the respondents had been active in coaching for just over 15 years and invested an average of 37% of their annual working time in coaching. Our sample is comparable to the German coaching market (cf. Middendorf, 2018, 2019, 2020; Philipps University of Marburg, 2017) in terms of age, gender, experience as a coach, and share of coaching activity in total working time. According to the coaches interviewed, the difficult situations described occurred between one and 17 years ago; on average, the situations described occurred about 2.5 years ago.

1.4.2 Results

In accordance with the order of our research questions, we first address the findings on the type of situations that the coaches experienced as difficult (RQ1). We then show how the coaches dealt with these very situations (RQ2) and how these situations turned out (RQ3).

1.4.2.1 The Range of *Difficult* Situations

Based on the answers to the first open question, we identified seven categories of overarching content aspects that made the situations difficult. These categories can be understood as a *taxonomy of difficult situations*. They are:

- *Behavior of the coachee*
- *Challenges with psychological problems of the coachee*
- *Expectations of the coachee towards the coach*
- *Demanding working or living conditions of the coachee*
- *Demarcation of the coach*
- *Behavior of the coach*
- *Influence (from) the commissioning organization*

The first four aspects of content came from the coachees, the fifth and sixth from the coach, and the seventh from the commissioning organization.

Behavior of the coachee. In this context, respondents frequently mentioned coachee behaviors that mainly made it difficult to work on content or methodology during the coaching. To be mentioned here in particular are:

- inhibitions of coachees to engage in reflection and change processes,
- the disruptive intervention of the coachees in the planned course of the coaching.

In addition, the interviewees named behaviors which, in their view, mainly impeded interpersonal cooperation. This was expressed particularly in

- a high need for speech on the part of the coachees,
- violations by the coachees of the coach's values,
- assaults against the coaches,
- the unreliability and unpunctuality of the coachees.

Challenges with psychological problems of the coachee. Several respondents assumed in the course of coaching that a mental disorder might exist on the part of the coachee; however, a mental disorder was not expertly diagnosed in any case. In this context, respondents most often reported the challenge of differentiating their coaching from psychotherapy and the challenge of referring coachees to psychological help.

Expectations of the coachee towards the coach. Often respondents mentioned inappropriate expectations in this context, which were directed at their own way of working. For example, coachees expected the coaches to work in a way that contradicted the coaches' ideas or possibilities. In addition, respondents cited unreasonable expectations regarding the scope of coaches' responsibilities. Accordingly, some coachees expected coaches to provide tasks that were not part of coaches' responsibilities. These included expectations of help with mental health problems and expectations of services from other service areas.

Demanding working or living conditions of the coachee. Some respondents indicated situations in which they were confronted with destructive and demanding working or living conditions of the coachee.

Demarcation of the coach. In this context, the interviewees often reported a low level of internal demarcation, which they saw as caused by existing background information. This background information referred either to knowledge about the organization in which the coachee worked or to knowledge about a person who was the subject of coaching. Low internal dissociation was also reported by respondents due to the following:

- there was an erotic interest in the coachee,
- there were reservations about the coachee,
- there was emotional involvement on the part of the coach.

Behavior of the coach. Some respondents mentioned situations related to their way of working. For example, in the case study (see Sect. 1.1) it becomes clear that it can be experienced as difficult when the coach has to deviate from his/her usual way of working.

Influence (from) the commissioning organization. In this context, respondents frequently mentioned that the coachee was obliged to take part in the coaching. They also stated that the coaching assignment was incorrectly or incompletely recorded by the organization.

1.4.2.2 The Situational Characteristics of *Difficult* Situations

Based on the results of the S8-I scale (cf. Rauthmann & Sherman, 2016), we were able to take a closer look at the situational characteristics of the situations described. Thus, with the help of the DIAMONDS taxonomy, we were able to determine how the interviewed coaches experienced the described situations. The acronym *DIAMONDS* stands for *D*uty, *I*ntellect, *A*dversity, *M*ating, p*O*sitivity, *N*egativity, *D*eception, and *S*ociality. This relates to eight dimensions: How work-related is a situation experienced as? Does work have to be done, a duty fulfilled, or a problem solved? (Duty). How high are the intellectual demands experienced? (Intellect). How conflictual is the situation? (Adversity). And how romantic or erotic? (Mating). As pleasant (pOsitivity) or unpleasant (Negativity)? As deceptive? (Deception). But also: As how social? (Sociality).

With regard to the collected DIAMONDS values, it was found that the dimension *Negativity* was on average the most pronounced in the situations described. *Negativity was* followed by the dimensions *Intellect* and *Duty*. The dimensions *Sociality*, *Deception*, and *pOsitivity* were rather less pronounced. The dimension *Mating* was the lowest in the situations described.

In order to examine the extent to which these expressions differ from expressions identified in the context of daily situations, we conducted a comparison with a comparison sample (cf. Rauthmann & Sherman, 2016). The results of a statistical group comparison show that the mean scores of seven of the eight DIAMONDS dimensions differ significantly between the sample of the present study (difficult situations) and the comparison sample (daily situations). With regard to the mean score of the *Duty* dimension, there is no significant difference in means. These differences are also evident in Fig. 1.1.

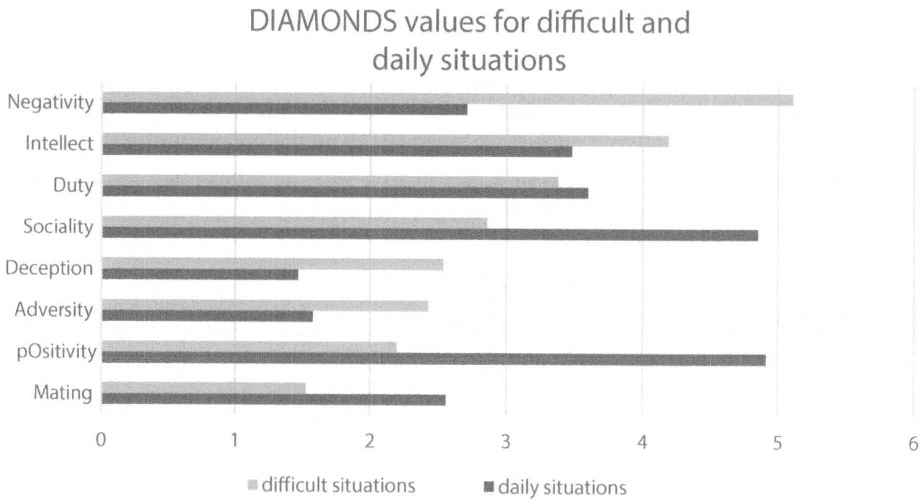

Fig. 1.1 DIAMONDS values for difficult and daily situations. Independent-sample *t-tests* were calculated for comparison. Seven-point response scales (1 = not at all to 7 = completely) were used to elicit DIAMONDS. These were used to record the extent to which individual statements apply to a described situation. The data on difficult situations were taken from the present study, S8-I scale. The data on daily situations are taken from Rauthmann and Sherman (2016), S8-I scale, aggregated values for *M SD*

1.4.2.3 Dealing with Difficult Situations

On the basis of the answers to the second open question, it was possible to obtain more detailed insights into how the situations described were dealt with. In order to be able to record the coping strategies used in their full breadth, we adapted the *higher-order families of coping* (cf. Skinner et al., 2003) to the field of application of coaching. The correspondingly adapted categories and definitions can be seen in Table 1.1.

Along these adapted strategy groups we sorted the reported strategies and summarized them. Overall, the strategies used by the coaches were by far the most frequently used to adapt individual actions to the difficult situation. Strategies for matching individual and social resources were mentioned much less frequently.

It is also worth mentioning that the use of supervision or intervision was only mentioned relatively rarely in the free-text answers. If we follow the answers of the research partners to closed questions, however, in almost all cases a discussion of the situation took place in supervision or intervision. The individual strategies identified are shown in Table 1.2.

1.4.2.4 The Coaching Process After Difficult Situations

In many cases, the answers of the interviewees made it possible to learn more about the respective course of the coaching process after the situation described. In just under a

Table 1.1 Groups of coping strategies for dealing with difficult situations

Adjustment of individual actions to the difficult situation	
Problem solving	Strategies aimed at adapting individual actions in order to deal effectively with difficulties
Information seeking	Strategies aimed at learning more about the difficulties and thus finding additional ways of dealing with them effectively
Narrowness	Strategies aimed at finding the limits of one's own actions
Escape	Strategies aimed at withdrawing from the difficult situation
Matching individual and social resources	
Self-reliance	Strategies aimed at using individual resources more effectively when one reaches limits
Support seeking	Strategies aimed at drawing on social resources
Delegation	Strategies aimed at referring to social resources when individual resources are limited
Matching own preferences and available options	
Accommodation	Strategies aimed at flexibly adapting individual preferences to the available options
Negotiation	Strategies aimed at working towards a compromise and thereby creating new options
Submission	Strategies aimed at abandoning individual preferences and positions in principle or completely in the short term
Opposition	Strategies aimed at removing constraints

Annotation. Following Skinner et al. (2003)

Table 1.2 Coping strategies for dealing with difficult situations

Adjustment of individual actions to the difficult situation	
Problem solving	Use of intervention methods Adaptation of one's own working methods Adjusting one's own attitude Change in framework conditions
Information seeking	Self-reflection Consultation with the coachee Use of supervision or intervision Consultation with other professions (e.g., legal advice)
Narrowness	Self-criticism Concerns
Escape	Psychological defense Restriction to another subject Termination of cooperation
Matching individual and social resources	
Self-reliance	Reinterpret Self-regulation
Support seeking	Use of supervision or intervision Involvement of other professions
Delegation	Referral to another coach or coaches Referral to another profession or body
Matching own preferences and available options	
Accommodation	Lowering of one's standards
Negotiation	Consultation with the coachee
Submission	Giving up one's own positions
Opposition	Expression of one's own protest or defense

Notes. The categories are the result of qualitative content analysis, carried out on the basis of information on 96 difficult situations from job-related individual coaching sessions, described by 66 coaches. Own survey and analysis. Based on Skinner et al. (2003)

quarter of the descriptions, more detailed information about the respective progress was missing. In just under 30% of the situations, the coaching was terminated before the final phase of the coaching process was fully completed.

The termination of the processes was most often initiated by the coachees, in rare cases the coach him- or herself terminated the coaching. Overall, the coaching process was most often continued after the difficult situation or ended as planned. In the fewest cases, a difficult situation was followed by a questionable continuation of the coaching, i.e. the coaching process paused and was probably resumed at a later point in time.

1.4.3 Discussion

As was also made clear in our considerations, coaches encounter different situations at various points during the coaching process which they themselves experience as difficult. The study presented here provides a theoretically sound insight into these situations on the basis of 96 situation descriptions of experienced coaches from practice.

With regard to the range of different situations, it was possible for us to design a taxonomy of difficult situations. Four of these seven identified overarching content aspects of difficult situations originated from the coachees:

- *Behavior of the coachee*
- *Challenges with psychological problems of the coachee*
- *Expectations of the coachee towards the coach*
- *Demanding working or living conditions of the coachee*

Two aspects from the coaches' side:

- *Demarcation of the coach*
- *Behavior of the coach*

And one aspect on the part of the commissioning organizations:

- *Influence (from) the commissioning organization*

As we show, in most cases the interviewed coaches met these situations with coping strategies that served to adapt their own actions to the respective difficult situation. Furthermore, our results show that in almost 30% of the reported cases a premature termination of coaching followed the difficult situation.

Interestingly, the categories of the *taxonomy of difficult situations* we formed from the material resemble aspects in which coaches see causes for negative effects of coaching (cf. Schermuly et al., 2014) or also "breakdown factors"[9] (cf. Marshall, 2006). Even if all these cases are only the subjective perception[10] of the coaches, these results indicate the practical relevance of difficult situations. Situations experienced by coaches as difficult, it seems, highlight factual situations that can be critical to coaching success. The high number of dropouts following difficult situations or the determined dropout rate of almost 30% further underlines the practical relevance. Therefore, we strongly recommend that the topic of *difficult situations* be increasingly integrated into the training and continuing education of coaches. The taxonomy we have designed offers a starting point here.

Based on our findings, it was not possible for us to analyze patterns in dealing with difficult situations in more detail or to determine which coping strategies are effective and

---

[9] Breakdown factors are factors that lead to failure in coaching.

[10] It cannot be ruled out that respondents answered in a socially desirable or biased way (tendency to present oneself better than one actually was; incorrect memories, etc.).

which are not; further research is needed here. There is also the limitation that we focused exclusively on the perspective of the coaches. We know from coaching research that the perspectives of coach, coachee, and other parties involved can be very different (cf. d Haan & Nieß, 2018). Future studies on difficult situations should therefore also take a closer look at the perspectives of other parties involved. The same is true with regard to the setting we considered. In other settings and counseling formats, other aspects of content may well be experienced as difficult that did not play a role in an individual setting in a professional context.

1.5 Conclusion and Outlook

In their professional practice, coaches can encounter a wide range of situations that they experience as difficult. The *difficulty* of the situations, as we were able to show, can have various sources and originate from the coaches themselves, the coachees, or the commissioning organization.

On the basis of the presented study and the previous findings from psychotherapy research, we propose to regard difficult situations in coaching less as something to be avoided. Rather, it seems to make sense to accept them also in coaching as something that happens regularly and that requires a reflective approach. It can help to be aware in such a situation which parts of oneself one brings into the situation and which parts come from the person of the coachee or other parties.

The introductory case study gives an idea of how the coach dealt with his or her difficult situation. The extent to which this difficult situation was also solved well remains largely open. When reading, it becomes clear that there are various possibilities of intervention to react to a difficult situation. It does not necessarily have to be a direct confrontation, but can also involve working on one's own attitude. Depending on the specific case, it seems to be helpful to expand one's own competencies, to work on one's own blind spots, but also to consciously make use of the support and help of third parties, e.g. in supervision or intervision.

With the *taxonomy of difficult situations* we have presented and the *groups of coping strategies for dealing with difficult situations* we offer a first roadmap for addressing difficult situations in training and further education of coaches, but also for personal reflection and the development of one's own skills as a coach.

References

Böning, U. (2005). Coaching: Der Siegeszug eines Personalentwicklungs-Instruments – Eine 15-Jahres-Bilanz. In C. Rauen (Ed.), *Handbuch coaching* (pp. 21–54). Hogrefe.

Bozer, G., & Jones, R. J. (2018). Understanding the factors that determine workplace coaching effectiveness: A systematic literature review. *European Journal of Work and Organizational Psychology, 27*(3), 342–361. https://doi.org/10.1080/1359432X.2018.1446946

Cox, E., & Bachkirova, T. (2007). Coaching with emotion: How coaches deal with difficult emotional situations. *International Coaching Psychology Review, 2*(2), 178–190.

d Haan, E., & Nieß, C. (2014, January). Critical moments. *The Training Journal,* 65–69.

d Haan, E., & Nieß, C. (2018). Kritische Momente im Coaching: Wie Klientinnen, Coaches und Interessengruppen Veränderungen wahrnehmen. In R. Wegener, M. Hänseler, M. Loebbert, & A. Fritze (Eds.), *Coaching-Prozessforschung: Forschung und Praxis im Dialog* (pp. 56–66). Vandenhoeck & Ruprecht.

Davis, J. D., Elliott, R., Davis, M. L., Binns, M., Francis, V. M., Kelman, J. E., & Schröder, T. A. (1987). Development of a taxonomy of therapist difficulties: Initial report. *The British Journal of Medical Psychology, 60*(2), 109–119. https://doi.org/10.1111/j.2044-8341.1987.tb02720.x

Day, A., d Haan, E., Sills, C., Bertie, C., & Blass, E. (2008). Coaches' experience of critical moments in the coaching. *International Coaching Psychology Review, 3*(3), 207–218.

Diochon, P. F., & Nizet, J. (2015). Ethical codes and executive coaches: One size does not fit all. *The Journal of Applied Behavioral Science, 51*(2), 277–301. https://doi.org/10.1177/0021886315576190

Duff, M., & Passmore, J. (2010). Ethics in coaching: An ethical decision making framework for coaching psychologists. *International Coaching Psychology Review, 5*(2), 140–151.

Fliegel, S., & von Schlippe, A. (2005). "Grenzliches" – Schwierige Situationen im therapeutischen Alltag. *PiD – Psychotherapie im Dialog, 6*(2), 207–213. https://doi.org/10.1055/s-2005-866847

Funder, D. C. (2016). Taking situations seriously: The situation construal model and the riverside situational Q-Sort. *Current Directions in Psychological Science, 25*(3), 203–208. https://doi.org/10.1177/0963721416635552

Henkel, M., Michel, S., Gaubatz, S., Keymer, A., Brakemeier, E.-L., & Benecke, C. (2019). Schwierige Situationen in der Psychotherapie und wie Therapeuten mit ihnen umgehen. *Zeitschrift für Psychosomatische Medizin und Psychotherapie, 65*(4), 372–383. https://doi.org/10.13109/zptm.2019.65.4.372

Jacob, G., Lieb, K., & Berger, M. (2009). *Schwierige Gesprächssituationen in Psychiatrie und Psychotherapie.* Urban & Fischer.

Korotov, K., & Bernhardt, A. (Eds.). (2018). *Cases in executive coaching: From the annals of the ESMT coaching colloquia.* ESMT Center for Leadership Development Research.

Korotov, K., Florent-Treacy, E., Kets de Vries, M. F. R., & Bernhardt, A. (Eds.). (2012). *Tricky coaching: Difficult cases in leadership coaching.* Palgrave Macmillan.

Lazarus, R. S., & Folkman, S. (1984). *Stress, appraisal, and coping.* Springer.

Lazarus, R. S., & Folkman, S. (1987). Transactional theory and research on emotions and coping. *European Journal of Personality, 1*(3), 141–169. https://doi.org/10.1002/per.2410010304

Marshall, M. K. (2006). *The critical factors of coaching practice leading to successful coaching outcomes.* Unpublished Doctorial thesis. Antioch University, Los Angeles. https://etd.ohiolink.edu/!etd.send_file?accession=antioch1160858983&disposition=inline. Zugegriffen am 10.05.2020.

Mayring, P. (2014). *Qualitative content analysis: Theoretical foundation, basic procedures and software.* https://nbn-resolving.org/urn:nbn:de:0168-ssoar-395173. Zugegriffen am 10.05.2020.

Middendorf, J. (2018). *16. Coaching-Umfrage Deutschland 2017/2018.* https://coachingumfrage.wordpress.com/startseite/umfragen/. Zugegriffen am 02.06.2020.

Middendorf, J. (2019). *17. Coaching-Umfrage Deutschland.* https://coachingumfrage.wordpress.com/startseite/umfragen/. Zugegriffen am 02.06.2020.

Middendorf, J. (2020). *18. Coaching-Umfrage Deutschland.* https://coachingumfrage.wordpress.com/startseite/umfragen/. Zugegriffen am 02.06.2020.

Milner, J., Ostmeier, E., & Franke, R. (2013). Critical incidents in cross-cultural coaching: The view from German coaches. *International Journal of Evidence Based Coaching and Mentoring, 11*(2), 19–32.

Möller, H. (2016). Theorie und Methodik der Beratung an der Universität Kassel. *Organisationsberatung, Supervision, Coaching, 23*(1), 1–4. https://doi.org/10.1007/s11613-016-0448-2

Noyon, A., & Heidenreich, T. (2020). *Schwierige Situationen in Therapie und Beratung: 34 Probleme und Lösungsvorschläge*. Beltz.

Odyniec, P., Victor, P. P., Berner, A., & Willutzki, U. (2016). Schwierigkeiten in der psychotherapeutischen Arbeit. *Psychotherapeut, 61*(3), 216–221. https://doi.org/10.1007/s00278-016-0105-4

Philipps-Universität Marburg. (2017). *Coaching-Marktanalyse 2016/17: Kurzfassung*. Philipps Universität Marburg/MAFEX.

Plutchik, R., Conte, H. R., & Karasu, T. B. (1994). Critical incidents in psychotherapy. *American Journal of Psychotherapy, 48*(1), 75–84. https://doi.org/10.1176/appi.psychotherapy.1994.48.1.75

Rauthmann, J. F., & Sherman, R. A. (2016). Ultra-brief measures for the situational eight DIAMONDS domains. *European Journal of Psychological Assessment, 32*(2), 165–174. https://doi.org/10.1027/1015-5759/a000245

Rauthmann, J. F., Gallardo-Pujol, D., Guillaume, E. M., Todd, E., Nave, C. S., Sherman, R. A., Ziegler, M., Jones, A. B., & Funder, D. C. (2014). The situational eight DIAMONDS: A taxonomy of major dimensions of situation characteristics. *Journal of Personality and Social Psychology, 107*(4), 677–718. https://doi.org/10.1037/a0037250

Rauthmann, J. F., Sherman, R. A., & Funder, D. C. (2015). Principles of situation research: Towards a better understanding of psychological situations. *European Journal of Personality, 29*(3), 363–381. https://doi.org/10.1002/per.1994

Safran, J. D., Muran, J. C., & Shaker, A. (2014). Research on therapeutic impasses and ruptures in the therapeutic alliance. *Contemporary Psychoanalysis, 50*(1–2), 211–232. https://doi.org/10.1080/00107530.2014.880318

Schermuly, C. C. (2018a). Nebenwirkungen von Coaching für Klienten und Coaches. In S. Greif, H. Möller, & W. Scholl (Eds.), *Handbuch Schlüsselkonzepte im Coaching* (pp. 415–424). Springer.

Schermuly, C. C. (2018b). Client dropout from business coaching. *Consulting Psychology Journal: Practice and Research, 70*(3), 250–267. https://doi.org/10.1037/cpb0000112

Schermuly, C. C., Schermuly-Haupt, M.-L., Schölmerich, F., & Rauterberg, H. (2014). Zu Risiken und Nebenwirkungen lesen Sie . . .-Negative Effekte von Coaching. *Zeitschrift für Arbeits- und Organisationspsychologie A&O, 58*(1), 17–33. https://doi.org/10.1026/0932-4089/a000129

Schreier, M. (2014). Qualitative content analysis: In practice. In U. Flick (Ed.), *The Sage handbook of qualitative data analysis* (pp. 170–183). Sage. https://doi.org/10.4135/9781446282243.n12

Schröder, T. A., & Davis, J. D. (2004). Therapists' experience of difficulty in practice. *Psychotherapy Research, 14*(3), 328–345. https://doi.org/10.1093/ptr/kph028

Sherman, R. A., Nave, C. S., & Funder, D. C. (2013). Situational construal is related to personality and gender. *Journal of Research in Personality, 47*(1), 1–14. https://doi.org/10.1016/j.jrp.2012.10.008

Skinner, E. A., Edge, K., Altman, J., & Sherwood, H. (2003). Searching for the structure of coping: A review and critique of category systems for classifying ways of coping. *Psychological Bulletin, 129*(2), 216–269. https://doi.org/10.1037/0033-2909.129.2.216

Smith, A. J. M., Kleijn, W. C., & Hutschemaekers, G. J. M. (2007). Therapist reactions in self-experienced difficult situations: An exploration. *Counselling and Psychotherapy Research, 7*(1), 34–41. https://doi.org/10.1080/14733140601140865

Turner, E., & Passmore, J. (2018). Ethical dilemmas and tricky decisions: A global perspective of coaching supervisors' practices in coach ethical decision-making. *International Journal of Evidence Based Coaching and Mentoring, 16*(1), 126–142.

Wegener, R. (2019). *Bedeutsame Momente im Coaching*. Springer. https://doi.org/10.1007/978-3-658-25687-6

Zimmermann, J. (2019). *Tricky coaching: Schwierige Situationen während des Coaching-Prozesses aus Sicht der Coaches.* Unveröffentlichte Masterarbeit, Universität Kassel.

Behavior of the Coachees 2

2.1 Practical Example 1

Case Description
I remember a supervisee who worked in a prison. The theme that ran through the entire supervision[1] process of close to a year was the supervisee's unpunctuality and unreliability, with permanent postponements and cancellations of appointments. It wasn't until I was clear and charged for an hour that his employer made him pay for himself that our working relationship changed.

How Did the Supervisor Proceed?
At first, I was sympathetic to him. I took my time (at my expense) and postponed my appointments at short notice. It annoyed me, as I was thus always adapting my working day to his way of doing things. Since I was still new as a supervisor in this place at that time, I did not want to lose the process. So my attitude was also ambivalent. At some point, I reinterpreted his behavior and began to address his behavior as content within the supervision. I motivated him to think about whether this behavior could have something to do with his work in the prison. Thereupon an exciting part developed in the supervision—also concerning the strict working conditions, the time schedules, and the fixed structures of a penal institution. The supervision ended after 1 year and I think I worked well with him on this topic.

[1] The term *supervision* is used and understood differently depending on the country and the context. In this book, it primarily refers not to oversight but to various counseling/consulting formats.

H. Möller, J. Zimmermann, *Difficult Situations in Business Coaching*,
https://doi.org/10.1007/978-3-658-35087-1_2

Tom Levold

As is often the case, clarification of the contractual framework is at the heart of the case history. What is interesting to me is the question of why the process went on frustratingly for such a long time. Did it make any difference at all to him whether he came on time or not? Did he see himself as a client for supervision at all, or was he just taking up an offer that the employer expected him to accept? Did he possibly derive a certain satisfaction from not having to abide by the rules in a system that is subject to very strong regulations, including time regulations? What motivation did the employee have? What value did the supervision have for him? Were there motives to deal with the phenomena rather passively and tolerantly? Were there other orders on the part of the correctional facility that suggested a cautious approach to the subject? Did conflict aversion or own insecurity play a role? Was it too difficult to put a spin on it after it had been going on for a very long time?

On the part of the supervisor, it is interesting to see whether and in what way these questions were even made an issue in the course of the process.

After reading the described procedure, my assumptions regarding the uncertainty of the contract on the part of the supervisor have been partially confirmed, as well as the assumption that the behavior of the supervisee can be classified differently against the background of the restrictive, regimenting context of the penal institution. The case study confirms the necessity of dealing clearly with the framework conditions from the beginning, so that one does not get into such a stalemate with an uncertain outcome. This should be particularly taken into account when the supervisor notices that her own motives, which are not related to the process, are involved: Uncertainty about keeping an assignment or the desire to secure follow-up assignments, uncertainty about the value of one's own work, fear of not being able to provide clarification or confrontation, etc. If one's own interest in an assignment is greater than that of the client, this leads to an unfavorable distortion of the working relationship, which in the long run cannot do justice to either partner.

I already inform my clients about my conditions in the appointment confirmation email. Cancellations four or more days before the appointment are not subject to a cancellation fee—if I can't reschedule the appointment, it is at my expense. Between two and four working days before the appointment you pay half the fee, less than two working days the full fee. This is then considered to be agreed in writing. I have done well with this clarity so far. I consider this to be a reasonable balance of risk—since I tend to make long-term appointments and don't have any walk-ins, I can't reschedule all appointments that are cancelled in good time. Quite exceptional circumstances also make it possible to make exceptions to the rule—but this must be made explicit in each individual case. If the clients are late, I call after five minutes to clarify whether they are on the way and late or whether they have forgotten the appointment.

Ullrich Beumer

The central theme of this case is dealing with rules, agreements, boundaries, and jointly created orders as a solid basis for prosperous cooperation and human coexistence in general. One can interpret the unpunctuality as an attack on the authority of the counselor.

There are several facets to the case presentation, possibly including a gender element in which the female counselor cannot be accepted as setting boundaries; an experience more common in prisons where women are more likely to be psychologists or social workers. Clearly, however, at the forefront is the question of how to appropriately deal with boundaries. Our emotions and affects, our libidinal desires and psychic energies are regulated by appropriate boundary management. Skillful boundary management is needed to close or open boundaries when appropriate.

Boundary management, as it is called in the tradition of the so-called Tavistock conferences, is one of the central tasks and competencies of counseling, along with containment and generativity (as an attitude of enabling and promoting the new). This also applies to the supervisor, who has fundamental boundary responsibilities in terms of maintaining time limits, ensuring a space conducive to consultation, and working towards the shared task and goal. We are now at the end of a long historical phase in which, both socially, in organizations and in the field of counseling services, the expansion, transgression, and dissolution of boundaries have been among the central dynamics and implicit orientations for action. This also applies to the correctional system, where the rehabilitation mandate has long been in the foreground and sharp boundaries and sanctions are sometimes frowned upon. The supervisor, for example, speaks of the penitentiary, and in doing so undercuts the *correctional system*, which, understood in terms of depth hermeneutics, must be seen as a denial and lack of consciousness of a social reality. This also becomes clear in the present case, which can undoubtedly be seen as a reflection of an institutional dynamic.

If this supervisor came to me for supervision, it would be important for me as supervisor to work with the counselor on all three relationship levels: First—and this is what she finally did by issuing a default invoice—the real level of the business relationship between supervisee and counselor needs clarification and tighter handling. Then I would work more intensively on what the driving forces are in this dynamic. What about it is institutional (counter-)transference, what is concern for the assignment, what is possibly professional habitus? I know in the counseling field, as far as it is professionally biographically shaped by a culture of nonprofit thinking or social work attitude, a rather avoidant attitude of boundary setting, an idealization of relationship, emotion and boundary extension. This does not have to be fundamentally bad, but it does require awareness and clarification as to whether this is more conducive or obstructive in the case at hand.

Finally, it would also be useful to look at a possible level of one's own transmissions: What is the learned way of dealing with boundaries? To what extent does this influence the rather avoidant form of behavior that is visible in the case? What about the development of a clearer professional orientation toward boundary management instead of too much emphasis on containment? Finally, to what extent is clear boundary management a prerequisite for the emergence of something new, of new insights and behaviors? Motto: Understanding is over, from now on there are consequences!

Agnes Büchele

The theme running through supervision seems like being locked into a theme about nonconformity. If you act out of conformity you are held accountable, if you criminally overdo the non-conformity you are locked up. The supervisee does not like to be locked up by rules, so he keeps exposing them and interpreting them as needed.

In my effort to imagine the course of the supervision over a year, the image of a wrestling match and power play between the supervisor as a woman and free but dependent self-employed person and the man, employed in the powerful institution of the prison, arises in my mind. The struggle for payment, for money, is symbolic of power and influence. *He is in charge*, acts with time, postponements and payment and makes *her* squirm. There are also gender roles acted out according to the classic: "Me Tarzan, you Jane." When the woman succeeds in demanding time structure and payment, she manages to get on professional track in supervision and into a more authentic counseling relationship. She goes on to leave the reader, and arguably herself, in the dark about *when*, throughout the year, the moment of billing arrived and how *exactly* she was then able to navigate the process well. In order to arrive at productive insights, it would be important to be able to capture, through concrete examples, how she proceeded in particular situations and what issues were worked through that ultimately made for good work. Without being aware of these themes in the dynamics of the process and the consultation, the supervisor would always remain Jane in the relationship.

If this supervisor came to me for supervision, it would definitely be a matter for me to understand the meaning of the long concession and patience under the aspects of transference and counter-transference. It would be necessary to find out from her what—apart from the understandable interest in keeping the assignment—prevents the supervisor from negotiating with the supervisee his concerns, his goals as well as the conditions for the supervision and to address any ambiguities that arise as directly as possible. Making the implicit gender issue conscious seems to me to be a necessity in the process and a good chance to understand unconsciously effective gender patterns in the counseling relationship: What is she thinking as a supervisor *and* as a woman, what is the supervisee thinking in her position *and* as a man? What *does she do* as a woman in the role of supervisor and what *does she not do* because she is a woman? What does he *do* as a supervisee and a man and what *does he not do* because he is a man (cf. Scheffler & Baumann, 2011)? These implicit issues touch on each person's identity, role understanding, and agency; they are at work in every organization (cf. Wetterer, 2002). Role understanding and gender identity have become moving values, with gender role-models remaining relatively constant. They are all the more in need of clarification and the ability to bring up gender in contemporary counseling and communication and to be aware of mechanisms of action in this regard (cf. Abdul-Hussain, 2012). The supervisor could be encouraged, among other things, to put these issues into words with the aim of also strengthening her role in a gender-competent way.

Achim Mollbach

There is a conflict between supervisor and supervisee for almost a year about behavior or behavioral expectations around the supervision process. It is not so much about the client's behavior in supervision, but about the client's behavior toward the supervisor as a contractual partner of the organization. The supervisee exhibits behavior that the supervisor considers inappropriate.

In the case description nothing is said about whether explicit agreements were made at the beginning of the supervision in the context of the clarification of the assignment on how to deal with last-minute cancellations or postponements of appointments. Such agreements have, among other things, an economic purpose: they regulate services and considerations in a business relationship. It is possible that the lack of such an agreement or the supervisor's failure to use the agreements indicates that the supervisor does not see or does not want to see the relationship with the client or client system as at least also a business or economic relationship.

The fact that the supervisor does not charge a cancellation fee until after 1 year may also be due to the fact that at the beginning of the process with the client system the supervisor tacitly assumed that the values and rules of the game in dealing with each other were congruent, so that from the supervisor's point of view there was no need for any regulation in this regard.

A conflict arises when the client acts differently from what the supervisor expects of him and consequently also reacts differently to the supervisor's interventions than the supervisor assumes from her system of values and actions. The conflict remains, even if further interventions are basically only repetitions or only variations of previous interventions.

The supervisor chose two interventions: On the one hand, she addressed the client's behavior in the context of supervision, but not by directly confronting him with her expectations as a supervisor and contractual partner, but rather by using the behavior toward the supervisor as material in supervision to stimulate a process of reflection in the client regarding his activities in the prison—possibly in the hope that the client would also reconsider and change his behavior toward the supervisor via this route. If this supervisor came to me for supervision, building on this very indirect approach, I would consider with the supervisor what prevented her from formulating her expectations directly and clearly without this detour. Furthermore, it could be reflected upon with the supervisor whether a more direct and clear position as a party to the conflict having expectations of the other party's punctuality and reliability would have been a reasonable alternative. As a second intervention, the supervisor decided—albeit after a year—to be paid for the hours of absence. Here it is useful to work with the supervisor on why she did not come to this decision until after a year. Admittedly, she states that she was new to the place and did not want to lose the supervision. This is quite understandable. Nevertheless, it might be interesting for the supervisor to ask how it is that it took her so long to make this decision.

Edeltrud Freitag-Becker

The supervisee unconsciously and thus unplanned confronts the supervisor with the core issue of the penal system: breaking the rules can lead to a stay in the penal system. His closeness to the inmates leads to an unconscious identification with their misbehavior: Daring to cross boundaries, bending them to one's own liking, making one's own rules, collecting broken rules like trophies.

The supervisor allows herself to be involved in this relationship structure for a year and thereby becomes complicit. Together, supervisor and supervisee betray the agreement with the client. Only the supervisor's detachment from this role and her revealing behavior enable a change. She changes roles and becomes the punisher, the perpetrator. The transference dynamic takes up a lot of space and influences the respective role shape. The drama triangle (persecutor–rescuer–victim) was, so to speak, the inspiration.

It is striking that there is no named topic of consultation. The struggle for compliance with the rules is the focus of supervision. Counseling situations from the penal system are reflected: The main thing is that the rules are observed and appropriate rule behavior is trained; there is little room for dealing with the reasons for breaking the rules. Rules provide support—the possible issues behind them are unsettling. Analogously, the real place of the counseling event remains unclear: Covered, in the dark, shadowed, unclear, unrecognizable, etc.

It could be helpful if the supervisor and supervisee were to exchange views about their images of organizations: About the real ones as well as the internalized ones ("organizations in the mind") and about the understood patterns of relationships and behavior in this context. The transference analysis could provide access to a deeper understanding of the respective willingness to break one's own rules: Clarification of the attraction to break rules as well as the fear of discovery of the act.

Heidi Möller

The phenomenon of mirroring comes to mind. The negative evaluation of prisoners is transferred to those who work there. They, too, are called guards and are not particularly recognized socially. In the sense of Balint's mirror-phenomenon theory and identification with the clients, the supervisee behaves like a hoodlum. Like an inmate he is unpunctual, cheats the employer. It almost comes close to a refusal of supervision, similar to a refusal of treatment in prison.

The metaphor of prison as a substitute for a father (cf. Pecher, 1989) expresses an unconscious longing for stability and rules. Only in this way can it be explained that things are surprisingly quiet in German prisons. The paternal principle of rules and norms responds on a deep level to the longing of many prisoners for a father, since they have mostly grown up with a father-deprived upbringing. Moreover, it is possible to rebel against rules in prison and still enjoy them at the same time.

Ultimately, the community of the good (cf. Roth, 1991) does not care what happens behind the walls. The main thing is that no one breaks out.

2.2 Practical Example 2

Case Description

A coachee comes with a crisis-like, close-to-burn-out professional situation. Already in the first interview, it turns out that she is basically proud of her overwork and the symptoms of an approaching burn-out. The only thing she really wants to change about her professional situation is that she suffers from all the work. Narcissistic and perfectionistic tendencies are present in her, which increases the likelihood of burn-out. She denies the need for therapy. The goal of the coaching is to help her cope better with the stresses of work. In addition, a strategy is to be worked out that will prevent the coachee from being burdened with even more work in the case of an upcoming restructuring of the department (fewer personnel with the same, rather increasing workload). The coachee strives for recognition. The coaching narratives also describe heroic situations in which she always ultimately triumphs through extra work, excessive diligence, and perfectionism. For me as a coach, the dilemma arises of whether to feed the narcissist or to challenge her and offer other perspectives on her behavior. The latter is not very successful, the former is not in line with my understanding of coaching and would, in my view, be a task for a therapist. As a result, we go around in circles for quite a long time in coaching.

How Did the Coach Go About It?

From the beginning I had a funny feeling as a coach, because it quickly became clear that overwork and personal suffering from the professional situation function as an essential part of the ego. The professional perspective proved to be a dead end in my reflection after the first session. Then in the second session the issue behind the issue emerged. It was in the family and partnership realm: Helplessness in the face of system structures versus securing self-efficacy. Only in this change of topic was reflection and insight gained by the coachee possible. First strategies for self-care also in the professional area could be developed. The coaching will be continued.

Carla Albrecht

When reading the case description, I notice that the coach tends to devalue her client and finds few positive aspects about her. This becomes clear in her remarks; she does not name any qualities that she finds acceptable about her and no aspects of her behavior that she appreciates. The coach seems to have a rather negative countertransference reaction to the client. This probably makes it difficult for her to establish a positive relationship with the client. However, this is a fundamental requirement for the success and effectiveness of coaching, as evidenced by many studies in the field of coaching and therapy research (e.g., Bordin, 1979; Hubble et al., 2001; Ryba, 2019).

To get out of this difficult situation, as a coach I would first take a detailed history to get a better view of the client's system. Guiding questions to clarify the personal background could be, for example: How did she become who she became? Where did the demand to always perform well come from? What would happen if she stopped doing that? What would she lose then? Regarding the current professional situation, I would ask: What is the constellation in the organization with managers, with colleagues and, if applicable, with employees? What is the culture in the organization? How did the restructuring come about?

A good diagnostic procedure at the beginning of a coaching process often also helps to establish rapport and to get an all-encompassing picture of the overall system without running the risk of overlooking essentials (cf. Möller & Kotte, 2013). The information from the case history can then be used to generate hypotheses for the behavior of the counterpart and as a coach one develops more understanding for the coachee's attempts to find solutions.

For me, establishing a stable relationship is the basic prerequisite for further interventions. These are manifold, depending on what the case history and a further clarification of the task have yielded. On a private, more personal level, one could begin to work on the client's behavioral patterns and inner core beliefs, on what she would also lose if she changed her behavior. Alternatively, one could start by working on the professional situation, e.g., with a detailed analysis of her role in the organization (cf. Giernalczyk & Möller, 2018).

- What are her responsibilities in her role?
- What isn't she allowed to do?
- What scope for action is there for her?

If my countertransference reaction continued to be strongly negative after the case history, I would do a countertransference analysis on myself to better understand what it is that triggers feelings and impulses to act in me and why. If there is concordant countertransference, I can see how she herself is probably feeling and why she is behaving the way she is (unconsciously) as a result. If the relationship is stable enough, there is then the possibility of making these countertransference feelings available to the client and working in the here-and-now: "I'm just getting the impression that you don't want to change your behavior at all. Whenever I make a suggestion about what you could do, you explain to me why there's no way you can do that and it's actually good the way it is."

Thomas Giernalczyk

My central starting point would be the analysis of my countertransference. By this we mean all thoughts, feelings and impulses for action that arise in the coach in the context of contact with the coachee (cf. Giernalczyk & Möller, 2018). She notices an either/or attitude in herself, which she cannot easily transform into a both/or attitude. Our countertransference reactions always invite us to reflect on the client and on ourselves: As a coach, am I experiencing the situation in the same way as my coachee? This question assumes that the coach's experience is sometimes a mirror image of the coachee's. Is the either/or issue a building block that creates the problematic situation unnoticed? Turned more to me as a coach, this would mean: Is it my coachee's situation that creates tightness in me as a coach?

Is the specific mixture of suffering, clinging to the situation and self-exaltation calling up the either/or relationship pattern in me?

These questions aim at the personal equation of the coach. What does she bring to the table in terms of transference tendencies that she has developed as her own relational patterns in her biography? In general, one can say that transference is a component of counter-transference to the coach.

My second starting point would be the issue of narcissism: With a narcissistic issue as described here, I would accept the need for feeding. The battered self-esteem requires specific attention, through which the capacity for emotional reflection and insight is made possible in the first place. Various theories of narcissistic disorders agree—despite differences—that behind the façade of grandiosity and self-presentation there is a part of the self that is in need of recognition and mirroring, and that mirroring and insight into neediness is developmentally beneficial (cf. Volkan & Ast, 2002).

My third consideration relates to change in the organization: The change-related desire (not to work even harder) is an understandable, defensive reaction to imposed change. According to the concept of the change curve, impending change often generates resistance and fear. If we think micropolitically, it is quite normal to think about one's own advantages in the organization. Neuberger (2002) describes in the concept of micropolitics that we must assume that all members of an organization pursue both the interests of their organization as well as, often covertly, their own interests.

Based on the countertransference analysis, I would try to address the conundrum that the coachee suffers from her work pressure on the one hand and is proud of her symptomatology on the other. Together with her I would consider what her symptoms stand for. It is likely that the symptomatology is seen as unbeatable evidence of her work pushed to the edge. I would be interested in other evidence that also demonstrates her prowess. In this way, we would create a space where the accomplishment can be appreciated and the narcissistic neediness seen. The reference in the vignette to refusing psychotherapy is significant to me. The suggestion of psychotherapy at the beginning of a coaching session also contains potential for mortification. If the coachee feels offended by this, she will probably find it more difficult to accept help in coaching as well.

Exploring the restructuring of the organization together could be a topic area where I can both validate the coachee's needs and explore her interest in the tasks and the department. In the vignette, brackets indicate that coach or coachee see some employee hostility in the restructuring. This leads to the question of how both relate to the company. Coaching is usually a triangular contract between coachee, company, and coach and requires reflection on the togetherness (cf. Giernalczyk & Möller, 2018). Presumably, there is again an aspect of either/or in the initially only negative attribution. I would be interested to know whether legitimate, positive aspects, such as ensuring the continued existence of the company or improving the competitive situation, can also be discussed.

Klaus Eidenschink

The initial situation described appears as if the coach evaluates negatively both the survival strategies developed by the client and her work situation, but also the counseling request. Therefore, it is no wonder that the coach also quickly finds herself between unfavorably classified alternatives. For the coach, the way out of this dilemma is obviously to refuse the desired rescue on the one hand, and on the other hand to find ways to convey to the client that she is narcissistically using her suffering to stabilize herself.

The coach and the client have in common that they feel exploited. Both oscillate between resisting and conforming out of fear of not meeting the expectations of the environment. This consonance in pattern is an indication that the coach has become entangled and consequently she will have difficulty making a favorable contact offer to the client. This creates a counseling relationship in which the client is again expected to conform to expectations—this time to those of the coach. This threatens to stabilize a presumably narcissistic basic structure of the client, because the coach does not want to feed her. However, this is not about feeding, but about building a relationship in which the client can have the experience of an unintentional counterpart and thus experience what it is like to really be herself.

The coach sees the solution in improved self-efficacy and consequently works toward it. From my point of view, this is not wrong—especially if she focuses on self-care. My fear at this point, however, is that the inner foundation for much-needed self-care is not yet in place. If so, the coach's strategy would fall under the rubric of "doing the right thing at the wrong time." For me, the symptoms of helplessness and overexertion point to a deep inner isolation of the client. In any case, it is important to examine this differential diagnostic consideration so that the counseling does not build on sand and ultimately lead to renewed excessive demands and a lonely struggling with oneself.

Mathias Lohmer

In this case situation, the coach–coachee entanglement is striking, leading to a stalemate in the coaching process. The coach gets into an acted countertransference resistance in the face of seemingly contradictory orders of the client (better deal with professional stresses; maintain pride in overwork). The coach finds herself in a self-constructed and unsolvable either/or dilemma: Feed or question.

As a first step, a countertransference clarification would be helpful here to clarify for the coach what brings her into such a negative-devaluing attitude toward the client.

One hypothesis would be that the coach, in general, might be a more business-critical person and thus vulnerable to a perpetrator–victim view with the demands of the company as the perpetrator side and the threat of the client being overwhelmed as the victim side. From this perspective, it would be understandable that the coach would like to protect the client from the demands of the company and is frustrated that the client does not take on the role of the victim and allow her to take the position of the savior.

The coach's critical attitude toward the hero stories would suggest—in the context of the countertransference analysis—the question whether she is skeptical of the client's success, in line with the above hypothesis.

One could suspect a collusion (an unconscious interaction on the couple level) in which a coach—presumably coming from the psychosocial and less from the economic spectrum—would like to connect with the client's tendencies to emancipate herself from a classical orientation towards success, and because she does not go along with this in this way, comes into a critical and disapproving attitude. In the context of this collusion, the client would then for her part unconsciously pass on her own shares of feelings of having excessive demands placed on her and critical of the work to the coach, could relativize her own critical attitude in her and let her—and thus her own side of ambivalence toward the demands place on her—run aground.

On the topic of implication and collusion, in a supervised work with the coach, it would first be necessary to clarify what might correspond to the coach's own transference onto the client, what she would have liked to see realized in her, and how her own ideology contributes to this impasse.

In general, this case confronts one with the peculiarities of coaching narcissistic personalities. Here it is of central importance to mirror the coachee's desired self-image (being able to work hard; being successful), i.e., to mark it positively. After sufficient trust has been established in the relationship, it is appropriate to also confront the coachee with the costs of this self-concept. In doing so, the coachee must always take into account the narcissistic sickliness and longing for recognition and affirmation, without connoting this negatively for herself as feeding. On the other hand, she must not allow herself to be used as a self-object for the uncritical confirmation of grandiose self-concepts.

Peter Uffelmann

In the case vignette, descriptions are used that refer on the one hand to the individual situation and on the other hand (rather marginally) to the challenges in the professional activity.

Individual phenomena	Organizational phenomena
Crisis	High workload
Burnout	Restructuring of the department
Narcissistic	Staff shortage
Perfectionist	Strategy development
Proud of the symptoms	
Suffering due to work	
Striving for recognition	
Excessive diligence	
Heroic situations due to overtime	
Helplessness	

It is not clear from the vignette what the coachee's job is, what position she holds within the organization, what her tasks are in the context of restructuring and strategy development. The focus on the personal level, which is a little too quick for my liking, neglects the inclusion of the organizational context. Here a careful exploration of the coachee's embedding in the organizational structures and dynamics of her company would be useful and helpful. Especially in the diagnosis of possible burnout phenomena, circumstances, and behavior should be considered in equal measure. The personification of the client's suffering may seem sensible from the point of view of strengthening self-efficacy, but the additional analysis of the coachee's options for exerting influence prevents an approach that is too strongly centered on psychopathology. Furthermore, it could be helpful, especially in the sense of self-efficacy, to offer a differentiated resource check that considers personal, social, and organizational support aspects.

My suggestion would be to carry out a renewed clarification of the coaching assignment, according to the motto: Go back to the start. I favor such a process reflection with clarification of the assignment as a fixed component of both the formal and psychological contract in coaching, even without major irritations. The following questions could also come into play during the process:

- What did we find (phenomenological perspectives)?
- How did we think about it (hypotheses)?
- What have we set out to do (goals, intervention planning)?
- What did we do (intervention)?
- What was the outcome (evaluation)?
- What's next?

Heidi Möller

A triangular contract of this kind is quite unusual. We coaches are used to a company saying: "Please help the client to cope better with stress." But for the client's company to say: "Help her not to let so much get on her plate," that is unusual. The client may have a very central role in the company or the company may be described as quite employee oriented and caring.

I am concerned with the question of where the devaluation by the coach comes from. My hypothesis is: Assuming that the coach's perception is correct, that the client frames herself as a heroine of the work, then the question of the subjective meaning of this arises. The coach's anger may be understood as fear of what would happen if the client stopped trying so hard. The coach may preconsciously fear a violent decompensation of her client. The anger that feeds the devaluation would then be an expression of her fear of coming close to a mental crisis in the coaching process. Here it could help her to look at the client's need to be successful.

2.3 Practical Example 3

Case Description

The team leader of a small team comes for coaching three to four times a year over 2 years. He repeatedly reports his frustration with some employees and complains about them. At the same time, he complains about his supervisor who does not give him any leverage to deal with these difficult employees. In the course of coaching, the coachee talks himself more and more into his dissatisfactions with his job. He immediately invalidates and dismisses various ideas for change and solutions that are developed during coaching. At the same time he complains that he is burnt out and listless. He is no longer happy in his job, but he does not want to change his situation because he only has 13 years to work until retirement. As a mandate for the coaching he mentions the wish to be able to experience more joy in his work again. After the coachee has vented, he states that he feels relieved. For me, the difficulty in this process lies in the coachee's endurance of this negative spiral and this supposed infatuation with problems. Although he claims to be satisfied with the output, as a coach I am not.

What Was the Coach's Approach?

I ask questions about what he enjoys in his job, what interests him, what keeps him on the job; ask who in his environment might support his ideas and concerns. I let the coachee choose images that symbolize his resources and that he carries with him. In order to regain strength and motivation and to be able to activate his resources, the coachee decides to apply for a time-out in the form of a visit to a health resort.

Sandrina Lellinger

There are a couple of points here that I'm paying attention to. The coach describes that the client comes for coaching three to four times a year. This leads me to believe that he always comes when the pressure is high and he needs relief. In coaching, what the coach describes as "venting" happens. Afterward, the client is satisfied and the coach is not. This leads to the question: Who actually needs to be satisfied with the coaching at the end of the lesson or process?

If the client comes with wide time intervals and always only with situational need for relief, a real work process can hardly develop. Instead, the client uses coaching as a service, the coach plays along with this game, behaves accordingly and is dissatisfied with feeling like a service provider. No solution or action orientation emerges, coaching is reduced to the relief function. In order to develop a real working process in coaching, in which learning and change become possible in a sustainable way, continuity and usually several consecutive appointments are needed. This allows the coaching relationship to mature and develop depth. The time between appointments is then part of the process and supports the impact of each session. Therefore, I would encourage the coach to design not only the individual sessions but a process, to promote continuous cooperation and, if necessary, to make it a condition.

One starting point would be to explore what image and concept of work this client has acquired socializationally. He may say that he would like to experience more joy in his work, but can he really think that work is joyful? Possibly his concept of work includes that work is oppressive, restrictive, joyless, and that regular relief is a necessary remedy for this. Superiors may be fundamentally in the way in his experience, the relationship with co-workers always difficult.

I find the coach's impulse to work with the client in a resource- and solution-oriented way appropriate. In my view, work with images is needed, an approach that moves away from the struggle for solutions. However, since this has not led in the past to the client achieving his goal of having more joy at work, it may need a different approach. I would intervene here paradoxically and open up a scenario for the client of what it would be like if things went on like this for 13 years now: The supervisor leaves him with nothing to do, the employees are difficult and simply not amenable. I would look at what images arise in him, because it is described here that all solution approaches that are developed in coaching are immediately invalidated and discarded by the client. So, instead of continuing to focus on solution options with him, I would do the exact opposite and see if this creates motivation and energy for change in the client. The client seems to have a lot of experience in invalidating and discarding suggestions that are offered to him. To do this, the coach should offer a real difference that allows new things to emerge and strengthens the client's self-responsibility. The prerequisite for this is a sustainable and trusting counseling relationship.

Sebastian Kunert

My look at the genesis of the difficult situation described tells me: This is a typical case in coaching: Clients whose frustration energy is sufficient to seek professional advice, but not to dare a profound change in their lives. They are trapped in the gilded cage of their job; they are held in by the position, the pay, the employer's reputation, the relaxed work routine, the lack of complexity. At the same time, they are deeply dissatisfied and project this onto colleagues, employees, or the manager. Since they hardly experience relief elsewhere, they need coaching as a place of catharsis. The coach from the case study asks the right question: Can *I* take this? Am I making myself an accomplice to the situation and ultimately acting to stabilize the problem instead of solving it?

My methodological approach in such a coaching assignment would be to listen patiently in the sense of being present in a nonthreatening way. I think it is also important to "recontract" with the client at regular intervals, i.e., to ask whether the format is still perceived as helpful and supportive.

An alternative could be to leave the level of everyday patterns and go even higher to the meta-level of inner drivers. Here, desires, longings, and goals can be addressed. The focus is then on the question: What am I looking for in life and what role does my profession play in this? To facilitate this view from the very top, I once scheduled a session in the café of the Berlin TV Tower: A great view, out of the lowlands of everyday life; a bird's eye view in the truest sense of the word. On sticky notes I queried various drivers (fame, money, power, etc.); none of which applied. In the end, I asked, "Then what is it?" A blank card remained, "I'm moving in perpetual loops here because I'm actually dancing around a nothing." This realization of inner aimlessness was then the starting point of a personal learning journey.

Thomas Bachmann

This is a typical case for me: The client is in a "stuck state." If we understand the professional situation described as a force field, then there is only one positive valence in the client's life space, namely retirement. Before that, the barrier is time: The 13 years until then. There are a few areas that the client wants to avoid: The difficult leadership situation in the team, problematic organizational circumstances and conflicts, represented by his manager. Changing jobs also seems to be one of the things he wants to avoid. No energy for change can be detected in this field. The negative forces cancel each other out, the positive psychic energy is weak, due to the still longer period of time until retirement. This question often comes up in coaching and is a typical occasion with which people come to coaching. If there were sufficient life energy, they would not choose this support model at all.

I conclude from the way the client is described that a lot of frustration, if not bitterness, plays a role here, which the coach also picks up on linguistically and resonates with it. The client has settled into his problem world and probably wants to maintain his view of things and confirm his worldview again and again. The sentence "Better familiar suffering than unfamiliar happiness" by Tucholsky adequately describes this phenomenon. For the familiar suffering, the client has developed lots of coping strategies to live with it. If the stress level rises, he gets some relief from the coach or he tries to change a few small things. But the sessions are not enough to really bring about a big change, i.e., to make a bigger leap, e.g., to really tackle the issue with the superior, to act more forcefully, so to speak. The unfamiliar happiness is just not known, uncertain, not tangible enough to really move in this direction and to take risks.

I would like to look in the direction of the coach. For me, in coaching there is always the question: Who has the greater interest in change? And here it seems to me that the coach has more interest in change than the client. For the coaching contract and the question of who actually wants to make a difference here, this constellation is interesting. The energy for change has obviously landed on the wrong side here. Now one can speculate how it came to this. In any case, we still know too little about the client. What is his family situation? Any house payments? What about children? Therefore, it would be too early for me to hypothesize about his personality structures, resistance to change, or attributions such as "won't take responsibility." We have a relatively thin fact base from the case study, and all we know is that someone is stuck. I know from my coaching experience that change sometimes takes a long time. The client has been coming to the coach three or four times a year for 2 years, so he's been through six or eight sessions now. And sure, you can assume a usual coaching session is usually shorter. But practice shows that especially in career coaching, changing professional situations often takes a very long time. So I would say that is fine, it takes time. Nevertheless, I would look to see if at least smaller steps are happening. Is change on the horizon? How can you release more energy for change? And maybe sometimes it's okay to just be stabilizing because a private situation is a way it is. Then our stabilizing function in coaching is enough. You should decide as a coach, if you are frustrated about the course, when and how to discuss this with the client, i.e., renegotiate the assignment.

In order to find the energy for change, I try to stimulate the client's sense of possibility in such cases. This succeeds, for example, with the question: "Imagine that we meet in five years in a street café. What story of your life will you tell me then? Where will you be working or what will you be doing then?" The answer is usually the same: "Yes, well then, it must be different. Then I won't have the current situation anymore, then I'll have made up my mind, etc." Then I say, "Okay, and between five years from now and today, where is the decision point when you take a different turn? Three weeks from now, four years from now, six months from now?" We circle the decision in the conversation in a way that creates emotional pressure to find the reason for the change. From polarization to contraction—that is how Gestalt therapist Frank Staemmler would put it.

After reviewing the approach of the coach, I consider the decision to visit a health resort as good, the client takes care of himself. And it is, at the same time, more of the same. Before the coach was the treatment and now there is a real treatment. It could be that the client remains in his pattern and does not take responsibility for his life, he still lacks the energy for change following the treatment. But one could also think in the other direction: Consider the health resort as a time-out in which clarification, contemplation, and thus perhaps also new ideas and visions can develop. I do not want to venture a prognosis at this point.

Beate Fietze

The client's infatuation with the problem gives the impression that he has settled into a state of dissatisfaction and would rather remain there than actually tackle a change. The client only comes to coaching at long intervals to relieve himself of too much pressure and thereby integrates coaching into his ritualized restoration of the status quo. This leads to a feeling of disruption and mirror phenomena for the coach: The coach is now just as dissatisfied as the client. Instead of being able to help overcome the dissatisfaction in accordance with the mandate, he experiences himself instrumentalized as a stabilizing factor of stagnation.

The client does not go into conflict: Not into conflict with the superior, not into conflict with the employees and not into conflict with himself. He does not put himself in front of the decision or change question. This is exactly what he seems to avoid and delegates the responsibility for change to the coach.

This description of the relationship figure and dynamics between coach and coachee is not yet a diagnosis that already provides the reasons for the conflict avoidance and derivable measures. Therefore, as a first intervention, further explorations are required.

One of the challenges of coaching is to find out on which level the issue is primarily located. One can start close to the person with the psychological question, e.g., with the dynamics of transference and counter-transference, or go into the reflection by looking at the organizational structures and cultural concepts.

I would start here from the disturbing feeling and provide the transference of the feeling of dissatisfaction in order to step out of the ritual as a coach and make the client's avoidance behavior visible. The goal would be to make the previously unconscious coaching concern conscious and to recontract the working alliance. My intention would be to initiate a process that starts from an explicit mission and goal formulation and that—if the client engages with it—could be guided through different stages. The issues raised by the client could be taken up again, e.g., on the basis of the three dimensions of *person—function—profession* of the wonderful concept of career coaching by Kornelia Rappe-Giesecke (2017) and spelled out on three different loops of a rope. This way I would get access to the professional career, the career perspective, and the life story of the client. It would be possible to see where the client reaches a boundary that opens up a new perspective for him. For example, the question here about personal responsibility in professional life can be answered in very different ways. In the concrete case, I would ask in which type of organization the client is employed, what room for maneuver his position allows at all and which dilemmas are inherent in his position. A further approach would be to ask what understanding of work he starts from. The longing expectation of retirement age as a liberation from externally determined work, for example, is a widely accepted sociocultural pattern of interpretation and not necessarily a case for the psychologist. After all, personal biographical questions can be used to work out formative patterns of behavior. If, on the other hand, I feel that the client is not engaging in reflection on my perceptions and that I continue to be repeatedly instrumentalized, I might pull out of the coaching process. The working relationship is voluntary on both sides and terminable from either side.

Heidi Möller

I was puzzled by the description "only 13 years to work until retirement." This refers to an early termination that was completed internally. It begs the question to me, where does something like this come from? As a Freudian, I would look for the secondary gain of illness. What is the psychological gain and how can someone be stuck with dissatisfaction? Even behaviorally, thinking about reinforcement, the dissatisfaction must weigh more heavily than the interest in change. Loosely based on Tucholsky, "Better the old hell than the unfamiliar happiness." Change seems to trigger a lot of anxiety. The status quo is highly stabilized. One approach that Kauffeld was able to show as impactful for coaching is the technique of Motivational Interviewing (MI; cf. Miller & Rollnick, 2015), a procedure that comes from addiction therapy and is now considered valuable and used for organizational consulting and coaching (cf. Klonek & Kauffeld, 2012). In MI, the benefits of the status quo and the costs of change are contrasted with the benefits of change and the costs of the status quo. If the "change talk" succeeds, then a desire to change may emerge (cf. Endrejat et al., 2017).

External factors can also be important: How satisfied is the client with his family life, his circle of friends? What interests him beyond work?

The focus would be the client's mental model about work. On the radio on Fridays you hear: "Only three more hours until the end of work." Here it is suggested that work is toil and pleasure takes place exclusively beyond work. This model is echoed in the debate about work–life balance. Here, too, the assumption is made that work and life are irreconcilable opposites. Taking responsibility for one's own state of mind even while working would then be a goal for this coaching process. How do I ignite joy and passion (cf. Hirschhorn, 2017) even within my working hours?

Another question that concerns me is that of the client's basic relationship to the world. Does he see his environment (people, working conditions, etc.) as responsible for making sure he is happy and satisfied? This is what we in psychodynamic counseling would call an oral pattern. If so, he lacks the idea of adult responsibility, the idea that everyone has to make their own life according to their needs in order to live well. Perhaps he also lacks self-efficacy beliefs and optimism. In the sense of the feeling of coherence (cf. Antonovsky, 1997), one should ask where his belief in the manageability of his happiness has disappeared to? What gives his work meaning?

2.4 Practical Example 4

Case Description

The coachee came on the recommendation of a colleague and emphasized at the first appointment that she had asked the colleague for someone *really* good. I experienced her as very self-confident in her appearance and above all demanding. The first appointment was preceded by a phone call in which she said that the coaching session was too expensive for her. However, she still decided to have a free initial meeting. What I found difficult from the beginning was the repetitive question: What should I do? Usually, I don't experience this question as difficult because I am usually successful in getting the coachee into a reflective mindset and facilitating a reflective process. However, this coachee proved to be extremely persistent. In addition, I experienced her as very rude and cool in her manners, which did not facilitate the process. This situation occurred again and again in the further coaching process and was unsurprisingly related to the coachee's stress level and sense of constriction.

What Was the Coach's Approach?

I did not respond to the demanding and sometimes desperate question of what she should do, in the sense she meant. If she asked the question rather at the beginning of the session, I went into the exploration and said that I still needed information about this. In this way, she came out of the closet a bit and was already formulating options for action herself. I summarized these again for her at the end of the process and added any recommendations. If she asked the question toward the end of the process, the exploration process, including her own options for action, had already taken place and so I could again summarize her ideas for her. If she asked the question feeling particularly constricted, I explored this feeling of constriction with her phenomenologically and she was able to relax a little in this way. Her feelings of tightness and also the pressure she felt, which she conveyed through her behavior rather than verbally, were always understandable to me. These feelings often transferred to me and I felt pressured by them. As things progressed, I prepared myself particularly well for this coachee, taking care not to be under pressure myself and to ensure as little stress as possible in advance, so that I did not absorb the pressure and tightness too much. As the coachee's working conditions steadily improved and she gained more and more confidence in her work, she generally became more relaxed and the question hardly ever came up after about a year. Her behavior towards me also became softer and more open.

Sandrina Lellinger

In the description of the initial contact, the client appears like a demanding customer who, with her statement that she expects a *really* good coach and her simultaneous feedback that the fee is too high for her, creates a "double bind" for the coach, i.e., a communicative situation with contradictory messages. Ambiguity is also expressed in the behavior further described: The client's question to the coach about what she should do reveals uncertainty and neediness as well as an attempt to shift responsibility from herself to the coach. On the other hand, her behavior, described as brusque and cool, conveys a devaluation of the coach.

In this case study we do not learn what the client's specific concern was. Together with the described effect of the client, the assumption arises in me that there is an issue in the background that the client may not yet be able to reveal. The client's attitude could then be understood as a rehearsal for the coach: Is the coach proving resilient? Does he stand by me even when I am dismissive and demanding? Is he really interested in me? In the background, there are often larger personal issues that clients only bring into the coaching once they have experienced that the coach, despite the behavior described, remains approachable and proves to be a reliable partner. These clients often experience great insecurity in their relationships with others; their biographies are marked by hurtful breaches of trust and experiences of abandonment. In working with these clients, the relationship is of particular importance, even more so than in other processes. Therefore, I would start exactly at this point and clarify what the client needs in order to get involved.

Sebastian Kunert

On the part of our clients, there is often confusion with instructional formats, such as expert consultations. Often coaching is equated with a training measure, a training, or a professional continuing education. The special feature would only lie in the one-to-one format. This assumption is not completely wrong, after all, a coaching process can definitely contain educational elements. Many people find the Johari Window (a scheme for comparing self-perception and perception by others according to Luft & Ingham, 1955) helpful when it comes to feedback, the Four Ears Model (a theory of communication analysis according to Schulz von Thun, 2010) for overcoming communicative difficulties, or statistics on the distribution of tasks among managers to sharpen their own understanding of their roles. However, these professional psychological contents are rarely the focus of the conversation, but only serve to stimulate the client's self-reflection. An important first step is not to allow oneself to be driven into the performance corner, i.e., to have to achieve something measurable, didactic. Demanding clients create a doubting atmosphere with their attitude, in which coaches feel compelled to prove themselves and justify their worth. Coaching is a co-creative process in which both sides contribute something so that something new emerges from the interaction. Those who only want to be trained should look for a training provider of their choice.

Methodologically, good contracting is required here. Together with the client, one should clarify what the idea of coaching is, what it can achieve, and where the limits of the format are. If, in the course of the coaching process, wishes for instruction still arise, they can now be discussed at the meta-level. In extreme cases, the coach is also free to end the joint work by pointing out that the client seems to need a different format. A final service could then be to assist in finding a suitable provider.

Thomas Bachmann

I recognize here a typical contact behavior for *visitors* in coaching, as Steve de Shazer (2014) called this type of client: Passive, examining, interested. "Do something with me!", one could call the guiding principle. The contradictory nature is interesting: On the one hand coming to coaching, paying money, having problems and on the other hand being passive and waiting and not wanting to take their own part in the initial situation into reflection.

For me, the question is how I as a coach can create a space in which the coachee can get involved and open up, where she does not have to show this closing-off behavior. I interpret this as protective behavior, but also a little bit of testing out expectations: A *really* good coach, recommendation, high fee, etc.

Now comes the excruciating first trial session, where you as a coach are supposed to show how you work. The client is still in test mode: "*Let's see if I get involved here. Show me what you can do!*" The challenge is to show yourself professionally without really being able to work, because there is no formal and also no psychological contract yet. Some colleagues then try to do just a little coaching. I have had better experiences with separating the getting-to-know-each-other and the coaching process. As a coach, I try to keep the process of getting to know each other short. Either we clarify it on the phone or really just in a half-hour face-to-face meeting. Then the client should decide whether he wants to work with me or not.

I find the frequent practice of having two or three free initial conversations with different coaches problematic. If you're the third person, you're already hearing it then because it sounds so automated. After the three appointments, the clients have often already had so much input that the topic has already been clarified a bit and not a single euro has been spent on it. This is an unsatisfactory situation for both sides—also for the clients: They have to sit down with three coaches, find appointments, travel around and then make a difficult decision at the end. But what do they want to decide on: On likeability, competence, the right questions, the coach's clear approach and his explanation of how he works? The result could be the cementing of defensiveness: If he has asked me unpleasant questions, then as a coachee I prefer to avoid them.

The first session in coaching is always very valuable. That's when we coaches can be effective. There is still a lot of strangeness and therefore more effective. Offers of reflection and resonance from the coach can be quite effective, especially at the beginning. It's a shame to blow those opportunities prematurely. In this case, for me it is a matter of designing the initial contact in such a way that I do not serve any client patterns and do not put myself in an application situation. Central guiding questions for me are: How do I design the clarification of the assignment? Where does the recommendation come from? I do context clarification. How does someone come to me and what expectations guide them? My determining attitude is: This seems to be the appropriate way for the client to get into contact at this moment, and I will see if we can find other ways to work together.

Beate Fietze

The case presentation does not introduce us to the client's concrete concerns, but begins abruptly with a demonstrative demand for quality from the client to the coach. He should be *really* good. Provocative text questions occur often in coaching as an opening figure. I interpret it frequently and also here as an expression of a psychological resistance to the feared insecurities in the coaching process: On the one hand, the client appears very self-confident and demanding and on the other hand the coaching is too expensive for her even before any admission to the coach. This is a dissonance, it doesn't really fit together.

I would like to comment on the debate about a free initial session: In this case, I actually find the granting of a free initial session irritating because the difference in fees actually precludes a coaching process.

In the meantime, I have largely moved away from offering a free initial consultation, not least for methodological reasons: The first session has a very high information content and is extremely time consuming for me in the follow-up. In the initial consultation, the main motive is usually named, which usually remains an important point of reference throughout the process, "in the overture lies the motif," so to speak. Often the client's first presentation of the situation is also particularly impressive and in many cases significant behavioral patterns emerge, e.g., avoidance behavior and a provocative behavioral style.

When a client decides to come to me for coaching, she rightly expects me to have the content of the initial meeting present. However, I can only guarantee this if I reflect intensively on the first session and record it in detail.

I find it very helpful to call up the different positions, i.e., the organizational context and the role expectations. There are professional roles in which competitive behavior is expected in order to be able to occupy them at all. I, therefore, advocate not immediately personalizing or even pathologizing the behavior, but being open to the fact that it may have a highly functional aspect in its organizational context. In this case, however, my perception of a particularly pronounced need for security predominates. I would therefore try to convey security and stability to the client, so that she can, as it were, largely take off the armor of her brusque defensive behavior and enter into the relationship.

Heidi Möller

If I follow the concept of scenic understanding (cf. Giernalczyk & Möller, 2018) as a specific psychodynamic approach to coaching, I would get stuck on the question of landing with "someone really good." I would immediately be beset by the question of whether I am really good. In the sense of countertransference analysis, this inquiry and my inner resonance (my own inner valence analysis) points to a self-esteem issue on the part of the coachee. Should this hypothesis be confirmed by further exploration and analysis of thc working relationship, then in the sense of self-esteem work according to Stavemann (2011) I would work with the Socratic dialog to destabilize the mental model about valuable and less valuable people. Afterward, it could be worked out how the coachee manages to be the one who stabilizes her self-worth.

Countertransference analysis (cf. Lohmer & Möller, 2019) could also lead me to the topic of rivalry as an anthropological premise: "The working world is a shark tank and I have to constantly assert myself." This basic assumption about the nature of human beings would show up in the coachee's relationship formation with me, in that the question in the room is always being negotiated as to who is actually better here. In the work context, such an attitude can also become a defensive routine of always making sure you don't get eaten up. Certainly, part of a healthy psychological makeup is the competence to compete. If this behavior becomes entrenched and there is serious rivalry, I would see a coaching need in being able to let go of this behavior and instead build up modes of cooperation.

If the working relationship is resilient, I would provide my impression of the whole situation and look at it under defensive aspects with the coachee. What is this appearance, this mode of contact, protecting her from? What would happen if she allowed emotionality and closeness? If coaching enables an emotionally corrective experience, it could be experienced that softness, accessibility, and affectivity do not have to be dangerous; then the coaching process would have made a difference to automated behavioral readiness.

2.5 Practical Example 5

Case Description

An employee repeatedly reports how much other colleagues annoy her and what they would do wrong. She is being coached in order to increase her job satisfaction and possibly avoid constant sick days. She herself only makes small mistakes, but the others make big ones or lie and cheat. She herself is close to retirement. It is clear that she has been placed in a position in the company where she cannot do much harm. She needs the last few years to retire, even though she is very unhappy with the lack of appreciation she is receiving. As the coaching progresses, it becomes clear that she has a hard time with self-reflection and can barely put herself in the shoes of her colleagues. I have a constant impulse to shake her and roughly confront her with reality; at the same time, it seems unhelpful. The coaching ends after five sessions as planned. On the surface, some insight has been gained, but a short time later I hear that nothing has changed.

What Was the Coach's Approach?

I kept my distance and tried to work very precisely on individual situations: What was it like exactly? What did you think, feel and say then? How did that resonate in your opinion? This felt laborious and a little futile, because it was clear that it was also about her personal attitude, which she will not shed in the last few meters of professional life. At the same time, I also felt sorry for the coachee because she has to hold out like this for another 5 years.

Eric Lippmann

Presumably, this is a person who did not come to coaching voluntarily. She may have been referred because she has so many sick days. This puts her at risk of being a visitor or complainer who would not have sought coaching on her own initiative—certainly not to question and reflect on herself. It is not so clear to me what her mission in coaching is. For visitors (cf. Schlegel, 2002), coaching is often a potential insult: Why do I have to go to coaching and not the others, who need it at least as much, if not more than I do? Therefore, it is important to contract well, to pay attention to the referral context, and to "pacing" well with the coachee, i.e., to consciously adapt one's own behaviors to the behaviors of the person being counseled in order to build trust (cf. Dannemeyer & Dannemeyer, 2018).

Based on the hypotheses made, I would look again at the referral context: With the coachee, I would explore what the coaching event means to her. If she turns out to be a complainer, I would dignify with her the desired goal: To want to change the others. But since we can't change the others in coaching, I would ask her if she would also be willing to work on the second-best goal, which is her interaction with the others in terms of making the most of the time she has left at work. In working out solutions, one must always expect the coachee to fall back into the complaining pattern. One possible course of action would be to "pace" again and remind the coachee that we are working on the second-best goal. This helps to have the coachee as a client in front of you again.

When working out a solution, I would ask about patterns from the past, whether it was different in this context before and if so, what she did differently then. You can also ask about the problem pattern of illness, when the increased sick days would have started and what changed then. In addition, I would ask how many sick days there were or are and who thinks that there are too many. Getting sick can also be seen as a solution pattern, but it also has its effects, its price. As a coach, we are usually given a so-called killer assignment, namely to advise away a problem behavior or symptom. Even though this assignment may not come directly from the coachee, but from the referral context, the killer assignment could be called a "double bind" for the coach. The thesis behind this is that the coachee probably also had reasons for calling in sick or becoming sick. If these aspects were not taken into account, then at least one side of her would not be appreciated, which favors getting sick as an option. This is why working with the inner team is a good idea (cf. Schulz von Thun & Stegemann, 2004). This could be introduced, for example, as follows: "It is not you who sees illness as a solution, but one side of you sees it as a perfectly valid way of solving problems in order not to be constantly at the mercy of unpleasant situations at work. Does it make any difference to you if I address you in such a way that it is not you, but a side of you?" Subsequently, the different voices in dealing with the situation at work could be elaborated and possible solutions could be worked out with them.

Finally, I would like to point out the aspects of perception and self-fulfilling prophecy: The case writer reports that the coachee is "close to retirement." When I read that, I thought—and I am 60 myself—that the coachee was 63 or 64 and still had a year or two to work. From my perspective, you're not *close* to retirement at 60, but from the case-maker's perspective, you probably are. He is probably quite a bit younger. If the coach then talks about attitude that she won't "shed in the last few meters of professional life," I would point out the danger of the self-fulfilling prophecy. I had a manager in coaching just recently who was able to get an employee two years away from retirement to the point where she was motivated to come back to work and was less sick. We worked out in detail how she was able to lead the employee to do this. But if you no longer believe in it yourself—and pity doesn't help—then there's not much chance that you can guide the coachee to a different pattern.

Robert Wegener

Whether voluntarily in coaching or prescribed, this client appears to be in a predicament according to the case presentation. The coaching themes discernible in the text are, on the one hand, the client's dissatisfaction with her work and the vaguely formulated wish—or the requirement—to reduce the number of sick days she takes or even to avoid them altogether. Further, there seems to be some indication in the text passage that the client—in the sense of Steve de Shazer and Inso Kim Berg (see also Shazer, 2014)—has a strong tendency to complain. *Complaining clients* are characterized by their acknowledgment of having problems—unlike, say, *visitors,* another form of client type—and also suffering greatly from these problems. However, everyone else is to blame for their problems. *Complaining clients* thus see themselves as victims of their circumstances, often failing to recognize the opportunity available to them to approach life as an actively shaping subject. In this way, they deprive themselves of the possibility of solving problems in a self-determined way, whatever the solution may be. To put it somewhat exaggeratedly, complaining is the solution to their problems, or rather the attention they receive as a result.

With regard to complaining types of clients, it is essential not to make the mistake of failing to acknowledge their situation, which they experience as unfortunate, as correspondingly *difficult.* This means that when *establishing contact* with the complaining client, it is also important to first acknowledge her decision to complain—instead of, for example, adopting an attitude of actively tackling problems. This is often not easy for inexperienced coaches. Accordingly, this coach is also struggling with his own counter-transference: He seems to react inwardly irritated to the client's behavior and would perhaps prefer to tell her not to be surprised that she is doing so badly. In such situations, it helps to become aware that complaining clients actually suffer from their situations, or rather their interpretations, even if they *could do* something about it. Since strong complaining is often a biographically acquired pattern that was once useful at an earlier point in the biography, e.g., to prevent something worse in the family of origin or to be heard at all, it is often not easy for clients to change this pattern. Therefore, the principle in dealing with complaining clients, in the spirit of psychotherapist Carl Rogers (e.g., 1951), is to invest enough time in building a sustainable *working relationship* in order, as Rogers puts it, to earn a confrontation first. In the present case, this would mean listening with compassion and without judgment to the client, and encouraging her to talk at length about her predicament. As already mentioned, it is important to show understanding for the situation that is experienced as difficult and to signal to the client that the client is taken seriously and understood. In coaching jargon, this is also referred to as "pacing", i.e., resonating in the client's world. Only by building up such a sustainable relationship and appreciating the situation that is subjectively experienced as difficult will the door probably open to exploring with the client the question of the extent to which it is possible to become active oneself in the awkward situation and, with respect and appreciation, to discard her dominant pattern of complaining and explore new paths (cf. on the central effect of coaching in the sense of changing dysfunctional patterns of interpretation and action: Schreyögg, 2012).

It seems—as can already be seen in the catchy case presentation—that the coach did not succeed in establishing a good contact with the client during the coaching. Instead, a very early analysis was made in the sense of a cognitive approach and little or nothing was achieved. It is not surprising that the effect of this coaching failed to materialize. Without the central impact factor of relationship (cf. also Mannhardt & d Haan, 2018)—as both coaching and psychotherapy research has already repeatedly demonstrated—the best techniques and approaches generally have no effect.

Claudia Beutter

Here, a coach is annoyed with the coachee; the evaluative choice of words is striking. There are hardly any statements about the coachee in the case description in which the empathy of the coach is clear. In contrast to empathizing, empathy means behaving in a way that helps or at least can help the other person because of empathy (cf. Bischof-Köhler, 1993). The place where empathy on the part of the coach can be assumed is that of the impulse to *shake the coachee*. However, an action in the helping sense was then missing. The coach's going along with the coachee could also have led to a sympathetic reaction, with the consequence of a clearly different description of the situation: The narrative would then rather contain the coachee's predicament, namely the circumstance of having to deal with a difficultly experienced situation for a while longer instead of being allowed to retire. Following this idea, it is also conceivable that the coach does not really immerse himself in the situation as the coachee sees it.

The coach seems to experience his coachee as rather static, unchangeable. He uses attributions that describe less a temporary experience of the coachee (e.g., she *is,* she *needs*, she *does*), instead of focusing on the coachee's experience and asking about this experience ("colleagues annoy her") in different situations, e.g., with the help of scaling questions and expressions (cf. Schmidt, 2016). In this way, he possibly underlines a gained impression of being stuck: Is so, remains so. This would explain a possible self-perception of not being able to do anything or move anything. This in turn would possibly be a similar experience to that of his coachee (cf. Bauer, 2011). His constant impulse to want to "shake" his coachee can be interpreted as an affective reaction. Also, the statement that nothing changed with his coachee suggests that the coach may have felt angry or helpless against the background of not becoming effective. The coach writes of *some insight* from the coachee *on the surface* which suggests a more cognitive approach based on an idea of how the problem could be solved.

The described approach of the coach suggests that he formed an accurate opinion of *how* the coachee's situation was. He possibly wanted to lead her to a different point of view with his questions. In the description the words "*felt sorry for*" *and* "*has to hold out*" speak for an empathy of the coach into the situation from which he wanted to get his coachee out. Possibly the coach lacked the confidence that something could be changed. *In* any case, having to persevere suggests that he found it similarly arduous to experience his interventions with the coachee.

Heidi Möller

I am particularly interested in the coach's intense affective reactions. If, according to our research (cf. Müller et al., 2020), coaches are in particularly good health, are highly motivated and more than satisfied with their lives, the confrontation with their own shadow in the client's inner mood is a challenge. Such disparate feelings about life and the maximally different life concepts behind them must be transformed into a sustainable working relationship. Self-employed, successful coaches meeting inwardly resigned clients—this is not easy. Pre-conscious envy on the part of the coaches may play a role. Just letting themselves go maybe a defensive attitude on their part. Especially since coaches with a fair amount of self-efficacy expectation are confronted with feelings of powerlessness by this type of clientele. These clients want to make us experience with all their might: Nothing works anymore! Impressions of a lack of manageability can also be highly infectious. Getting angry is then a way for professionals to keep these feelings at bay.

The coaching community at least pretends to be highly self-reflective: So what to do with a person who tends to externalize problems? An attitude of "I'm okay and everyone else is so-so to miserable" is very challenging for coaches. How do we ignite variability or change mental models in such a constellation?

The incompatibility of value systems also plays a role: Only interventions that are compatible with the value structure of our clients will be effective.

"On the surface, some insight has been gained," writes the colleague in the case study. It is an old Freudian idea that insight heals, along the lines that when things are understood, behavior, and experience change quasi-automatically. Through neuroscience research (see Ryba & Roth, 2019), we know this is not so. If the coaching was very cognitive, where situations are explained and coaching is insight mediation, the affective anchoring is missing. The theory of somatic markers (cf. Damasio, 2004) makes clear the importance of physical markers of past events. Only when the mind and somatic markers can be brought into harmony can change take place (cf. Storch & Weber, 2019).

If I understood the affective charge of the colleague—the shaking and wanting to be rough—as a countertransference reaction, it would be an aggressive reaction to a passive-aggressive behavior of the client, because that is what being constantly ill can also represent. Only the coach has his vital life expressions available—the client does not. In the concordant counter-transference, the coach feels like the client, this power could be mirrored and together we could search for more constructive processing modes that *empower*.

Understood differently, as complementary countertransference, the coach feels like the client's significant others, the question can continue: How might the client seem to her colleagues? Maybe she annoys the colleagues? Maybe she generates rejection with her passive-aggressive behavior and longs very much for appreciation? Then the approach would be: How can I become appealing to my colleagues and bosses?

Depending on the hypothesis, different strategies would be offered, which, however, would not exclude each other, but could complement each other in a meaningful way. In this way, the countertransference feelings would be usefully turned around.

However, the colleague's solution idea suggests that the distance remained, the client remained lonely.

2.6 Practical Example 6

Case Description

This is a one-to-one coaching process with a male, 42-year-old manager. The coachee is the head of a controlling department with complex controlling projects in an internationally active production company. He is married and father of a still small six-year-old daughter. Four appointments have taken place so far. My difficulty as a coach is that although the coachee formulates his central needs and concerns (working less, more time with his daughter, "Father's Day" once a week, sabbatical) in the first and subsequent appointments and sets out his next steps accordingly at the end of the coaching sequence, he forgets these at the start of the next sequence. He then starts each time with work-related challenges at the beginning and it takes a few rounds of deepening again until his core concerns are again the focus. In the last sequence, I addressed this difficulty and perception on my part and asked if perhaps these core concerns were not so central after all and other things were more important to him. He said, "No, no, that's true, that is most important to me, I just forget."

We then discussed how he could manage not to let these personal concerns take a back seat and what he needed to be able to stick to his core concerns. He then said that he needed pressure to remain true to these concerns. I asked him how he could build up this necessary pressure. He did not really know the answer to this. At the end of this fourth sequence, something interesting happened: A different or new difficulty. The coachee decided to ask his superior whether it would be possible to reduce his workload to 80% and at what point this could happen. This also seemed like a good next step. Again he slightly doubted whether he would then not forget it again. Rather as a joke I said: "You can let me know in two weeks what the result of the conversation with the boss was." To which he replied, "Oh, that's great, now that's the pressure I need!" In retrospect, in reflection, I realized that I'm not really comfortable with this pressure-giving role. The coachee is thus assigning me a role that I, as a coach, cannot and will not take on. I will discuss this difficulty of taking on too much responsibility for the client's goals with him next time. I am convinced that the inner drive for an action cannot come from external pressure, especially not from the pressure from a coachee, because there is a danger of transference here.

How Did the Coach Go About It?

As a coach, I find this alternation of content levels (personal concerns or wishes versus professional role issues, organizational aspects) in coaching challenging, because on the one hand I don't want to control the coachee too much in terms of content and at the same time I want to remind him of his inner motives. I then sense in myself an inner restlessness and also a certain lack of interest in these rather superficial remarks, which in my opinion miss the point. In these cases, I make remarks like, "Now, do these issues have anything in common or to do with your concern for spending more time with your daughter or your concern for working less?" For me, mirroring as well as addressing irritations with me as a coach are also promising interventions in such cases. With the above case, I am also very open about the content direction, as it is unclear what the coachee's core issues are. I think he is searching and it could be, after all, a completely different issue that is really bothering him. For the time being, I support him more in searching than in implementing solutions.

Eric Lippmann

My first hypothesis in this case again concerns the referral context: His wife may have suggested coaching to him so that he can achieve a better balance between the fields of life. I've often seen men not necessarily want to go to counseling themselves, but wives advise them to or even tell them they need it. Another hypothesis is that it is an ambivalence. There are voices within him that say he needs to work 100%, if not 120%, to be successful at all in his career. That is, after all, why professional issues are burning on his mind. Then I'm sure there are voices that say he should have more time for his daughter. Interestingly, the wife is never an issue, only the daughter. That raises other hypotheses.

Besides clarifying the referral context: Who has what concerns about the coaching and who would see what as a good outcome of the coaching? On the one hand, I would ask about the inner voices that come up in the coachee regarding the concern "more time for the daughter, less work." On the other hand, I would explore with him whether he has already had similar situations in his life where he should have decided and then actually pursued his solution—without external pressure. How did he deal with such situations at that time, when perhaps a voice inside him also said: Without external pressure it won't work. If he reports successes, the next step would be to ask whether and how he could transfer this pattern of success to the current situation.

If he can't report a pattern of success, then I would look to see if there are external people or even voices within him that could take on the role of pressurer if that seems to serve him well. As a coach, I would avoid getting into that role because it risks making the coachee somewhat dependent on the coach.

In the concept of hypnosystemic counseling (cf. Schmidt, 2004, 2005) it is always central to ask about the effects of all solution patterns:

- What would happen if he actually worked only 80% with correspondingly less pay?
- What impact would this have and on whom: Wife, daughter, superiors, career, colleagues, etc.?

The question about the effects usually brings good explanations as to why someone tends to focus on pursuing a goal or give it up. This is based on the hypothesis that there were previously good reasons for not pursuing the reduction of the workload.

Regarding solutions of the case maker, two points stand out to me:

The coach's statement regarding disinterest "in these rather superficial remarks": If the coach makes an assessment of which topics are superficial and what could be possible core topics, then he takes too much responsibility. In the concept of inner voices, which are obviously present in the client, it is precisely important that the client sort out his inner voices and brings them into an optimal line-up with regard to his concerns. Exploratory questions on the part of the coach can be very helpful. Should the client come to the conclusion that the reduction to 80% is not the right way after all, then this is a result that the coach can question for possible effects. However, a judgment would be out of place.

Addressing irritations from me as a coach can certainly be a helpful intervention, I agree with the case giver. In this way, the original assignment—to have more time for the daughter—can be questioned once again. A further exploration of what the client is actually about can be supported. Only when it is clear what the client's core concern is, does it make sense to start exploring solutions.

Robert Wegener

In the case presented, the impression arises that the coach is working with her client unilaterally on a block of topics, although the client is possibly caught in a conflict of goals with other topics. For example, the coach talks about central needs, namely "working less, more time with the daughter," Father's Day" once a week, sabbatical". However, the client apparently finds it difficult to work on these in the time between coaching sessions. Concerns that the client brings in at the beginning of each new session are then often of a professional nature, which irritates the coach. In the case description, it remains unclear to what extent the coach has differentiatedly clarified with the client in the *contract phase* what importance and significance these topics actually have for him.

In the following, I introduce a content hypothesis as to why the client is not succeeding in effectively working through his issues. The argument for this content hypothesis is that the client holds on to these issues during several sessions and, when asked by the coach whether the concerns are perhaps not so important to him after all, counters: "No, no, that's true, it is most important to me, I just forget about it." If one follows the assessment that the issues are indeed important to the client, it can be assumed that he is caught in a conflict of goals in the sense of the *content hypothesis* (cf. Grant, 2018; Locke et al., 1994). This would mean the client wants to address the stated issues, but other concerns pointing in a different direction are getting in the way. As a result, the client is correspondingly ambivalent: He wants to achieve the goals described, but is not really committed to doing so.

As a classic solution-focused *intervention,* it would be appropriate to scale the stated goals to their importance and difficulty and to ensure that they are goals and not vague issues, e.g.:

- How important is this goal to you on a scale from 0 (not at all important) to 10 (maximally important)?
- On a scale of 0 (not at all difficult) to 10 (maximally difficult, but achievable if I apply myself to the maximum), how difficult do you consider it to be to achieve this goal?

In the sense of a diagnostic value, it could be checked in this way how motivated the client is for his goals. The importance would indicate the attractiveness of the goals, while the difficulty would indicate the client's self-efficacy, i.e., the degree to which he is convinced that he can achieve the goals. If the values for importance were rather low or for difficulty rather high, both would be diagnostically relevant indications for the coach. If one follows my above case assessment, the *hypothesis* suggests that the client rates his goals highly in terms of importance and difficulty.

Based on such a hypothesis, the question would become central as to what makes it so difficult for the client to achieve his private goals. In the sense of a *methodological hypothesis,* there are now various suitable *interventions for* this. Following the coaching concept underlying Geißler's virtual goal-achievement coaching (cf. Wegener, 2019, p. 126ff.), there are two fundamentally different possible answers to this question. Either the client does not have the necessary skills to achieve these goals, or something is holding him back and slowing him down. Clients are usually good at deciding which of the two possibilities applies. The client's answer would then be the starting point for working out a learning and development goal that can help the client to achieve his formulated outcome goal (cf. above) and overcome the existing ambivalence in his behavior.

An alternative, but related approach would be to work with the affect balance according to Maja Storch and Frank Krause (cf. Storch & Krause, 2017). The affect balance is used to clarify how much positive (maximum 100%) and how much negative feelings (maximum 100%) a client feels toward a topic. Storch and Krause (2017) argue that only when someone experiences 100% positive and 0% negative feelings toward a goal can they pursue it with full vigor. In the present case, it is reasonable to assume that the client also has negative feeling components. The central question in coaching would then be to what extent the client can succeed in reducing his negative emotional components. Last but not least, the work with the inner team (cf. Schulz von Thun, 2019) through the identification of inner voices in the sense of *hypothesis formation* would also provide information about which forces in the client have a positive effect on his goals and which have a more restraining effect.

In this case study, the coach has not (yet) succeeded in sufficiently grasping all aspects relevant to the coaching topic at hand as well as the client's inner dynamics. However, the statement "I think he is searching and it could be, after all, a completely different issue" indicates an opening. It will now be important that the coach does not throw out the baby with the bathwater, i.e., that instead of an either/or position she adopts a both/and perspective. This means that she invites the client to consider all the issues that are relevant for him.

Claudia Beutter

The coach perceives the recurring circling around the core concern as demanding. What the coach sees as the difficulty in concrete terms is not clear to me. The obstacle on the way to the solution for the coachee? The obstacle to effectively accompany the achievement of the agreed goals as a coach? Perhaps both?

In the case described, the coach discloses her perceptions and learns that her coachee considers pressure to be necessary in order to stick to his personal goals. The coach's question about ideas on how the coachee could build up this pressure himself remains without an answer. It would be interesting to ask where the pressure comes from in the work context (there seems to be enough here) or where the pressure for his goals could come from in his private life. The coach does not want to control her coachee "too much" in terms of content, but would she like to? She might assume that—instead of external pressure—there should be intrinsic motivation to achieve a change. The coach's lack of interest could be investigated: perhaps through non-targeted communication (circling around the core concerns)?

Based on the assumption that the coachee always behaves sensibly, it could be considered what function circling fulfils for him. The question of the role a coach should have in the implementation of plans can be part of the coaching contract or declared in one's own understanding of coaching. The fact that it preoccupies the coach could be an indication to pursue the issue of goal orientation. The described solution to support the coachee in the search suggests that a "recontracting" (in the form of negotiating a new goal) was undertaken. Whether this was done explicitly with the coachee or is implicitly intended as a solution for maintaining the coach's interest remains open in the account.

The juxtaposition of the terms work-related challenges and core concerns suggests that the two issues are to be considered separately and that the work-related issues are to be addressed only in the service of the core concerns (time with daughter, time, etc.).

However, the issues are interconnected, at least through the aspect of time. If more time is spent on one issue, less is available for the other.

It could be the coachee's unconscious other goals or needs that contradict their core concerns. Kegan and Lahey (2009) have developed an interesting approach to this. They believe that such concerns are about identifying why a person repeatedly engages in behaviors that contradict the serious and openly declared goal. They call this the "immunity to change," behind which is a kind of belief system. They recommend an approach designed to identify this predicament and to gradually review and update the beliefs involved.

The fact that the coachee suggests his coach as a source of pressure suggests to me that he thinks he can't do it on his own. The coach suggests as a joke to put pressure on him, but then does not pursue the topic of pressure further. Exploring the pressure needed by asking questions might yield insights for implementation or for obstacles to implementing the core concerns. The coach could thus approach the support of the search hypnosystemically and thus systematically make the inner processes tangible, conscious, and ultimately changeable for the coachee.

Heidi Möller

The case vividly shows that it is an illusion to sharply separate work- and life-related counseling. The client's concern can only be understood from the perspective of the role bearer and the private person. The diverging goals of the two inner instances call out to be integrated.

The example also shows a typical, normative discourse. The change in the world of work goes hand in hand with a change in values. Many of the young employees want to live and work. In order not to be different from the mainstream, they need a demonstration of a value structure in front of their own superego: I want to have time for the family and work less. In coaching, the resilience of this attitude would have to be tapped. Does the coachee really want this or is it perhaps much more interesting to work than to deal with the growing daughter? *In dubio pro libido*: In coaching, a space has to be made possible to get to know the real needs, to possibly detach oneself from superego messages of having to be a faithful family father and to name things as they really are. Admitting to oneself that one prefers to work and to accept the private conflicts that come along with it can also be a topic in coaching. Completely different levels of intervention would then open up. If he had the need, then it seems to be difficult to implement it. An unclear need seems to me to have to be clarified first. Perhaps the coachee is not seeking a changed gender ratio. Coaching means ideological openness.

The coach in the case study refuses to act as an implementation supporter. Why actually? If we follow a concept of coaching influenced by behavioral therapy (cf. Greif & Benning-Rohnke, 2015), this element is part of it. Action goals are often not practically implemented. Research and experience suggest that the insufficient formulation of concrete implementation intentions as well as the lack of support in the stabilization of new behavioral routines are decisive for this. According to a panel survey, in projects with implementation support, target achievement in the area of profitability improved by 29% and in the aspect of growth orientation by as much as 105% (cf. Greif & Benning-Rohnke, 2015, p. 25).

A look into the future of coaching makes me claim that the combination of face-to-face coaching with digital implementation support tools (texts, apps) is promising and can increase the effectiveness of coaching.

I can well empathize with the coach's hesitancy to be a tamer if the source of this desire is a Theory X view of man: "Man is unwilling and fundamentally has an aversion to change and tries to avoid it." Theory Y, on the other hand, states, "Man is intrinsically motivated and committed to shaping his life toward greater satisfaction" (cf. Schreyögg & von Werder, 2004). In the case of the existence of a pessimistic anthropological premise, the biographical background of such a mental model would have to be examined in order to allow a possibly more useful view of man to gain space.

2.7 Practical Example 7

Case Description

A coachee reports on her work at the Youth Welfare Office in legal counseling for unaccompanied minor refugees. Her dedication and commitment were not really recognized by her superiors. Standing up strongly for the best interests of the child was not a top priority. The priority was rather not to stand out and to get along with the courts and the political will of the current government. She had worn herself out over time and was already showing symptoms of exhaustion. In the beginning, she had such a tremendous need to talk that I, as a coach, almost couldn't get a word in edgewise. This helplessness also paralyzed me. In the following sessions, it was helpful that she could learn to respect her own limits again, to take a step back in her commitment with regard to superiors, team, and cooperation partners. We discussed possibilities and developed things that were relieving for her, and she learned to deal with herself in a mindful and kind way. But the resignation about work remained. Since she has only one year until her retirement, this situation is very difficult for her to bear.

How Did the Coach Go About It?

As I mentioned, the need to talk almost overwhelmed me in the beginning. She had such a strong need to get things off her chest that interventions on my part did not really reach her. I then discussed this case in an intervision with colleagues and was much more confident in dealing with it afterward. Focusing on herself and being less fixated on the outside was a key that allowed her to come to peace. This was also reflected in her statement: "With you I always become so calm."

Eric Lippmann

The first thing that is important for me here is also in which (referral) context this consultation takes place. Is it supervision in the context of the organization, so supervision of these social workers? And then do I have the mandate of the organization and what is that? Like: Make sure that the social workers regulate themselves better and sit here not as political citizens but as role bearers of an authority. Or is it a client who comes to me of her own accord and pays me? What would be her mission? I would incorporate the answer into my work. The predicament described would probably be reflected in the assignment to me: "This helplessness also paralyzed me." This focus of helplessness runs through as a theme. Refugees are often helpless and then there is the client. That is already this mirror effect, which would be central for me.

What resonates particularly with me, in this case, is the age-old debate I know from psychotherapy: Are we more supportive of people enduring difficult situations? So we are oil in the gears of difficult situations. Or are we also a bit of a disruptor in the whole system? What is our task in the helping professions? And the question: What is the concern of this person who has come here? And depending on the context, her statement "Her dedication and commitment were not really recognized by her superiors" would not be interpreted as a success.

When I read the approach of the coach, the thought that I have already expressed comes to mind: Are we a sedative to the clients as well? Is it our job to keep people calm so that they function well?

Robert Wegener

In the sense of the *contract*, the goal in the present coaching case is obviously to help the client to adapt to the situation given by the Youth Welfare Office. The client should learn to come to terms with the guidelines of the Youth Welfare Office or to come to terms with them and to better respect her own limits. This contrasts with the client's original strategy of working for the best interests of the child to the point of exhaustion. It seems clear that the coaching did not reach far enough and important facets were not captured. It is difficult to explain the client's professional dissatisfaction and resignation at the end of the coaching in any other way.

In accordance with the objective, the client probably did not engage in any in-depth discussion of her own professional identity in the present coaching session. Furthermore, it was probably not clarified to what extent the client could use existing leeway in the design of her professional role in order to create at least a certain fit between the demands of the organization and her own demands, and she would not have had to completely renounce her own demands, as is the case now. Connected to this is the *content-related hypothesis* that the client does not have a differentiated, elaborated idea of her professional role. In a role-playing coaching (cf., e.g., Lippmann, 2013, p. 24ff.; Eck, 1990) such a differentiated discussion would take place precisely. In the process, the client would have been able to recognize for herself, for example, that in certain cases she can prioritize the best interests of the child, and in other cases she should follow the restrained official strategy; with an overall positive effect also on her professional sense of meaning and self-image. In a role-playing coaching session, the client could have further discussed how she can have a positive impact on how she is perceived by her professional environment. Standing up for the best interests of the child does not have to mean making a fuss per se.

Another *content-related hypothesis* could be that the client does not have a clear enough professional identity and that it could be useful to work with her on this. A possible *intervention* for this would be the Logical Levels Model (cf. Dilts, 1994). The logical levels model distinguishes six different levels of human action and being: Environment, behavior, skills, values, identity, and meaning. On the basis of this model, the client might have been able to identify what is particularly important to her professionally on the different levels—for example, in the sense of values guiding her actions, professional identity, or sense of purpose. It may have provided options for how she could realize these ambitions outside her current workplace, for example, in the form of committed volunteering. A more mindful and friendly, or at least more relaxed, approach to herself in her current workplace might then have come about of its own accord.

In the sense of an evaluation of the coaching, the coach was able to help the client with regard to the symptoms of exhaustion described at the beginning. However, the impression of having had a calming—if not already sedating—effect should not obscure the fact that the client's professional motivation (cf. Schmidbauer, 1977) to champion the issue of child welfare was not really addressed. It looks quite as if the client, speaking in the language of orthodox medicine, had been given a sedative pill, which apparently also took away some of her vital energy.

Claudia Beutter

In the case described, it seems that someone is wearing herself out over time to the point of exhaustion and has an "tremendous need to talk." To me, this suggests that the chafing is not verbal, but internal. This is where it might be helpful to relieve the pent-up friction via talking. I see a similarity between the coach's experience in coaching (barely getting a word in edgewise, feeling paralyzed) and her coachee's helplessness. The coachee can't change things, can only decide for herself to do things differently. This seems to be condoned rather than appreciated. Working with the coachee seems to focus on managing one's own resources. What strikes me in the description is that *this situation is very difficult for her to bear*—not because retirement is a long time away, but because it's *only* a year away. It sounds to me like she doesn't has enough time to fundamentally change anything. Resignation at the end of such an intense and personally committed job can have a negative impact on the time afterward.

There is no statement of where the coaching idea comes from, who gives the order, and what goal the coachee herself has brought in. What does the woman want now? How does she want to shape her last year, how does she want to transition into retirement? She seems overly committed to the best interests of the child. My hypothesis is that, via a greater awareness of the connection between her professional identity and her values, she might loosen the connection with her supervisor's values and esteem. That the coachee has, at best, a longing goal that her supervisor be as value-oriented in content as she is seems understandable to me. Another issue that seems important to me is the very high degree of overlap between person and role. She puts her professional heart and soul into it, so to speak—after all, life and limb are at stake. This could mean that she perceives her personal being and her professional role as a unity, which is doubly difficult with such an explosive topic. Fatigue, also as a result of a lack of opportunity to distance oneself, is quite conceivable.

I can imagine that the client can be won over to a path that is oriented toward the best interests of the child. In my opinion, this would be possible for addressing her tiredness and also if it is about a reinterpretation of the non-recognition of this superior.

Heidi Möller
I could create two different scenarios: What would my assignment be if here is a woman, exhausted in work that is meaningful to her, sitting in front of me? What would I do then? That would certainly be very different than if there was a mandate from the organization that said, "Watch out that people don't get sick on me. See that not too much is decided here contrary to the government option!"

With such a highly explosive, current, political topic, the coach's abstinence is particularly difficult. All of us, regardless of our function, are always citizens and political people, and we have to balance that well. If I'm reading between the lines correctly, the coach has a guiding principle: It's good to take a step back. There's a prevailing notion: If you're exhausted, then you need to work less. Is that the answer?

Also, in her role as a youth welfare worker I have leeway in making decisions: Do I want to be rebellious? Then I have to pay the price for not getting recognition. Then I get the recognition from my moral superiority. I can choose to do that. But here we are talking more about the amount of work, less about the attitude. To me, the coaching client makes herself very sympathetic by struggling to find the right path. The coach could support her in that: How does she want to hold it? I see something very vital in this, to strengthen the client to find her own style of working and not to dictate mine.

However, I would first ask about patterns in the relationship with superiors. The client has a long career history and if she has repeatedly struggled with the requirements of a job, this could be an indication of an unresolved Oedipal conflict. Then the there-and-then could be looked at and how it is reenacted in the here-and-now of the current work situation. Resolving the transference could make a major developmental step possible. The question could be asked: Why do I need the recognition of the organization? The question could be redefined: I work with joy, without someone constantly having to say: "You did that beautifully." Then, beyond the working period, a wonderful development of autonomy could be possible, which is also useful in the private sphere. In the transition to retirement, the challenge arises to live in the future without someone to mirror the performance. The client can learn to become independent and this seems to me a good preparation "out of the job."

I really like that the coach didn't fall into the trap of replacing the boss and giving the missing credit. That's a trap you sometimes fall into as a coach. That didn't happen in this case, instead here she was able to abstain from this.

2.8 Practical Example 8

Case Description

The coachee came with the concern that overall she was overloaded with her professional and private situation. She had a 30-hour job as a project manager, but worked about 50 hours a week. Even after she had put the three small children to bed, she would sit down at the PC again. The au pair is not a real relief, as she also has to be managed closely. She is constantly pressed for time and can't really get involved even when she is with the children, and her thoughts easily drift off to work. She blocked my attempts to question her professional self-management with the following remark: Everything was already optimized, but there were simply too many meetings that she absolutely had to attend. She was also very pressed for time in the coaching sessions and the progress of the coaching process was too slow for her. She could not carve out two hours or more for coaching so often. She was only able to take my approach that it was important, especially in her situation, to slow down her life and question her current job as well as other elements of her system to the extent that she started conversations about changing jobs at her company. She did not have time for mindfulness exercises and meditations. Ultimately, she discontinued the coaching by not signing up for another appointment and forfeiting the remainder of the package fee she had already paid.

What Was the Coach's Approach?

My attempts to make it clear to the coachee that her concern could not be solved with an even faster coaching process, she could not accept. In the course of the process, she became more and more demanding for advice on how to change her situation quickly. She did not want to engage in solving her concern with the resources she already had. My partial refusal to present her with solutions laid out made her more and more dissatisfied. My guess is that she then came to believe that I, as a coach, could not help her.

Wolfgang Knopf

An extremely stressful situation in which the gender issue immediately catches my eye: If she came to me, the question arises in my mind whether she chose me as a man and what significance that has. First thesis: Whatever this is about, the inequalities between women and men in the world of work and in society as a whole are an important background detail.

"The coachee came with the concern that overall she was overloaded with her professional and private situation," the coach reports. This concern describes the situation, but not a wish, a mandate for coaching. One can assume that a change is desired, but in what direction, in what form, remains unclear. Thus, coaching joins the other tasks to be accomplished, and like all other demands is a task to be done efficiently. Coaching does not represent a break in the lived pattern. Like everything else, coaching is evaluated for quick effectiveness. Since this was not given from the coachee's point of view, the coaching was discontinued.

The establishment of a sustainable working alliance is a challenge and difficulty here. A first impulse to offer a totally decelerated space in coaching, to simply do nothing as a coach in order to let something emerge, however, seems to be overtaxing the coachee and not appropriate. It seems very difficult in the traditional setting not to be seduced into further misguided self-optimization in coaching. Any verbalization, visualization, ultimately any traditional method remains locked in the mode of efficiency because—I assume—the coachee knows these methods and uses them as a project manager.

In this specific case, I would suggest a method that I learned from Peter Heintel and that I use repeatedly in coaching with managers: Walking together. Peripatetics[2] recognized the support of walking for thinking and reflecting ages ago. The option of adapting to the subject at the speed of walking while thinking and reflecting can open up new and different levels of experience. Point of entry is the body. By always being in motion, something is happening—whatever it may be. It may open up a slowed-down space for reflection for coaching.

Kornelia Steinhardt

The coachee's situation is not an isolated case for women in management positions. A social contradiction can be discerned that places women who want to reconcile both demanding professional activities and family in an almost irresolvable double-bind situation: Either the professional commitment or the family suffers—it is the woman's fault who fails to manage both. The support systems that should benefit both sexes are still not sufficiently established. Similarly, there is a lack of societal willingness to develop a different attitude here. The way many organizations deal with these double burdens for women reflects this dynamic. The coachee described here seems caught in this contradiction and probably unconsciously experiences herself as guilty of not living up to the demands, which triggers shame that in turn must be warded off. Apparently, no space is allowed to be opened in which to reflect on why the coachee has to torture herself so much in order to perform as perfectly as possible in both areas of life.

A counter-transference analysis makes it clear that the coachee's pressure is so high that one can only fail as a coach in the end: Never meeting the coachee's conscious and unconscious demands, just as she herself never meets her excessive demands. Therefore, the essential first step is to build a trusting and stable working alliance. This can only be achieved if the coachee's overload and pressure are sufficiently acknowledged and the coach can, in a sense, become the container of the coachee's unbearable feelings. This includes taking the coachee's unbearable feelings and translating them into acceptable

[2] Followers of the teachings of Aristotle.

thoughts. By this, it is meant that the coach conveys a lot of understanding and meets the coachee's needs first. This could mean, for example, not holding two-hour coaching sessions, but arranging shorter sessions. Once a trusting working alliance has been successfully established, work can be done to better understand why this pressure does not seem resolvable for the coachee. Work can also be done on how she can grant herself relief—both in the work situation and in the family situation. Thus, in a first step, more self-enlightenment could take place without massively affecting the coachee's functioning defenses. Based on this, possibly smaller and larger strategies of self-relief can be worked on together with her.

The temptation in this process is great to either exert pressure as a coach and thus confirm the coachee in her unconscious feelings of guilt or to get stuck in the process of recognizing and understanding the personal mechanisms. The balance between insight and strategy development must be kept in mind.

Ursula Hermann

Here, a coachee is reported to have high expectations of herself as a manager, mother, household manager, and woman, which overwhelm her. Counseling is always a place where socially explosive questions are focused on. The compatibility of work, family, and private life is one such issue: It is discussed in the media, politically framed by measures and legal regulations. In coaching—as in this case—it is reduced to an individual problem of supposedly correct optimization.

The mechanistic view of optimization is countered by the coach with deceleration. A look at these different word images makes it clear that they are opposites and mutually exclusive. While deceleration may give particularly stressed people space to reflect, in this case it must be questioned how an optimization of needs can be decelerated, which only functions with a certain degree of speed and for whose success something like mindfulness is only sand in the gears.

The coachee comes with the request to find relief both professionally and privately. It must be very frustrating when everything has already been optimized and yet there is still what seems to be an unattainable optimum to be achieved. This frustration, incomprehensibility, and despair must be given a space in coaching, taken up and held, as Bion's model (1992) of container-contained describes (cf. Lazar, 1994). In this way, a working alliance can be formed that gives space ("container") to fears, insecurities, and exhaustion as well as a foothold ("contained") and from which the coachee can develop something that actually suits her.

I would try to create this space and access to the coachee through the terminology she uses, such as the linguistic image of optimization. Metaphors (cf. Lakoff & Johnson, 1997) permeate our everyday life, our language, our thoughts, and our actions. In working with metaphors, it is possible to pause and at the same time look at the coachee herself and her actions and ideas without her finding herself in a complete deceleration, doing nothing. Because this idleness can trigger something very unsettling, especially in people who are extremely tense.

Language images, which are conceived and articulated by the coachee, connect perception, bodily experience, emotions as well as rational thinking and establish a social context (cf. Kohl, 2007). This is relevant in this coaching process, as not only the demands and requirements from the coachee find an expression, but also her environment and social imprint become clear. Thus, in addition to functional optimization, feelings, wishes and resources can be added that the coachee does not directly mention. It is not easy to find joy about achievements and successes in a life that is experienced as a constant toil of optimization. It is precisely the ambiguity and subjectivity of language images that is a valuable intervention method (cf. Münch, 2001) and resource for giving these parts of the coachee's life a space.

Heidi Möller

How can lust and passion return to such a joyless life? The burden of the coachee touches me strongly. For this client, life is nothing more than working through problems. The entire daily routine resembles a to-do list. Nowhere do real encounters seem to take place, not even in coaching, one appointment of many to be worked through. She also can't play with the children without thinking about work or perceiving the game itself as work.

As is well-known, stress does not exist, but only evaluations of situations lead to the experience of being overwhelmed. The dominant mental model here is the individualization of a societal problem, the fact that we are still far away from the principle of gender equality in organizations (cf. Möller & Müller-Kalkstein, 2014).

The coachee individualizes this social problem: If only she controls, manages, and organizes everything properly, the stress is fixed. With the idea of coming to rest through self-optimization, the client must remain trapped in chronic feelings of insufficiency. Role-related demands on the modern woman cannot be met by her (cf. Möller, 2012). They are contradictory and unattainable and do not infrequently lead to mental illness if these paradoxes cannot be seen. Thus, the coachee remains a hamster in the wheel.

To renounce, to cut back, to say no offensively; what would happen if the coachee tried this? What would she then come into contact with? Breaking the prevailing pattern could risk decompensation: What happens to her once things go quiet and there is no problem to solve? Externalized, this would mean she would appear unfemininely aggressive in the company. In internalizing mode, she might become depressed. This seems to be what the coach is afraid of and so the two have not been in contact. The working relationship cannot be addressed: "What's going on here with the two of us?"

A burden for the working relationship is the, I suspect, passionate occupation of the topic of excessive demands. It seems to me that the coachee is also proud of her commitment. Who is she apart from diligence and commitment? The risk of facing this question seems too high for both participants.

2.9 Practical Example 9

Case Description

A department head felt very stressed because he had an above-average staff-to-management ratio and did not feel supported by his boss. The coaching process went in the direction that I supported him to work less with algorithms and process definitions, but to focus more on the self-direction competence of his teams and to develop it. In a coaching session, he suddenly told me he was highly spiritual, deeply steeped in Buddhist ideas, and could solve many problems through meditation. In fact, I was completely surprised and have to admit to myself that I didn't think he was authentic at this point. The coaching ended after one more session. He still assigned me to talk to his group leaders. Afterward, we conducted a joint supervision with him and his group leaders. In the end, all the measures led to him avoiding "sandwiching" himself quite cleverly. He left employee management to his group leaders, and strategic management to his supervisors. Basically, he has made himself superfluous.

What Was the Coach's Approach?

I discussed with him how his spiritual strength and activities in this regard could help with his leadership problems. He did not elaborate on this. His answers seemed to me to be scripted.

Kornelia Steinhardt

The head of the department describes the typical difficulties as a middle manager in the "sandwich" position. For managers on the second or third level, shaping their role is a particular challenge, as they have leadership responsibility toward their employees and at the same time experience demands and often pressure from their superiors. In this area of tension, it is important for managers to shape their own role in such a way that pressure coming from above is not passed on unfiltered to the employees and, conversely, that they do not become the mouthpiece for the employees' concerns upwards.

In the foreground of the case described is the clarification of the function as middle manager: What demands are made on the design of this function in the company and how does the coachee design his role against this background? What causes him so much stress and how does he interpret and shape his role differently? This has to be considered from both sides: How does he lead the different teams and their group leaders? To what extent is it his job to lead the members of the individual teams? Or can this be delegated to the group leaders and he supports the group leaders? The coachee would thus take on the responsibility that he misses with his superior. On the other hand, it is important to work out what expectations and support he himself needs from his boss. How is it possible to convey to her what level of leadership and support he himself needs? With this approach, the coachee might experience that his rather technical design of the leadership position ultimately increased stress. With this other form of role design and implementation support in coaching, it could be possible in the positive case to get out of the stress spiral. In this respect, the strategy of supporting the self-direction competence of the teams is a way in this direction.

The mention of spiritual competence could be understood as the coachee's self-awareness of not merely having technical competences, but also of knowing an approach to himself that brings out other aspects of his personality. Even if it seems incoherent at first, this could be taken up in the way of considering in coaching to what extent he can use his Buddhist ideas and meditative competences constructively in the context of his understanding of leadership and his attitude in the sense of coping with the leadership tasks. It could be worked out which abilities he perceives in himself in this segment and what significance they can have for the professional role.

Ursula Hermann

A head of the department with very extensive leadership responsibilities has solved in the coaching process all the things that originally led him into coaching: The leadership responsibility is shifted to other hierarchical levels, the stress is gone, he still has his job. A successful coaching process? No, at least not from the coach's point of view. Because the coachee's confession of being "highly spiritual" is questioned by the coach and perceived as inauthentic. Moreover, the coachee ultimately makes himself "superfluous" as a leader. What is actually irritating here? The coachee's desire to highlight his or her special characteristics at the end of the coaching process? That not only the coachee has made himself superfluous as a leader, but in the end the coach is no longer needed either? How much non-understanding is actually allowed to remain in a coaching process?

Much has been accomplished in this process. Relying on the self-direction skills of the teams and thus minimizing the staff-to-management ratio has had the effect that the coachee hoped for. A fitting intervention. Also, despite irritation, the working alliance does not seem to be completely out of kilter, because other assignments still took place and could be implemented well. The very sudden introduction of spirituality caused incomprehension on the part of the coach. Sometimes it is enough here to admit to oneself that even as a coach one doesn't understand everything. Geißler (2011) described two phenomena in his essay on understanding and also not understanding in counseling, which are also evident in the case described: First, a coachee can only present himself as a subject in the counseling setting if he can be sure that he has not been understood in *everything*. In this coaching process spirituality is such a point, which is not comprehensible for the coach, but obviously important for the coachee. Further work assignments are not affected by it, so the spirituality can remain as something that has meaning for the coachee. The coach does not have to understand this, on the contrary, Geißler (2011) sometimes sees in the coachee a wish to intervene with the coach: "Please don't understand every little bit of me!" On the other hand, this shows that the coach is a necessary superfluity. The superfluous coaches are remembered because they have ensured that one has developed further, experienced a *greater degree* of autonomy and can now enjoy this without advice (cf. Geißler, 2011).

Wolfgang Knopf

At first, stressed by the high management margin and the lack of support from the boss and then completely relaxed. This relaxation did not come about through the coach's interventions, but through spirituality, which apparently suddenly appeared, solved all the problems and thus also made the coach superfluous.

It is striking that the coach does not know what to do with the coachee's confession that he can solve all problems from now on through spirituality and mediation, and is even surprised by this statement and cannot accept it. It seems almost like a break-off of the working relationship by the coach. The coachee's reaction to the question of how his spiritual strength could help with his leadership problems confirms the break in the working alliance. The coach still seems distant, even dismissive of the coachee's attitude, but does not address this.

One repetition stands out: The boss does not support the coachee, has withdrawn support. In personal coaching, the coach withdraws support from the coachee once the topic of Buddhism comes up. In the end, the coachee withdraws his support from his group leaders and no longer takes his responsibility in the sandwich position.

The thesis and question that arises is: How is leadership responsibility lived out in this organization? Are there really superfluous levels of leadership? Since I assume his coaching is paid for by the organization, the result of a triangulation would be intriguing. How would the boss formulate the coaching assignment for her department head?

Heidi Möller

The named spirituality of the coachee leads to devaluation on the part of the coach. Yes, he seems almost angry. Might the quotation: Thou shalt have no other gods beside me! play a role? Even I, as an agnostic, would find it difficult to respect other models of effectiveness that are the opposite of what my scientifically based professional coaching theories say.

If the goal of the coaching was to develop the self-control competence of his team, then the coach was very successful after all. This high level of competence reminds me of a statement made by a board member of an automotive company: "My goal is to make the corporate processes so functional that my desk is empty." This is how the coaching process could be described as absolutely successful. The coachee managed to get his people working and he had time for strategic questions. It is a pity that the coach comments so critically on himself.

2.10 Practical Example 10

Case Description

On recommendation, the coachee turned to me because he could not manage a strategically important project well. In this project, he was supposed to get independent production managers of a corporation to cooperate more and in this way optimize the results of several subsidiaries. I was invited to conduct a participant observation during a meeting. In the following coaching session I was asked to give feedback on my observations. This session was exceedingly difficult for me because my impressions could not be shared in any way by my coachee. I reported back that he had pressured a production board member in a conflict situation without investigating what the reasons were for his actions. The production supervisor then ganged up on my coachee with a colleague and suggested that the work group be dissolved if an open exchange could not take place. My coachee then broke off the meeting and announced another meeting for the future. In my session, the scene from the meeting repeated itself. When he didn't feel understood, he suggested breaking off the session and offered to get back to me later.

What Was the Coach's Approach?

I offered to my coachee that we both obviously experienced and evaluated the meeting differently, and suggested that we examine our observations side by side. The coachee reacted angrily to this and said that I obviously didn't understand anything about such a power play. He felt that I had not understood him properly and that I had criticized him unfairly. I explained that I thought he had a very difficult job to do and that I was convinced that the other meeting participants would act very tactically. This intervention resulted in temporary reassurance. Later, when I described that he had been pressuring his meeting partner, he interrupted me and said it was pointless to talk to me about it. I offered that perhaps I had unfairly criticized or offended him, which he refused to accept. After that he broke off the contact prematurely.

Brigitte Fritschle

My first question is: Has the task of the coach been properly agreed and clearly communicated to all participants in the meeting? Does the group of production managers know about the task that a participant observation is supposed to perform? My first impression is: Probably not.

In any case, the coach is kind of a foreign body. I can hardly imagine a hotter potato than this assignment. This is where action-oriented and, as a rule, performance-oriented managers come together who can be very direct and clear in their reactions. The coach needs to be able to connect, which makes sense if he knows the tasks and the rules of the game of such a group.

A group of high-ranking managers will not allow themselves to be observed by a complete stranger without knowledge of the goal, task, and possible result of such a measure, even if the actual assignment should focus on one of the managers.

From the case description, I conclude that the coach expressed himself very authentically to his coaching partner, with clear and direct, possibly directive feedback. If that was the case, I think that would be a cardinal mistake. In my experience, no manager endures and accepts potentially critical feedback—certainly not at the beginning of a process and without a sufficient basis of trust. Managers at this level have a clear self-image of their position and role. Building trust takes time and personal commitment on the part of the coach.

The coach's desire to give feedback is not unusual. At this point, however, I think more attention needs to be paid to style, atmosphere, and the quality of communication. Feedback can be a sharp sword or an elegant foil. The latter is more appropriate here.

Uwe Böning

What remains unclear in the description of the initial situation is the role and task of the coaching partner seeking support: Is it a high-ranking board member? Is it the chairman of the board himself? Or an external consultant for the targeted cooperation project? Depending on this, the described process would have to be viewed and evaluated differently.

Three important aspects seem to me too little clarified for a meaningful intervention as a coach:

- Firstly, what is the cooperation problem and the cooperation objectives associated with it in the group or in this project?
- Secondly, what is the group dynamic starting point between the people and role bearers involved?
- Thirdly: What is the order situation and the relationship between the (session) leader to be advised on the one hand and the coach on the other? Here the case description possibly does not speak for a relationship at eye level, but for a skewed power relationship, which is likely to largely influence further diagnostic and intervention possibilities.

This leads to the central question: What should actually be the goal and focus of the coaching process at hand?

In any case, I would consider it a cardinal mistake for a consultant to take a company assignment literally and enter into a situation where task completion can almost only go awry: The real power issue hidden in the assignment foreshadows that there will either be winners and losers, or even only losers. In a corporate environment with clear roles and more or less clear internal role relationships as well as dependencies, the literal implementation of the task definition, even with an open agreement, is always a dangerous undertaking: This is because if, in this environment, one party feels like a loser or cannot assert his or her position in an open and fair process, retaliation or other power reactions must be expected. These cannot be resolved with trusting communication feedback. It should be borne in mind that changes in real power relations, which can be accompanied by a loss of validity and influence, cannot be seen purely as communication problems and solved with trust-based reflection processes.

In addition, I think it would have been useful to interview the other participants in the critical committee meeting before the coach gave feedback, in order to get to know the substantive positions of the production board members involved and to be able to better assess the group dynamic references. This might have been more likely to lead to an assessment of the power relations and thereby perhaps more likely to anticipate the possible leader responses. Before the participant observation, I think it should be clear: What is the exact assignment? Who is giving the assignment and who is responsible for it? To what extent are all participants informed about this assignment and agree to shadowing? To whom should the feedback be given? To what extent is the willingness to receive critical feedback actually given among those involved and not just predefined?

In any case, dangers and resistance are *always* to be expected in such an entaglement. Therefore it has to be considered: From which position of influence or power can the coach give his feedback? If this is not high: Be careful at the platform edge! This caution refers to the requested or also unconscious expectation of the coaching partner to have found in the coach a supporter who is to support him loyally. For such a difficult assignment, there should be an advance agreement on how to proceed in case of different assessments of the situation, in order to constructively intercept a critical collision that might occur.

It remains open: Is the break-off behavior of the coaching partner seeking to support a repetitive pattern that points to a personality-related problem behavior or rather a communication process (co-)caused by the critical feedback behavior of the coach? Possibly the behavior could also be related to a cultural feature within the group that when conflicts arise, communication can be broken off relatively quickly.

In critical cooperation situations, there is often a paradoxical situation: One of the participants (intensively) asks for open feedback—but woe betide if it is actually given and does not meet the expectations of the person asking for it! The truth in feedback must not only be understood, but also accepted. Truth is not always helpful, but can also be a sharp sword and an unbearable imposition, which has to be balanced with the processing ability of an affected person, so that it does not lead to the rejection of feedback or even to the breaking off of a relationship.

Heidi Möller

My structural view of the difficult situation described is similar. The mission to bring high potentials to a cooperation cannot succeed without a mandate. It is not easy to form a ringlet from isolated satellites. But since this book should first and foremost be preventively helpful in order not to let colleagues fall into traps or even shoot themselves in the foot, I am concerned with the question why the coach did not refuse this impossible assignment, why he did not say: "But I won't do that." My first thought leads me to the need to reflect on one's own relationship to power and influence. In coaching trainings it is, in my view, indispensable that the relationship to hierarchy is clarified biographically. Especially when coaches receive assignments in high hierarchical levels, it is important to reflect on the familiarity with the milieu. If a coach has had many milieu changes in his or her professional career, the inner attitude towards the "big shots" must be stable. There is a danger of being flattered simply by being hired by powerful holders of positional power, and of becoming unprofessional because of the narcissistic feeding that such an advantage of trust means. Finally, as a coach, you've arrived where you always wanted to be. In a world where x times my income is generated, robust self-confidence is required.

It is very flattering to be taken into a board meeting as a second. The seduction of the assignment may make us forget that someone only seeks a second if he feels weak, at least unconsciously. We don't know the interpretations of the other participants on the board, but it's not unusual in these contexts for the mere fact of bringing an advisor along to be labeled as weakness. If life at the top in this corporation resembles a shark tank, then the mere suspicion of weakness evokes annihilating aggression.

If the coachee leaves the session with the impression of weakness, so my second thought, asks for feedback and gets further failures reported back, an inner dynamic comes to a head. The desire for feedback is always ambivalent: We crave it and it terrifies us at the same time. Even though feedback is highly valued in organizations, not every feedback-taker is equally capable of using it constructively (cf. Budworth & Chummar, 2018; DeNisi & Kluger, 2000). For one group of feedback-takers, it leads to rumination, a dysfunctional brooding.

The coach's interpretation of the little further feedback (however true it may be) is that of Balint's mirror theory: The "scene from the meeting repeated itself. When he didn't feel understood, he suggested breaking off the session." This leads me to my third thought: All our analyses and hypotheses may be accurate, but they are of no use if they are not experienced as a helpful offer of understanding. The interpretation here helps the coach, but not the coachee. The old fishing law applies: The worm must taste good to the fish, not to the angler!

2.11 Practical Example 11

Case Description

A coachee from a company showed little willingness in the coaching to work on topics that had been discussed in advance with him and his superior. Before the start of the coaching and also at the beginning of the first session, the coachee communicated a great anticipation, almost euphoria. However, the actual conversations during the coaching process remained very much on the surface. Concrete courses of action that we discussed in the coaching were not implemented or even tried out. When asked about this, the coachee reacted strongly defensively and immediately broke off the coaching.

What Was the Coach's Approach?

I mirrored the coachee's reaction and asked him what had happened to cause him to break off. The answer was that the coachee had the impression that he had to work. He already had enough of that in his everyday professional life and did not need to load up on additional work.

Joachim Sauer

It seems that in the exploratory talks, which were obviously conducted jointly and resulted in a classic triangular contract (cf. Pühl, 2009), the common goals for the commissioned coaching were defined. Apparently, however, it was not possible to create a well-balanced consulting system (cf. Rappe-Giesecke, 2012, p. 64 f.), in which the expectations of the superior (as the commissioning system), the coachee (as the system seeking advice), and the coach (as the consulting system) were equally incorporated. Who has the power here? The question remains open whether the coachee was able to represent himself well in the clarification of the assignment or whether he was obligated to do this coaching process by the superior *and* whether the coach in this triangle followed a professional logic free of instructions or unconsciously followed a certain organizational logic of the superior after all (cf. Buer, 1999).

These possible discrepancies are perhaps more difficult to identify in the presence of all participants in the exploratory interviews than in individually conducted exploratory interviews (cf. Rappe-Giesecke, 2012). Thus, after initial euphoria, resistance to coaching emerges as a possible reflection of the working world.

It would help to clarify:

- Who gives what feedback to the supervisor?
- What is the risk associated with rupture?
- What does this resistance to coaching have to do with the coachee's job responsibilities in the organization?

A whole bundle of institutional reflection could be worked through in order to better understand the coachee's resistance. Ultimately, it remains the coachee's decision to continue the reflection process or—as in this case—to discontinue it.

Isabell Braumandl

In my understanding, the consequences of an unclean clarification of the assignment become quite clear here. Especially if the coachee is not the person giving the assignment, there is a danger that secret assignments and goals are agreed upon informally, but not explicitly formulated clearly in writing for all participants. This means that agreements are not transparent, appear unfair and possibly disadvantage individuals. In my view, this leads to an impairment of mutual trustworthiness up to distrust. However, a trusting interaction in coaching is central to coaching success. Therefore, I would look for causes with the participants during the clarification of the assignment and deduce that clarity is created for future assignments.

Could it be that the employee has been prescribed coaching as a deficit-oriented punitive measure? Then I am not surprised about the behavior: Socially desired behavior is the great anticipation and euphoria. The reactance is ultimately visible in the behavior until the coaching is terminated. Since the coaching is about the goals set by the manager, the reactance, i.e., the superficiality and the non-implementation are also understandable. Obviously, the client has reasons not to get involved more deeply and not to implement things that may contradict his own needs, values, and goals.

It reminds me of a kind of unclear triangular relationship: The client and payer are not the coachee. According to my understanding, it could be that the coach is instrumentalized as a proxy for the executive and thus the coaching consulting format is misused. In such triangular relationships, in my view, the following questions, among others, should always be addressed when clarifying the assignment:

- What is the coaching understanding of company, employee, and coach?
- Why is coaching chosen as a consulting format?
- Whose goals should be worked on, the coachee's, the executive's, or the organization's?
- What are the respective goals of the coaching for the participants?
- To whom is what reported at what time about the contents of the coaching?

The exact clarification of the assignment with framework conditions, communication behavior, etc. would *always be the* first thing I would do. Before that, as a coach, I should be clear about my values and attitude toward coaching in such a constellation. From my point of view this is especially important, because as a coach it is also important to think through negative financial consequences due to fewer follow-up orders in advance. Negative consequences could also be personal conflicts of conscience due to differences in values or a disturbed relationship of trust with the client.

From my point of view, individual supervision with the coach is a good idea here, in order to reflect on his professional role and his concrete behavior, but also to derive concrete future options for action that are in line with his attitude and values. Topics of such a supervision would be, for example, the clarification meeting with the client and the manager, the limits of coaching and the clarification meeting with the client.

Finally, it remains to be said: If the way of working desired by me as a coach is not supported by all partners, I would refuse the assignment. Even accepting possible negative consequences. This is also how I act in my coaching practice and therefore I only have a few such triangular assignments. In those cases, then the organization pays against invoicing and thus receives the information when the coaching took place and over which period of time. When it comes to the passing on of contents of the coaching, the client gets to decide what if anything gets communicated to others.

Eva Jonas

The first thing that comes to my mind here is that the coachee was initially very euphoric and then breaks off the coaching. What happened here? Was the initial euphoria just pretend? To what extent was the coaching obligatory? What say did the employee have? What are the consequences of breaking off the coaching?

In the case description, it is described that the coachee breaks off the coaching after he reacts strongly defensively to the question about reasons for the lack of implementation and the lack of trying out of developed options for action. Dropping out of coaching seems to me to be a very strong reaction. So the coachee clearly shows resistance here, which in social psychology would be called reactance. If people expect to be able to perform a certain behavior and if this freedom is threatened, they react with a motivational tendency to restore the freedom. They may do this directly or indirectly. It would be exciting to understand what *exactly* led to the resistance in the case described. Is the resistance directed against the mandate for coaching by the company, against the way of working in coaching or against both? Is the coaching a repetition of interaction processes in the company? Possibly this resistance was already recognizable before—a superficial way of working in coaching was reported—and could the resistance have been addressed by the coach earlier?

Overall, this coaching does not seem to have succeeded in establishing a commitment of the coachee to the joint work. Our research shows that the need for autonomy plays a very central role in coaching. Behavioral changes sought in coaching should therefore be linked to the autonomous volitional self. It could also be that the coachee finds it difficult to access the self. In this case, one could also make a shift toward more experiential methods that might involve the self more and thereby support change more than purely cognitive approaches. This could also be done in coordination with a previous diagnosis, e.g., according to the theory of personality–system interactions.

Sandra J. Schiemann

In the case described, it is difficult for me to make a precise diagnosis, since several parties are interacting here and various scenarios for the development of the difficulties are conceivable:

- The supervisor: The coaching was externally determined by the supervisor, although the coachee's self-determination would have been central to (successful) coaching. The coachee was restricted in his need for autonomy, which is why the motivation for the coaching was not maintained.
- The coach: As concrete options for action and their implementation did not come from the coachee himself, but from the coach, the coachee felt restricted in his autonomy by the coach (cf. Imel et al., 2011), which negatively influenced the course of the coaching.
- The coachee: The coachee was already not motivated at the beginning of the coaching and feigned motivation for coaching (cf. Schermuly, 2015).

Of course, certain personality traits of the coachee may also have caused difficulties in coaching (cf. Schiemann et al., 2020).

All three parties may have negatively influenced the coaching, but a mix of these scenarios is also conceivable, as social interactions are dynamic and influence each other (cf. Bierhoff & Jonas, 2011; Kelley & Thibaut, 1978). My recommendation is therefore that the coach uses supervision to explore what *exactly* the problem was in order to reflect on the dynamics that led to the break-off and to learn from these experiences for future coaching sessions.

Heidi Möller

Approximately two-thirds of all coaching processes are commissioned by companies (cf. Middendorf, 2019, 2020). The admission procedures into the respective coaching pool are often elaborate and are also experienced as humiliating by many coaches. Nevertheless, that's the way things are and coaching occasions often result from organizational necessities: Areas for development have been identified in an assessment center, a manager did not do well in an employee survey, conflicts in the team escalate, etc. So triangular or quadrilateral contracts are the rule in coaching, not the exception. My record is seven people who participated in an exploratory meeting. Thus, impartiality, abstinence, or else the ability to triangulate should be considered basic competencies for coaches. It goes without saying that the supervisor's goals and the coachee's goals do not coincide and that the HR manager has a completely different view of the issues in coaching. The claim of voluntariness as a prerequisite for successful coaching, which is hyped in the textbooks, must therefore be put into perspective. What employee can turn down coaching when it is offered to her? It is up to us coaches to create an experience out of this inevitability, so that the person who comes to the coaching less voluntarily can experience this setting positively and benefit from it. All that matters to me in triangular or quadrilateral contract meetings is that the coachee comes to me. In the course of the process, I have the chance to turn the compulsory coaching into an attractive offer for the client. Most of the time I succeed in turning it into a self-interest, a self-motivation, something meaningful.

2.12 Practical Example 12

Case Description

This case involved one-to-one coaching. Due to the physical distance, the coaching took place via the instant messaging service Skype. The coachee reported on his self-employed professional activity in the creative field and approached me with the request to support him in improving his client relationships. The main focus was on two major clients with long-term creative support contracts. They wanted to end the cooperation at a certain point. As has often happened with smaller business partners, the two client relationships ended in a dispute over the scope of services and fees.

In the course of the coaching, it turned out that the coachee mostly did not stick to the order volume in the creative area, but extended it independently by areas that did not correspond to his core competence and his order. Since the coachee had also completed a coaching training, he permanently tried to turn the coaching situation around (in the sense of "coach the coach") and furthermore questioned and boycotted all interventions.

How Did the Coach Go About It?

My experience: The coachee showed the same resistance towards me that his customers showed towards him. We subsequently limited ourselves to working on economically relevant facts of the customer relationships. This was accepted by the coachee due to my basic economic profession. Regarding the difficult interaction behavior of the coachee towards customers, friends, family, etc., which became apparent during the coaching process, I could not detect any significant change. The coaching process ended after five two-hour sessions of 60 minutes each.

Isabell Braumandl

In this case, in my view, there has been no clear clarification of the mandate, taking into account the issues of framework conditions, communication behavior, and cooperation in the process. This is associated with an unclear clarification of roles and expectations, which leads to a tussle over competencies. If the coachee is busy discussing his own role, there is no time to deal with the actual goals and contents. This is not conducive to a goal- and solution-oriented process. Such clarifications should actually take place before the start of the coaching process and, if necessary, be addressed immediately if a need for clarification arises in the process. A clear definition of both interaction partners is, in my opinion, a necessary condition to make the process trusting, binding, and transparent.

In order to keep the focus on the client and his important goals, the following questions should be clarified during coaching:

- What is the client's self-congruent specific goal for the coaching process?
- What exactly is meant by "improving his client relationships"?
- What has the client himself already done to improve client relationships, with what results?

As a coach, I would have various questions and thoughts about the medium Skype used. Maybe the chosen medium was not optimal for the coaching. What is the benefit to the client of using Skype? Could it be that financial limitations have led to the cheaper version via Skype? It may be that a hybrid of face-to-face and Skype sessions are better suited to successful coaching work. Skype in practice leads to media distortions in perception. This concerns eye contact, delayed reactions, and limited emotional perceptions of discrepancies between verbal and nonverbal signs. And: Does the medium possibly lead to show-related aspects in the sense of "impression management"? In my view, at least one or two personal appointments at the very beginning would have been very helpful in building up a trusting working relationship.

The client's own coaching education is a great resource for me. The coachee's knowledge of working methods and procedures should not block the process, but should be recognized and used by the coach.

In the case described, I would conduct individual supervision with the coach in order to reflect on her professional role and her behavior in the interaction with the coachee and to derive concrete options for action.

If I were to work as a coach with the client described, I would mirror the perceived behavior when the difficulties first arose and make the competence tussle an issue. For me, this would be a contradiction to the clearly made agreements on the design of the working relationship, the roles and expectations. I would make a corresponding new agreement with the client in order to be able to continue working with him on his coaching goals.

Sandra J. Schiemann

According to the case description, the coaching took place solely via Skype. Apart from the question of whether Skype is a safe server for coaching, in my opinion purely digital coaching can also make some coaching processes more difficult: For example, building trust and relationships at the beginning could be more difficult, or empathic feeling and behavior. With the help of *XING Coaches + Trainers,* we conducted a survey on eCoaching in the summer of 2017 and found out that although eCoaching is used due to spatial, cost- or time-related motivations, it is perceived to be less effective, less personal, and less trust building (see XING Coaches, n.d.). Therefore, in my opinion, it is important to work particularly sensitively and conscientiously as a coach in purely digital coaching.

Furthermore, I see difficulty in the goal operationalization. On the one hand, the coaching goal was not defined in a self-determined way: The goal is not solely in the hands of the client (but also in the hands of the customers) and therefore cannot be achieved by the client alone. Secondly, the goal was defined very vaguely: What does *"the request to support him in improving his client relationships"* mean? Therefore, I find it important in a first appointment to define coaching goals using SMART: i.e., Specific (Do both clients and I know what exactly is to be achieved and how with which intermediate steps? What, e.g., does "support" mean, or "relationship," or "improve"?), Measurable (When will this goal be reached? Are there clear numbers?), Attractive (Why is this goal important to the client?), Realistic (Is this feasible?), and Terminable (Can I set a date or a time period?) Accordingly, it is important to define goals precisely and to make them the client's responsibility.

In summary, I see a well-defined clarification of goals and expectations as well as a trust and relationship building at the beginning of the coaching as crucial to be able to lead the further coaching process successfully. In my estimation, although eCoaching is a modern, easy, and cost-conscious alternative, due to the importance of relationship building and clarity, the first session should take place in person. If there had been a face-to-face first session in this coaching case—so my assumption—the motivations, expectations, and dynamics would have been felt more quickly and the trust building in the competence of the coach would have been more successful.

Eva Jonas

In this case it catches my eye that two major customers want to end their long-term cooperation with the coachee. Since there is presumably an economic dependency on these major clients, this should present the coachee with a major problem and a certain, perhaps even existential hardship. Why is the coachee trying to turn the coaching situation around in *this* situation? How does it help him to coach and question and boycott the coach's interventions? Is this a defensive reaction because the underlying problem threatens the coachee too much? Or is something repeated here in coaching in the social interaction that would also be observed in the interaction with clients?

It seems to me that there is a power struggle between coachee and coach. Who determines what happens in the collaboration? Who is in charge? To me, as a coach, it seems difficult to communicate this impression directly back in a Skype coaching session. Therefore, I would rather try to identify the underlying need. If the coachee has an excessive need for autonomy, I would, for example, according to the model of schema coaching (cf. Handrock & Baumann, 2019), try to provide him with a cognitive model for classifying his behavioral tendencies and the associated cognitive and emotional patterns. Once he has comprehended this model, it would be a basis for classifying future difficult interaction situations, outside and inside coaching. In this way, a distance could be established that could support the coachee in self-reflection.

Heidi Möller

I share the skepticism about media-based formats in coaching only to a limited extent. Of course, the group discussions with the experts whose contributions are included in this book were conducted before the Corona pandemic. Many a colleague would probably take a different position today, as we have all been forced to increase our digital literacy. But the coaching market has long required an offering independent of space and time. And not just because we all need to review our respective carbon footprints in terms of excessive travel time. The advantages of asynchronous working are obvious. There are customer groups that appreciate more anonymity and come to self-disclosure much more quickly in this setting (cf. Berninger-Schäfer, 2018). Contacts can be offered more frequently, for shorter periods of time, and thus in a more needs-oriented manner. Intersession activities, whose significance has been clearly demonstrated in psychotherapy research (cf. Berger, 2018), can also be designed and keep the client engaged in the process of change work. Online formats hold some methods that long-acting coaches have forgotten since their training and are stimulated anew in this way.

Nevertheless, digitalization in coaching demands a lot of learning and unlearning from the community. And who likes to give up knowledge that has been tried and tested for a long time and has become dear to them? A whole new listening competence needs to be developed: Modulation of the voice, the frequency of breathing, the pauses, the quality of silence, all of these need to be used as diagnostic clues. The use of methods via Skype or Zoom requires a lot of creativity and a desire to innovate. In my view, the hybrid models of counseling will increase and I wish us all much pleasure in the further development of our offers, especially since the latest meta-analyses (cf. Jones et al., 2016) show no difference of face-to-face coaching with digitally mediated conversations.

To the case study: As a psychodynamically working coach I am happy when the coaching occasion is reactualized in the interaction with me. Then I don't have to worry about the there-and-then, but am in the here-and-now of the working relationship. Understanding the enactment that happens between coach and coachee may provide many clues for optimizing client relationships. Does the working relationship in coaching perhaps reveal a pattern of interaction design to the business? Here I see a possible understanding of the client's question, but this requires a high level of psychodynamic competence, which is often not present in coaches with a background in economics. To focus on the purely economic could be an evasion of the actual concern and an avoidance of the actual.

I would suggest, to improve customer relations, "Let's take a look at what exactly happens when you interact with people!"

References

Abdul-Hussain, S. (2012). *Genderkompetenz in Supervision und Coaching*. VS.
Antonovsky, A. (1997). *Salutogenese. Zur Entmystifizierung der Gesundheit*. dgvt-Verlag.
Bauer, J. (2011). *Warum ich fühle, was du fühlst*. Heyne.

Berger, T. (2018, Juni). *Online Beratung und Therapie im psychosozialen Bereich.* Unveröffentlichter Vortrag auf dem 5. Internationalen Coachingkongress. Coaching meets Research, Olten, Schweiz.

Berninger-Schäfer, E. (2018). *Online-coaching*. Springer.

Bierhoff, H.-W., & Jonas, E. (2011). Soziale Interaktion. In D. Frey & H.-W. Bierhoff (Eds.), *Sozialpsychologie: Interaktion und Gruppe* (pp. 131–159). Hogrefe.

Bion, W. R. (1992). *Lernen durch Erfahrung*. Suhrkamp.

Bischof-Köhler, D. (1993). *Spiegelbild und Empathie*. Huber.

Bordin, E. S. (1979). The generalizability of the psychoanalytic concept of the working Alliance. *Psychotherapy: Theory, Research, and Practice, 16*(3), 252–260.

Budworth, M.-H., & Chummar, S. (2018). Feedback for performance development. In S. Greif, H. Möller, & W. Scholl (Eds.), *Handbuch Schlüsselkonzepte im Coaching* (pp. 191–199). Springer.

Buer, F. (1999). Profession oder Organisation? Wem dient die Supervision? In H. Pühl (Ed.), *Supervision und Organisationsentwicklung. Handbuch 3* (pp. 70–103). Leske + Budrich.

Damasio, A. R. (2004). *Descartes' Irrtum: Fühlen, Denken und das menschliche Gehirn*. List.

Dannemeyer, P., & Dannemeyer, R. (2018). *NLP-Master-Lehrbuch: Die Magie der Veränderung mit Neurolinguistischem Programmieren*. Junfermann.

DeNisi, A. S., & Kluger, A. N. (2000). Feedback effectiveness: Can 360-degree appraisals be improved. *Academy of Management Executive, 14*(1), 129–139.

Dilts, R. (1994). *Die Veränderung von Glaubenssystemen*. Junfermann.

Eck, C. D. (1990). Rollencoaching als supervision: Arbeit an und mit Rollen in Organisationen. In G. Fatzer (Ed.), *Supervision und Beratung: Ein Handbuch* (pp. 209–247). Edition Humanistische Psychologie.

Endrejat, P. C., Baumgarten, F., & Kauffeld, S. (2017). When theory meets practice: Combining Lewin's ideas about change with motivational interviewing to increase energy-saving behaviours within organizations. *Journal of Change Management, 17*(2), 101–120.0.

Geißler, K. (2011). "Versteh mich bitte nicht so schnell!" Verstehen, Nichtverstehen und Intervenieren. *Supervision, 1*, 7–12.

Giernalczyk, T., & Möller, H. (2018). *Entwicklungsraum. Psychodynamische Beratung in Organisationen*. Vandenhoeck & Ruprecht.

Grant, A. (2018). Zielperspektiven in die Coaching-Praxis integrieren – Ein integratives Modell zielorientierten Coachings. *Coaching | Theorie & Praxis, 4*, 1–15. 5.

Greif, S., & Benning-Rohnke, E. (2015). Konsequente Umsetzung von Zielen durch Coaching. Praktisch nützliche Erkenntnisse aus der Grundlagenforschung und ihre Anwendung. *Coaching | Theorie & Praxis, 1*, 25–35.5.

Handrock, A., & Baumann, M. (2019). Schemacoaching. In A. Ryba & G. Roth (Eds.), *Coaching und Beratung in der Praxis. Ein neurowissenschaftlich fundiertes Integrationsmodell* (pp. 280–300). Klett-Cotta.

Hirschhorn, L. (2017). *Extending the Tavistock model: Bringing passion danger, dread and excitement into a theory of organizational process*. M19 Manufaktur für Organisationsberatung, unveröff. Manuskript.

Hubble, M. A., Duncan, B. L., & Miller, S. D. (Eds.). (2001). *So wirkt Psychotherapie*. Verlag modernes Lernen.

Imel, Z. E., Baer, J. S., Martino, S., Ball, S. A., & Carroll, K. M. (2011). Mutual influence in therapist competence and adherence to motivational enhancement therapy. *Drug and Alcohol Dependence, 115*(3), 229–236. https://doi.org/10.1016/j.drugalcdep.2010.11.010

Jones, R. J., Woods, S. A., & Guillaume, Y. R. F. (2016). The effectiveness of workplace coaching: A meta-analysis of learning and performance outcomes from coaching. *Journal of Occupational and Organizational Psychology, 89*(2), 249–277.

Kegan, R., & Lahey, L. L. (2009). *Immunity to change: How to overcome it and unlock the potential in yourself and your organization*. Harvard Business Press.

Kelley, H. H., & Thibaut, J. W. (1978). *Interpersonal relations: A theory of interdependence*. Wiley.

Klonek, F. E., & Kauffeld, S. (2012). "Muss, kann. oder will ich was verändern?" Welche Chancen bietet die Motivierende Gesprächsführung in Organisationen. *Wirtschaftspsychologie, 14*(4), 58–71.

Kohl, K. (2007). *Metaphern*. Metzler.

Lakoff, G., & Johnson, M. (1997). *Leben in Metaphern: Konstruktion und Gebrauch von Sprachbildern*. Carl-Auer.

Lazar, R. A. (1994). W. R. Bions Modell "Container-Contained" als eine psychoanalytische Leitidee in der Supervision. In H. Pühl (Ed.), *Handbuch der Supervision 2* (pp. 380–402). Edition Marold.

Lippmann, E. (Ed.). (2013). *Coaching. Angewandte Psychologie für die Beratungspraxis*. Springer.

Locke, E. A., Smith, K. G., Erez, M., Chah, D.-O., & Schaffer, A. (1994). The effects of intra-individual goal conflict on performance. *Journal of Management, 20*(1), 67–91.

Lohmer, M., & Möller, H. (2019). *Psychoanalyse in Organisationen*. Kohlhammer.

Luft, J., & Ingham, H. (1955). *The Johari window, a graphic model for interpersonal relations*. University of California.

Mannhardt, S. M., & d Haan, E. (2018). Coaching-Beziehung. In S. Greif, H. Möller, & W. Scholl (Eds.), *Handbuch Schlüsselkonzepte im Coaching* (pp. 85–94). Springer.

Middendorf, J. (2019). *17. Coaching-Umfrage Deutschland*. https://coachingumfrage.wordpress.com/startseite/umfragen/. Zugegriffen am 02.06.2020.

Middendorf, J. (2020). *[18.] Coaching-Umfrage Deutschland*. https://coachingumfrage.wordpress.com/startseite/umfragen/. Zugegriffen am 02.06.2020.

Miller, W. R., & Rollnick, S. (2015). *Motivierende Gesprächsführung. Motivational Interviewing*. Lambertus.

Möller, H. (2012). Sie kamen, sahen und siegten – der lange Marsch der Frauen in Organisationen. In T. Giernalczyk & M. Lohmer (Eds.), *Das Unbewusste im Unternehmen* (pp. 91–110). Schäeffer-Poeschel.

Möller, H., & Kotte, S. (2013). Integration und Ausblick: Ein Vorschlag zur systematischen Eingangsdiagnostik im Coaching. In H. Möller & S. Kotte (Eds.), *Diagnostik im Coaching. Grundlagen, Analyseebenen, Praxisbeispiele* (pp. 319–336). Springer.

Möller, H., & Müller-Kalkstein, R. (Eds.). (2014). *Gender und Beratung*. Vandenhoeck & Ruprecht.

Müller, A. A., Kotte, S., & Möller, H. (2020). Coach and no regrets about it: On the life satisfaction, work-related mental strain, and use of supervision of workplace coaches. *Coaching: An International Journal of Theory, Research and Practice, 13*(1), 16–29.

Münch, W. (2001). Metaphern und Analogien: Vom Zeigen und Weisen in der Supervision. In B. Oberhoff & U. Beumer (Eds.), *Theorie und praxis psychoanalytischer supervision* (pp. 83–105). Votum.

Neuberger, O. (2002). *Führen und führen lassen. Ansätze, Ergebnisse und Kritik der Führungsforschung*. UTB.

Pecher, W. (1989). *Das Gefängnis als Vaterersatz*. R. G. Fischer.

Pühl, H. (2009). Teamsupervision und Teamarbeit. In H. Pühl (Ed.), *Handbuch Supervision und Organisationsentwicklung* (pp. 161–193). VS.

Rappe-Giesecke, K. (2012). Sondierung – von der Beratungsanfrage zum Kontrakt. In H. Pühl (Ed.), *Handbuch der Supervision 3* (pp. 64–80). Ulrich Leutner.

Rappe-Giesecke, K. (2017). Triadische Karriereberatung. *Organisationsberatung, Supervision, Coaching, 24*(4), 379–396.
Rogers, C. (1951). *Client-centered psychotherapy*. Houghton Mifflin.
Roth, S. (1991). *Die Kriminalität der Braven*. Beck.
Ryba, A. (2019). Die Beziehung als Wirkfaktor. In A. Ryba & G. Roth (Eds.), *Coaching und Beratung in der Praxis: Ein neurowissenschaftlich fundiertes Integrationsmodell* (pp. 148–190). Klett-Cotta.
Ryba, A., & Roth, G. (Eds.). (2019). *Coaching und Beratung in der Praxis : ein neurowissenschaftlich fundiertes Integrationsmodell*. Klett-Cotta.
Scheffler, S., & Baumann, H. (2011). Gender und Beratung – das Geschlecht bei der Arbeit. In M. Hammerer, E. Kanelutti, & I. Melter (Eds.), *Zukunftsfeld Bildungs- und Berufsberatung. Neue Entwicklungen aus Wissenschaft und Praxis* (pp. 49–58). Bertelsmann.
Schermuly, C. C. (2015). "Ich brauche meine Zeit, um wieder offen zu sein" – Negative Effekte von Coaching für Coaches. *Coaching Magazin, 1*, 46–50.
Schiemann, S. J., Frey, D., & Jonas, E. (2020). Coach me if you can: How people on higher leadership levels are more dark triad and how they as a client negatively influence their executive coaches and coaching. *Coaching: An International Journal of Theory, Research & Practice*. https://doi.org/10.1080/17521882.2020.1784973
Schlegel, L. (2002). *Handwörterbuch der Transaktionsanalyse. Sämtliche Begriffe der TA praxisnah erklärt*. Freiburg im Breisgau.
Schmidbauer, W. (1977). *Die hilflosen Helfer. Über die seelische Problematik der helfenden Berufe*. Rowohlt.
Schmidt, G. (2004). *Liebesaffären zwischen Problem und Lösung. Hypnosystemisches Arbeiten in schwierigen Kontexten*. Carl-Auer.
Schmidt, G. (2005). *Einführung in die hypnosystemische Therapie und Beratung*. Carl Auer.
Schmidt, G. (2016). *Einführung in die hypnosystemische Therapie und Beratung*. Carl-Auer.
Schreyögg, A. (2012). *Coaching: Eine Einführung für Praxis und Ausbildung*. Campus.
Schreyögg, G., & von Werder, A. (Eds.). (2004). *Handwörterbuch Unternehmensführung und Organisation*. Schäffer-Poeschel.
Schulz von Thun, F. (2010). *Miteinander reden 1: Störungen und Klärungen: Allgemeine Psychologie der Kommunikation*. Rowohlt.
Schulz von Thun, F. (2019). *Miteinander reden 3. Das "Innere Team" und situationsgerechte Kommunikation: Kommunikation, Person, Situation*. Rowohlt.
Schulz von Thun, F., & Stegemann, W. (Eds.). (2004). *Das Innere Team in Aktion. Praktische Arbeit mit dem Modell*. Rowohlt.
Shazer, S. d. (2014). *Wege der erfolgreichen Kurztherapie*. Klett-Cotta.
Stavemann, H. (2011). *. . . und ständig tickt die Selbstwertbombe: Selbstwertprobleme erkennen und lösen*. Beltz.
Storch, M., & Krause, F. (2017). *Selbstmanagement – ressourcenorientiert: Grundlagen und Trainingsmanual für die Arbeit mit dem Züricher Ressourcen Modell (ZRM)*. Hogrefe.
Storch, M., & Weber, J. (2019). Das Zürcher Ressourcen Modell in Theorie und praxis. In A. Ryba & G. Roth (Eds.), *Coaching und Beratung in der Praxis. Ein neurowissenschaftlich fundiertes Integrationsmodell* (pp. 74–94). Klett-Cotta.
Volkan, V. D., & Ast, G. (2002). *Spektrum des Narzißmus*. Vandenhoek & Ruprecht.
Wegener, R. (2019). *Bedeutsame Momente im Coaching. Eine explorative Untersuchung zur Weiterentwicklung der Prozessforschung*. Springer.
Wetterer, A. (2002). *Arbeitsteilung und Geschlechterkonstellation. „Gender at Work" in theoretischer und historischer Perspektive*. UKV Verlag.

XING Coaches. (n.d.). *E-Coaching: Verbreitung und Wahrnehmung. Die wichtigsten Umfrage-Ergebnisse auf einen Blick.* https://swift.xingassets.com/v1/AUTH_xemail/production/xemail.xing.com/XING_Coaches/Umfrage_E-Coaching_XING_Coaches.pdf. Zugegriffen am 26.05.2020.

3 Challenges with Psychological Problems of the Coachees

3.1 Practical Example 13

Case Description

A 34-year-old coachee, male, teacher, reported on his problems with the management of the school after an accusation was made by a colleague that he had been found drinking in class. After the coachee described at length the situation in which this accusation had occurred, it quickly became clear to me that the accusations did not seem to be content-free. It was difficult to carefully develop the conversation to address this accusation. In the course of the conversation, the coachee suddenly wanted to leave the setting in a hurry. I—quite contrary to my usual working understanding—brusquely told him to either flee or turn himself in. After the end of the first session, the coachee came only once more for a short appointment, after which he broke off without giving any reason.

Carla Albrecht

The difficult thing about this coaching situation from the coach's point of view seems to be that he has let himself get carried away with acting, contrary to his usual understanding of his work. Whenever we as coaches behave differently than we are used to, this is a critical moment for the coaching process and indicates a strong countertransference situation or entanglement with the system. The goal as a coach is to adopt a meta-level through self-reflection and to feel free in actions or non-actions during the coaching process. Regaining this freedom can be ensured not only through self-awareness but also through regular supervision or intervision (cf. Giernalczyk & Möller, 2018).

In this situation, I think that the most important thing is to regain this inner freedom. In doing so, it can be helpful to be aware as a coach that the coachee himself decides whether he wants to face his problems or not. It is not the task of the coach to lead the counterpart to water. Coaching is an interactional process which, from a systemic point of view, is not

H. Möller, J. Zimmermann, *Difficult Situations in Business Coaching*,
https://doi.org/10.1007/978-3-658-35087-1_3

100% controllable by the coach. Sometimes the pressure of suffering has to increase, especially in the case of addiction problems, so that the person concerned admits their problem and really seeks help. I can address the phenomenon, but the client has the choice of what to do with it or not. Likewise, it can help to be aware of your own scope: I do not have to work with every coachee, I can also close processes, refer, etc. As soon as I have regained my inner freedom, I can also act more freely and reflect on this back.

Overall, with such a client a detailed diagnosis seems to be advisable as an elementary part of the initial interview—as in any other coaching process (cf. Möller & Kotte, 2013)—but with an even more thorough clinical case history. It is difficult to tell from the case vignette whether or not such a history has been taken by the coach. Diagnostics can help build rapport with the client. The client seems to have come with the expectation of finding a savior in the coach who will support and reinforce him that he is the victim and the colleague and the head teacher are the perpetrators. According to the drama triangle (cf. Karpman, 1968), this represents a classic constellation. If one does not take up the assigned role as coach, this can represent a strong intervention for the counterpart, which endangers the relationship. Now, this does not mean that one should assume the savior role. Rather, it invites more exploration of the system and the counterpart. Another intervention can be to invite the coachee to adopt perspective and help him/her to put him–/herself in the shoes of the other parties involved, e.g., the head teacher and the colleague, in order to adopt an alternative perspective to the victim role.

Klaus Eidenschink

Addiction is one of the psychological abnormalities that easily lead to reproach and withdrawal. All too quickly, the everyday mind judges and terms such as irresponsibility, indiscipline, and others come into play. Accusatory dynamics and shaming arise in interactions, which then hit old wounds internally in those affected (lack of self-worth, destructive own accusatory dialogues, old shaming experiences). Denial is therefore as much a part of addiction as the amen is of prayer. Therefore, even in counseling relationships, the ambition often arises in the counselor to break down this denial, loosely along the lines of "Admit it!", "Turn yourself in!" Such persecutory scenarios are unfavorable and destroy the counseling relationship or do not allow it to develop in the first place.

In such situations, it is important to find a way to avoid the detective game in the first place. This could look like this: "Well, if I assess the situation correctly, it's not exactly easy for you. From the outside, there are really only two possibilities: One is that you're being unfairly accused. The other is that there is something to it and you are trying to deny or minimize it. [...] What that means to us, as I see it, is this: Either you don't have a drinking problem, in which case we need to take a hard look at how it is that you fall victim to such an insinuation. You are welcome to get support from me for that. Or, you have a drinking problem and you deny that and then we need to look at why it's important for you to deny it."

Thomas Giernalczyk

This is a difficult case because there is a clinical issue in addition to the genuine coaching issue. We have evidence of an addiction problem here. I like to call this a "coaching plus X" situation. In these situations, there is evidence of psychopathological or psychosomatic symptoms that complicate the approach. Depending on the skill profile, the coach may explore this area herself or delegate it to clinically experienced colleagues, although it is clear that this delegation is also a sensitive moment at the relational level. The vignette suggests that the coachee had no motivation of her own to talk about this situation. I suspect some obligatory coaching. In that case, it is usually beneficial to talk about the problem and to develop an understanding of the fact that the client does not come to the session entirely voluntarily.

The colleague acted out his countertransference, his anger at the coachee's tendency to flee, by confronting his client abruptly, contrary to his usual approach. Apparently, this behavior overstrained the still-insecure working alliance. In terms of uncertainty about the impact of interventions, I would say that although the approach did not produce the desired result, forceful interventions do work from time to time. Critically, I would note that the source of the action here was probably an insufficiently reflective, one-sided identification with the manager, who was convinced that the teacher had an alcohol problem. The deliberative moment and lack of motivation within the triangular relationship fell short for a while.

In the coaching-plus-X situations, it is necessary to carefully explore the coachee's motivation: "Why are you here? What do you hope to gain from our work? How do you see your situation and what does your supervisor think of you?" Another focus for me would be reflecting on the situation with the colleague and mutual perspective-taking where the coachee perceives my openness to their view. In keeping with the triangular contract, I would bring the client into play later in mentalized form. I would offer to describe the situation from the executive's perspective, perhaps saying the following, "I would like to put myself in the position of your leadership. I mean, this assumes that you have a drinking problem. What are your thoughts on that?" I might also ask, "Why do you think management comes to this assessment?" And later, "How do you assess yourself in terms of alcohol use?" Depending on the course of the conversation, I would refer to the here-and-now: "I would like to share a perception with you. I have the impression that your breath smells like alcohol, do you have an explanation for this?" Having experience with this issue myself, I would explain to my coachee what common procedures are for employees believed to be abusing alcohol, "Typically, employees believed to be abusing or addicted to alcohol are presented with an alternative: Either they go to addiction counseling, in which case they are given a reprieve with regard to sanctions, or they do not accept it and very strict action is taken against observed misconduct. As a rule, the manager and the company doctor or social-counseling service work together. What do you expect for a procedure in your school and how would you face up to that?"

Peter Uffelmann

Here again the fundamental question arises: Who is the client, the source of meaning for the coaching? The coachee does not give the impression of coming of his own free will with a clear idea of what the coaching is supposed to achieve. He seems to be a person who is easily irritated, who quickly feels threatened in his professional self-worth and who gets into great stress when asked critical questions. The conflict that has arisen with the head teacher is possibly only the tip of the iceberg and primarily a leadership issue.

Especially in the context of schools, I experience that in similar situations, coaching offers are made to the colleagues by the head teacher as well as by the school supervisory authority, in the hope that the coach will do the job. In this respect I suggest, as far as other actors are involved in the coaching process as meaning-makers, to include them in the clarification of the assignment. Especially if the coachee does not pay for the coaching himself. The instrumentalization of consulting as compensation for leadership deficits is frequent in such contexts and then a careful exploration of the previous history is needed.

On the intervention level, it would be important to find out how the decision was made to seek coaching in the first place, who expects what effects from it, what is to come out of it and what financial and time resources are available. In such a clarification process, it could also be agreed who of the participants should be involved in the coaching process and when, and whether it would not make sense to offer a three-way discussion with the head teacher before coaching this coachee. In the case vignette, it becomes clear that a rash intervention practice on the relationship level without sufficient clarification of the contextual conditions of the coaching leads to difficulties which can leave frustrations on both sides.

Mathias Lohmer

Here it is not possible to illuminate the coachee's suspected addiction problem from a technically neutral stance. The psychoanalytical concept of *technical neutrality* refers to the coach's attitude of examining the coachee's attitudes and actions in a non-judgmental or trivializing way and exploring possible backgrounds.

Similar to other case descriptions, the first step here would be to notice and consider the pressure to act and counter-act, in order to then enter into joint reflection with an assessment of what has been observed—i.e., *containment* and *countertransference analysis* first, before further interventions are undertaken.

Mentalization-based therapy (MBT; cf. Döring, 2018) has also described this procedure as "stop, rewind and explore." Applied to the case description, this could be framed as follows: The coach stops the process courageously ("stop"), goes back with the coachee in the course of the hour to the moment when the coachee jumped up ("rewind") like a video that is rewound, and then the coach explores with the coachee what exactly was going on inside him at that moment and how the coach experienced the situation ("explore"). This is intended to stimulate the coachee's mentalization—that is, his ability to experience himself through the eyes of the other, quasi from the outside, and to be able to identify with the coach's perspective.

What can be observed in this case, but also in other case descriptions, is that crises often occur in coaching when the ability to enter the meta-level is lost. We know this from all forms of *entanglement* and *complication* (cf. Lohmer, 2019)—these are characterized by the fact that acting and counteracting are dominant and the jump into the meta-level is no longer possible. Here, the coach then either needs supervising help from outside or he can activate his own *self-supervising attitude* (cf. on this also "second-order solutions" in Watzlawick et al., 1979): What is happening to me right now? What is happening to us right now? Strange, why am I suddenly so strict? Strange, why am I so indignant? Why does he want to jump up right now?

Interesting in looking at the meta-level is also the question of how I can deal with myself in an error-friendly way and accept errors as an important indication and as an interesting fact. So not self-psychologically: "I have now made a mistake and offended you with it," but rather in the sense of Kernberg's transference-focused method (cf. Yeomans et al., 2015): "Interesting that I am reacting in this way right now and that we now have a tension between us. How are you doing with that?" So I first allow myself to be startled, upset, and ashamed of myself, do not trivialize it—but then move on. These sensations need to be used in the process of insight. And of course: If one has actually made a clear mistake, this should not be concealed, but openly admitted, regretted, and then examined!

Heidi Möller

I ask myself: Is the coach taking on a displaced leadership role? The coach threatens to become the boss through projective identification. Superiors have the (duty of care) to intervene courageously when an employee is suspected of addiction. This is quite difficult, especially in a psychosocial context. After all, those employees who have to deal with addicts day after day understandably want healthy colleagues. When helpers themselves become ill, this fact presents immense psychological challenges to a team and its leadership. All too often, professionals themselves end up in the role of co-dependents. Here too—as in the private context—denial and other defense mechanisms take hold. The social skin (cf. Ogden, 2006) of the team threatens to tear. The social order of the team is threatened: Those out there are sick and we in here are mentally healthy.

Unfortunately, the interaction described above fails to pick up on this explosiveness. Instead, the coach is asked to be indignant: "Now imagine, dear coach, what an impossible colleague this is, she actually says I'm drunk."

3.2 Practical Example 14

Case Description

The coachee is a successful division manager in a bank and in his late 50s. In his younger years, he was a competitive athlete in a single discipline. Now, for the first time in his life, he is developing symptoms of illness that somatic physicians cannot explain and that threaten to become chronic. At the same time, his and his team's motivation to work decreases. The (former) top performers no longer enjoy anything, they feel paralyzed. I coach him individually and also recently had a team development measure together with him. Despite his very cool and performance-focused, even tough personality, he trusts me and allows me to talk to him about psychosomatic symptoms, spiritual issues, and feelings of weakness and disappointment. However, every time his symptoms of illness arise, he focuses exclusively on those symptoms. His tenor: Dear coach, I need to get a handle on this first, I cannot focus on anything else before then. He has hired me as a coach because of his symptoms but says he must first get everything back under control from a medical point of view before my coaching can bear fruit with him. As a wealthy and influential man, he has access to several chief physicians and is now visiting them all. Afterwards he is disappointed because they are clueless. Of course, I cannot offer myself as a medical companion either and find it difficult that I cannot help him at the moment, although there would be starting points.

What Was the Coach's Approach?

The original coaching assignment was paid for through his employer. Therefore, team development and one-on-one coaching were included. I now approach my coachee to see if he would like to hire me for one-on-one coaching out of his own pocket. This allows me to either do a new assignment clarification with him or also end the coaching for now. The decision has not yet been made, but I assume a private assignment.

Sandrina Lellinger

In this case, the impression is created that not only the client is looking for something from the coach, but also the coach is looking for something from the client. The coach describes the client as a "wealthy and influential" person with a "tough personality". He vividly describes the client's neediness and proactively offers himself for further guidance even beyond the boundaries of the original assignment. Has he allowed himself to be seduced? What are his motives? Is this about recognition? Is it about the acquisition of further orders?

What is this client looking for in coaching? Apparently, it is for assistance and not only on a professional level but also on a health, emotional and spiritual level. Perhaps he is looking for a pastor, a companion, or a friend to guide and accompany him in front of his team, in his illness and in spiritual questions. In my understanding, such a form of accompaniment has nothing to do with coaching. Against the background of the client's health situation, I would encourage him to seek therapeutic support.

Sebastian Kunert

There are two relevant issues in this case study: Coaching in the therapeutic setting and package offers. Firstly, coaching in a therapeutic setting: As coaches, we work with our clients in a very personal way, i.e., the whole person always sits in front of us, not the isolated symbol of management. In this case, the somatic complaints seem to be endogenous, i.e., psychologically caused. This circumstance places coaching on the borderline of therapeutic work. The suspicion arises that the client's issues have already become chronic to such an extent that they are affecting his health. In my experience, the classic methods of our profession fall short here and there is a danger of not being perceived as effective (enough).

Secondly, the package offers: Once a relationship of trust has been (painstakingly) established with the client, it seems tempting to offer all the services that the professional spectrum allows and seem adequate as an in-house consultant. The range of most colleagues goes far beyond coaching and extends from mediation, team development, and training to complex organizational development. What seems unobjectionable from the coach's point of view can be highly problematic on the client's side. Package offers naturally carry the risk of loyalty doubts. If the executive's consultant also moderates the team retreat, the participants are justified in asking whose goals are being implemented here. If they cling to the suspicion of a "hidden agenda"—even if it is unjustified—the coach can still solicit trust as much as he likes, but it will not be possible to build a resilient working relationship.

There is also another risk: success and failure in one of the formats radiate into the other. If there is a crisis in the coaching process, the consultant does not enter the team development unbiased. Conversely, a very successful coaching can be sensitively disturbed by a negatively perceived moderation.

My methodical approach is: A good delimitation is needed here! What can coaching achieve, where are my professional limits? In case of doubt, coaching is limited to stabilizing the client, so that it becomes possible for him to devote himself to a deeper intervention. In the end, there may be a referral to a psychotherapist.

Package deals, i.e., work in several formats for the same client who is himself part of the consultancy, are in my view unproblematic if:

(a) Several processes are interdependently linked with each other. In this case, the work from a single source is of great benefit, since, for example, friction losses due to a lack of information flow, different consulting approaches or organizational difficulties are avoided.
(b) It is professionally appropriate, for example, because the counselor has a high level of professional competence or a special relationship of trust with the client system.
(c) There is a sufficiently long vacancy period between engagements to make the new format independent of the predecessor's history and to avoid confusion.
(d) Transparency is established, i.e., all participants know about the multiple roles of the consultant.

If in doubt, it is better to give a partial assignment to a colleague, which is definitely seen as a sign of strength and strengthens the image in the coaching scene.

Thomas Bachmann

For me as a coach, this case study is a hands-off case. However, we do not know exactly what complaints the coachee has. Psychosomatic symptoms can cover a wide spectrum up to life-threatening conditions. My first impulse would be to suggest psychotherapy to him. I would advise him on how to proceed in finding a good psychotherapist.

I also do not like the mixing of individual coaching and team coaching. Now also different levels (psychosomatic, psychotherapeutic, and spiritual) come into the process.

The coach's behavior is certainly well-intentioned, but to me, there are too many contexts mixed together and the coach is addressed in too many roles.

The keyword *psychosomatic* clearly indicates that we are no longer in the field of coaching here. The treatment of psychosomatic diseases is a different subject. Of course, psychosomatic symptoms can also be reduced by good coaching, but these cannot be the concern and their elimination the goal of coaching. After reviewing the colleague's approach to a solution, it depends on the type and severity of the psychosomatic illness how I proceed. If someone has already consulted all possible specialists, then there must be a high level of suffering and I would say: We have landed on the wrong subject. Coaching is the wrong address.

If I create a lot of context mixing in an organization, so coaching a lot of people, developing teams, and doing all kinds of things, it is problematic and it needs to be very well considered. The entanglement in dilemmas and the possibilities for failure grow with each new context; the contexts influence each other. So, I think it is okay to package, but only if it is transparent, if there are no conflicts, if everything is well clarified with both the team members and the manager. Because: If you dovetail the two, I experience the procedure as very fruitful. Nevertheless, it always remains a bit tricky, because the big question is—e.g., after the failed team development—how do I feel with my client when we sit together and he says: "Well, as a coach I thought you were quite nice, but as a team developer it wasn't so great"?

I am quite open-minded and relaxed about spiritual topics. People are quick to use the pejorative label *esoteric* in order to reflexively distance themselves here. I think that there are many approaches to the psychic system: Emotional, narrative, religious, symbolic, spiritual, shamanic, philosophical, or whatever. My point is this: As long as it helps to make things discussable or tangible and benefits the coachee in her process, I strongly welcome such approaches. It becomes difficult for me when such approaches trivialize or even manipulate client systems and the coachee's concerns. When everything is traced back to a cause, attempts are made to convey truths, and representatives of the same ideas are on the move with a sense of mission and missionary zeal. An example would be family constellations to initiate processes for subsequent therapies: If the method is promoted as an access to the truth about the family, from my side a very clear no!

Beate Fietze

Yes, one wonders, who is he actually addressing? The coachee comes with a multitude of overlapping problems. The starting point was obviously a psychosomatic symptomatology. Should his psychosomatic problem be the coaching topic, the overlapping work topic, or both? The case presentation of the coach is irritating. There is a clear medical responsibility for the psychosomatic problem. In my opinion, the coach would first have to work out together with the client which problems could be dealt with in coaching or refer to another counseling profession.

On the subject of spirituality, I would like to say that there are many different backgrounds from which coaching is practiced, different contexts of knowledge, but also different spiritual attitudes. So, there are also coaches who are able to deal with spiritual topics professionally in their coaching practice because of their own reflected spiritual anchoring. But this is not my approach.

Heidi Möller

Does this make sense for me to offer myself as a house consultant in a company? I do coaching and offer team development. Many colleagues like these multiple assignments, not just because of their bank balance, but also because they say they know so much of the organizational dynamics through different settings that they can be particularly helpful. I generally do not do this, because I fear for my abstinence if I support team and supervisor through different offerings at the same time. I rather follow the concept of networked consulting, where in consultation with the client, the different providers of the consulting formats exchange information with each other to generate the best for the company.

References

Döring, P. (2018). Persönlichkeit und Mentalisierungsstörungen in Organisationen. *Psychodynamische Psychotherapie, 17*(3), 168–180.

Giernalczyk, T., & Möller, H. (2018). *Entwicklungsraum. Psychodynamische Beratung in Organisationen*. Vandenhoeck & Ruprecht.

Karpman, S. (1968). Fairy tales and script drama analysis. *Transactional Analysis Bulletin, 7*(26), 39–43.

Lohmer, M. (2019). Der Umgang mit Verwicklungen und Verstrickungen – Abstinenz, Containment und Verantwortung im Beratungsprozess. In M. Lohmer & H. Möller (Eds.), *Psychoanalyse in Organisationen* (pp. 226–236). Kohlhammer.

Möller, H., & Kotte, S. (2013). Integration und Ausblick: Ein Vorschlag zur systematischen Eingangsdiagnostik im Coaching. In H. Möller & S. Kotte (Eds.), *Diagnostik im Coaching. Grundlagen, Analyseebenen, Praxisbeispiele* (pp. 319–336). Springer.

Ogden, T. H. (2006). *Frühe Formen des Erlebens*. Psychosozial.

Watzlawick, P., Weakland, J. H., & Fisch, R. (1979). *Lösungen. Zur Theorie und Praxis menschlichen Wandels*. Hans Huber.

Yeomans, F. E., Clarkin, J. F., & Kernberg, O. F. (2015). *Tranference focusssed psychotherapy for borderline personality disorder – A clinical guide*. American Psychiatric Association.

4 Expectations of the Coachees Towards the Coaches

4.1 Practical Example 15

Case Description

It was an individual supervision of a coach who was half employee and half freelancer. He wanted to have both areas supervised. In the employee relationship there were significant conflicts with the boss and a colleague. The freelancing was not as successful as the supervisee expected. The second session, surprisingly, was about the supervisee's pubescent daughter, and parallels to professional situations could definitely be worked out. At the end of the session I pointed out to the supervisee that I had an appointment in an institution about 120 km away before the next session and that it was therefore possible that I could not be on time to the minute—just so that he would not be surprised then. Unfortunately, I was then stuck in traffic and arrived four minutes late. The supervisand had already left me a voicemail five minutes before the meeting started saying that he was at the door and I would not open it for him, so he was going to drive back. I called him immediately and asked if he was still around. He was and he ended up coming to the meeting, complaining again about my tardiness. He did not accept my pointing out that I had warned him after all. I pointed out to him that I could not guarantee that the situation would not repeat itself, to which he replied that then I would have to plan differently. We worked unexpectedly well afterwards and made another appointment, which the supervisee later cancelled on the grounds that he did not agree with the procedure. He refused to have another conversation.

How Did the Supervisor Proceed?

I thought it was important to make it clear to the supervisee that I would not comply with his demand. I consider a four-minute delay to be quite acceptable. In general, I think punctuality is important, so I also announce it to my supervisees and patients if there is a possibility that I will not be completely on time. I was clear with the supervisee, friendly

H. Möller, J. Zimmermann, *Difficult Situations in Business Coaching*,
https://doi.org/10.1007/978-3-658-35087-1_4

and did not respond to his provocations. However, these did not resonate much with me either.

Tom Levold

In my opinion, the supervisor and the client have become entangled in a power struggle that was not resolved, but rather decided by the client breaking off the cooperation. What I find astonishing about this is that the supervisor obviously does not present this power struggle and the associated relationship dynamics as the difficult situation, but only the annoyance of her client and his breaking off of the relationship. Her own involvement in this constellation is faded out. This is particularly striking in view of the fact that the formulation of the client's request already referred to "significant conflicts." This should make the already important question of how one can come to a clarification with one another in the case of conflict even more significant.

The conflict itself concerns compliance with the agreed framework of the talks and thus the contractual basis of the joint work. As a rule—and rightly so—clients have to bear the agreed consequences in the event of violations of the agreement; the agreed fee must be paid whatever happens. Likewise, the supervisor has to guarantee the contractually agreed performance. I think it is important not to make adherence to the contract with regard to place, time, and fee dependent on aspects of content in the counseling process or on things that have nothing to do with the concrete counseling contract.

In the present case, in my view, the supervisor should not have offered an appointment in the first place where there was a likelihood that she would not be able to keep it on time. The reference to the possible unpunctuality and the distance does not cancel out this mistake—nor does the fact that the supervisee himself obviously did not ask for another appointment. The even bigger mistake for me is that the supervisor did not call the client when it became clear to her that time would be tight.

The fact that the client himself does not show any particular flexibility and drives back a few minutes before the agreed start of the appointment shows, as does his ultimate termination of the supervision, that his conflict behavior certainly contributes to the intensification of the conflict or to the lack of clarification or resolution—this could have been the subject of the substantive work on the client's conflicts and should have been reflected upon in this context.

The solution described by the supervisor confirms me in my thoughts that she feels in the right here and sees the responsibility for the failure of the cooperation only with the client. If punctuality is really important for the counselor in general, then one should only offer appointments that allow punctuality instead of preparing clients for unpunctuality.

Ullrich Beumer

What stands out in this description and the countertransference reaction are two things in particular: Firstly, one's own violent reaction, which suggests throwing the client out, i.e. getting rid of the problem, or morally insisting on a seemingly self-evident tolerance of the slight delay. The violent reaction suggests that there is an unbearable tension in the supervisee in the situation, perceived as offending, which one would like to get rid of by throwing him out. Questions of punctuality and lateness are of great importance in all counseling settings, as they offer space for dealing with rules and above all with authority and power.

In addition, there is the surprising reference here to the pubescent daughter, who probably does not appear at this point by chance, but can provide valuable clues to the diagnosis. Puberty is—similar to the professional situation of the client—a situation characterized by often unbearable tensions between the desire to break away and to go one's own way up to the point of moving out of the parental home and the often simultaneously existing dependence in economic and emotional terms. While in adolescence, however, the final move out is to be accepted as inevitable and necessary in order to live one's own life, this does not apply to the professional situation. Dependent employment and freelance work can certainly coexist and—depending on the situation and one's own wishes—be a sensible work concept. Often, however, freelancing is idealized already in education and leads to a devaluation of desires and necessities relating to dependency and care. In this way, a splitting tendency and a disposition for power struggles develop. The supervisor's own situation may not withstand such an idealization either and leads to a forced emphasis on her own role of authority in the relationship and the reference to her own greatness, symbolized by a significant assignment at a greater distance.

I think it is extremely important to use the situation that has arisen in a counseling way, since it clearly brings a central problem to the surface. If this supervisor came to me for supervision, I would find it important to clarify which parts are feeding the strong emotionality and the obvious power struggle. These are probably also tensions due to the supervisor's stagnating independence or aspired freelance work as a countertransference reaction, but also important dynamics on the part of the client.

I would find it exciting—in the sense of scenic understanding—to work more precisely on differentiation in the sense of the object-relationship triangle, i.e. to clarify, starting from the situation in the here-and-now of the counseling situation, through which dynamics of the professional situation and the family situation in the there-and-now and possible biographical influencing factors in the there-and-then lead to the experienced emotional dynamics.

In this context, it would be important to work towards pragmatic solutions by recognizing the psychosocial entanglement. In the counseling relationship on the real level, this could be a different way of dealing with punctuality issues, such as better planning on the part of the supervisor, an agreement on possible telephone notifications in the event of difficulties in keeping the appointment, and an overall milder way of dealing with such sometimes unavoidable situations. A second focus would certainly be the connection between the client's professional situation, his dissatisfaction, which also points to a severe assessment of the difficult detachment and the daughter's detachment situation. Here, too, it would be important to move from a divisive either/or to a both/and, which would allow for a more flexible and friendly approach to one's own further development.

Agnes Büchele

The supervisor seems ready to enter into all the supervisee's issues and problems with him. Within two sessions, these expand into a possibly existential crisis of professional *and* personal identity. An autonomy-dependency conflict is indicated, between the dependency as an employee and the aspired independence, which is currently repeated on the father-daughter level. This puts the supervisor more in a helper role than in a companion and supporter role, possibly guided by the narcissistic ideal: "In supervision with *me* you can discuss *everything*." However, the orders for the supervision have not even been clarified: time frame, payment, desired goals.

Containment is expressed in the organizational framing (cf. Lohmer & Möller, 2014). It is the basis of agreements and symbolically stands for trust in the counseling relationship in terms of presence, understanding, reliability, and the prospect of emotional support (cf. Fürstenau, 2001). All this does not have to be given immediately at the beginning, but a first good feeling for a good development of the working relationship should arise. However, by announcing a possible delay, which then actually occurs, the supervisor puts the uncertainty of the temporal organization before the beginning process. On the contact and relationship level, the values of trust and understanding are thus unsettled. The supervisor deals with the issue—at least in her description—in a formal and opinionated way. It becomes a wrestling match: "Who is in charge here—four minutes, that must be possible—I am in the right!"

The fact that it was possible to work well after the annoyance also makes the supervisee initially confident that the counseling process can continue. With the termination of the consultation and his criticism of the process, the supervisee then leaves the supervisor without a mandate. I see this as his questionable triumph in the wrestling match of the supervision partners. It probably also reflects the supervisee's defensive patterns in dealing with conflicts. This progression from the beginning to the end of the consultation vividly illustrates the importance of the initial contact and the framework conditions for the development and unfolding of a counseling relationship.

Break-offs—without further explanation—happen, they are part of the business. But they are suitable to understand in the retrospective analysis how people can behave in distressed situations and with a narrow view. The retrospective reflection is helpful and a prerequisite to complete the process for oneself in the—abandoned—position. To reflect would be, from my point of view, the connection between dealing with organizational correctness, the affects and their emotional meanings. Here the entanglement between the initiating organization and the presented contents and concerns is represented.

In supervision, the supervisor might be invited and supported to explore her emotional resonance with her supervisee and her supervisee's issues, and to allow for the hardened position. Her organizational correctness—one could also say entitlement—is at odds with the wealth of concerns and issues the client confides to her in two conversations. The task is to connect these issues with feelings and affects and thus to arrive at a subsequent understanding of the client. In reflecting on the termination and its unconscious meanings, the supervisor has the opportunity to recognize possible mistakes, to enrich her own experience and, in the aftermath, to be able to view the supervisee and his distress with respect. Thus, the termination of the consultation would not have to be remembered negatively, but can become a personal and professional resource.

However, the supervisor holds on to the value of punctuality in a rather obsessive way. At the same time, she justifiably admits exceptions. She holds on to her perspective in a bossy way from the point of view of the solution. She seems to have the attitude of having to make something clear to her supervisee, rather than entering into a process of understanding and offering nurturing frameworks. There is something condescending about the description of the solution. It develops in me a fantasy of a fighting cock who has to show who is the strongest. With this attitude, she may provoke even more frequent terminations. Therein lies a similarity to the client's conflicts. He has little or no interest in his own emotional resonances and sensations or in the meaning of behaviors and what inner processes might be expressed in them.

Achim Mollbach

In the present case, the conflict is about supervision. It is not about the behavior of the supervisor and the supervisee within the supervision, but about the behavior of both in the service or client process, in which the supervision process is embedded. A conflict between supervisee and supervisor in the service and client process surrounding supervision can arise from the fact that the supervisee sees the supervision process as embedded in such-and-such a service and client process and therefore has expectations and demands (e.g., on the supervisor's appointment management, etc.), but the supervisor does not see himself in such a process and accordingly has no process standards to which he aligns his own behavior. In addition, a conflict can arise from the fact that between supervisor and supervisee, just as between a coach and his client, there are no agreements and no transparency about the rules of the game in the interaction process, which encompasses the narrower coaching or supervision process.

It is not clear from the case description how the supervisor explains the situation, the client's behavior, and the outcome. The introductory remarks that the client had considerable conflicts with the boss and a colleague and that there were apparently also conflicts with the pubescent daughter can at least lead one to assume that she sees the explanation for the dynamics of the situation rather in the difficult client, who also has constant conflicts with others. This is not atypical for conflicts: The causes of the conflict are usually sought in the other party to the conflict. In a conflict, a professional helper may have the tendency to see the client's behavior as an expression of his disorder or his problematic personality, which immunizes the supervisor against looking at her own part in the conflict.

If this supervisor came to me for supervision, the goals could be, on the one hand, to make the situation understandable for the supervisee as a conflict process between two conflict parties, and on the other hand, to consider what she could learn from it for herself, i.e. what she could possibly do differently in the future or what she wants to do differently. In this context, supervision can follow the models of conflict coaching, i.e. coaching a person who is in conflict with another person (cf. Schreyögg, 2011). This also includes recognizing one's own share in the conflict dynamics, instead of more or less blocking out one's own share, if necessary, by psychologizing or pathologizing the client. For this, one aspect of intervention could be the introduction of the distinction between the supervision process and the service and client process. On the one hand, this distinction gives the supervisor a perspective to respond to different situations within her profession with different role models and processes to different contextual expectations. This also applies to the role attribution of the supervisor to the client. Within the distinction addressed, the client is a supervisee within the framework of the supervision process, and a service taker or customer within the framework of the client and service process surrounding the supervision process, who expects or negotiates service levels accordingly.

Part of this supervision would also be the stimulation of self-reflection on the part of the supervisor regarding openness or the opening of her self-definition with regard to such a distinction. In order to stimulate a change of perspective, a possibly provocative intervention for one or the other supervisor can also be carried out—the introduction of a decided business perspective: The supervisor as a provider of services in a market. Such a provider must constantly ask herself how she can design not only her services in the narrower sense, but also the service and customer processes around those services in such a way as to generate customer loyalty. From a business perspective, it is perfectly legitimate to set service limits and restrictions and not to respond to every service expectation of the customer.

Edeltrud Freitag-Becker

All persons involved are searching: The supervisee is searching to find himself in the different role requirements: Employee, Freelancer, Father. The supervisor is searching for herself, her authority and role in the context of different counseling assignments; and last but not least, the daughter, who secures a hidden place in the counseling setting, is searching to grow up. What they have in common is the search for a supportive framework for development, together with the associated processes of negotiating the various borderline experiences.

The framing of the supervision does not seem to be clearly contracted and instead the clarification is carried out via an adolescent-looking power struggle. Scenically, the pubescent pushes herself into the center. Infantility determines the events: Fight and flight as psychosocial forms of defense are alive. The process of searching for a framework that provides support and orientation for one's own development is reenacted in the struggle for responsibility for setting boundaries.

The supervisor divides the client in two ("half employee and half freelancer") in order to reduce the complexity of the client's problems and thus to find a way in. When, in the second session, the complexity is further increased by the narrative about the daughter's puberty, the supervisor identifies with the excessive demands to which the client seems to be at the mercy and which the supervisor can apparently only counter through distance (spatial and temporal distance). Also in puberty, the reduction to known behaviors of the child is an educational aid to be able to distance oneself from the unknown and thus threatening behaviors of the adolescent. The scenes additionally illustrate why the client's freelancing may not work and why the conditions for the supervisor's freelancing to succeed are also questionable.

Exploring the desires for distance and closeness and marking reliable boundaries are part of boundary and role management, which are essential for the design of professional and freelance roles. The supervisor should know the concept, the supervisee could learn it. In adolescence, it would help to mark one of the key points of conflict between growing children and their parents.

The start of the counseling assignment is characterized by the uncertainty of the protagonists involved. Supervisor and supervisee move in their own system logics, understanding, culture, values, etc., and dominate the process and contract design of the consulting assignment against this background. Everyone remains in their own safe territory and argues with and against this background. Consequently, clarification of the assignment and process control move between two poles of tension and require a holding, securing framework for the establishment of a constructive working relationship. Just as the frame holds a picture, allows it depth, sharpens the perspective, so the framing in the counseling design offers an orientation and foreshadows a reliability. Arist von Schlippe (cf. Schlippe & Schweitzer, 2016) speaks here of metastability. On the one hand, it is about the formal rules and agreements that secure the functional, formal part of stability; on the other hand, it is about the affective side of the framework that calls for the emotional part of stability.

The clarification of the order only enables part of the stability, but not an insignificant part, as it clarifies the handling of the same through the restrained tension in the order clarification phase. The supervisor already clarifies her ability to deal with critical process points at this start. The client gets the impression whether he can get involved in this counseling relationship with critical questions, topics, etc. A growing stability in the relationship would make it possible to face the instability of dealing with painful and negative feelings and not to have to follow the fluctuation tendencies.

In the first phase of the supervision process it would therefore be important to sound out and negotiate with each other the different approaches to understanding, wishes and expectations, so that each one's own uncertainty can find safety in this new place.

It remains hidden what the supervisor and supervisee worked on together unexpectedly well. In my opinion there was an unconscious pact of not wanting to go deeper. The search for reliability and the desire to be accepted, to be respected, was not redeemed by either. The disappointment could not be addressed. Young people would say: "It went well again and I got away with it again... Well, then I can also go—and take the longing for closeness and the fear of distance with me a part of the way—and thus remain on the search."

Regarding the case title *In Search of*: As long as the supervisor derives her authorization and her support from the parental, educative position, she remains seduced to remain in the power struggle structure. If she succeeds in letting go of this being bound, a different view of her own counter-dependency could take place through the distancing and the reflection of the various dependencies in the counseling relationship could gain in content. For this, the supervisor would have to understand the scenes with their transference offers, e.g. her own infantile desires, have an interest in wanting to get out of the puberty trap and the power struggle, in order to be able to offer the supporting role.

It would then be possible to address the following:

- Bringing desires for closeness, support, care into consciousness
- Show parallels between the different requirements and highlight differences
- Reflect on roles and their respective different dependencies
- Illuminate blockages that hinder self-authorization
- Illuminating limitations and their dynamics

Heidi Möller

I cannot let go of the theme of puberty because the customer is portrayed as unpredictable, like a pubescent. The parents think they are in good contact, but then a second later everything has changed. Possibly this supervision process also reflects the considerable conflict with the supervisee's boss. Such emotional instability may form the background of the supervision theme. Also the joy to get one over on the interaction partner can be seen as a mirroring phenomenon. Why should the supervisee behave differently in supervision than in the workplace? Puberty as a second chance (cf. Erdheim, 2002) offers the possibility to solve the oedipal conflict with authority figures.

The supervisee's dissatisfaction with his employment, which seems to be full of conflicts, and the difficulty of feeling autonomous as a freelancer, represents a professional development issue for anyone who becomes self-employed. The fantasy may arise: in freelancing, there I am pushing myself, there the clients are sitting and waiting for me. Analogous to the medical context, the waiting room is always crowded, humility is demanded of the patients to sit in the waiting room for hours, completely independent of what else they have to do. I float down the hall in my white coat. The fantasies that accompany self-reliance are important to address in the training context and to deconstruct if necessary. However, the subtle power motif must be illuminated in any case.

Self-employment, often idealized in educational contexts, presents itself as paradise: There I can do what I want and how I want. The similar professional situation of the two consulting partners in this case study may be the background of the strained working relationship. In the supervisee's fantasy, the supervisor may have made it and thus attract envy. She shows her client by her time commitment that she has a lot to do, the schedule is full. There is a relationship statement behind the fact of being squeezed into the supervisor's workday with tight deadlines. Preconsciously, the supervisee then shows her in response, "Don't think you're safe too soon!" It strikes me as slightly sadistic: "I'm already showing you the limits of your skies!" It would have been nice if this scene had remained useful for the counseling process.

Another triangulation can be seen in the case narrative: The research instrument, the online survey becomes a wailing wall and the researchers—hence the implicit appeal—may share my view of the clientele!

4.2 Practical Example 16

Case Description

The coachee asked me for help in taking action against his co-manager. He was unbearable. Therefore, he was looking for support to bring him down. He, the coachee, needed an advisor for conducting psychological warfare. Together with me he wanted to think about how he could put his colleague under more stress.

What Was the Coach's Approach?

I asked my coachee why he wanted to take action against his co-manager and what the *best* or *worst case scenario* would be. The reason he gave was that he was tired of sharing. *Best Case* would be that he would run the business alone. *Worst Case* meant for him to continue to align himself with the co-manager. I sensed negative countertransference and informed him that my role would not be to support him in waging a campaign against his colleague. My coachee then broke off contact with me.

Klaus Eidenschink

The coachee clearly states what he (consciously) wants. This is just as understandable as it is in need of clarification on which inner ground these aggressive ideas of dominance and competition germinate in him. It is a common phenomenon that in coaching consulting concerns are presented which—in whatever respect—are problematic. It is part of a coach's basic toolkit to tease out the psychological, contextual, or organizational issues behind the concerns presented by the coachee. It is rather rare that concern and issue are identical.

In this case, one can make many assumptions about what is going on in the coachee: He could feel inferior or sub-standard, it could be a reaction to slights or lack of appreciation, he could feel abandoned. Many other things are conceivable! It could be a fight for a fetish object (money) that compensates for the actual lack of connection with the world, it could be powerlessness that cannot be tolerated, it could be a lack of competence to use one's own aggression in a mindful way, and much more! This requires relationship building that allows and sustains moving from concern to issue. The coachee first needs to understand the distress that his concern carries with it. Therefore, the counter-aggression of the coach is unfavorable and leads predictably to a break off of the relationship.

Interventions that serve the principle described could be, for example: "A lot must have happened for you that you only solution you see is conducting a campaign. It sounds very much as if nobody sees what you actually achieve!" or "If we leave aside the unfair distribution of profits, is there anything else perhaps so grievous that it drives you up the wall?" This only helps, however, if the coach's attitude is one of approach and appreciation.

Peter Uffelmann

I assume that in this case the coaching was not financed by the company but paid for privately by the coachee. Otherwise, the coach would have to reject the coaching order. This is not exclusively a question of consulting ethics but also a formal legal question. Usually we are dealing with triangular contracts: The money comes from the company, the service recipient is the coachee. Thus, there is a double contractual obligation and loyalty, which may well have legal consequences in the case of business-damaging consulting processes.

So let us assume private financing. The coaching assignment, when viewed neutrally, contains the request: Let us develop strategies to remove the co-managing director from his position.

Basically, it would have to be considered diagnostically whether the coachee is a phenomenon of the "dark side of personality" in the triad of narcissism, Machiavellianism, and a mild form of psychopathy. This topic could only be dealt with once a sufficient relationship of trust has been established with the coachee and a personality diagnostic perspective could be considered for this coachee.

We do not know from what motivation this impulse arose in the coachee. Questions that arise here include: Is this a massive relationship breakdown? Is the co-manager incompetent or even damaging the company? Is it a question of sole domination of the company?

Before any strategic considerations can be made, these and other fundamental questions should be discussed. I would suggest this to the coachee, especially since an unreflective campaign—possibly based on a grievance—will not be very promising. A prerequisite for me would be that I would have no moral qualms about the assignment.

If there are no reservations, I would invite the coachee to look at the history of his or her plan, since clever disempowerment strategies require careful planning and an even more careful consideration of the opponent's weaknesses and one's own strengths. Usually, strong emotions are a hindrance in such a case. In addition, I would offer him to think about how he would see his role, function, and task as sole CEO and what additional benefit there would be for him besides seizing power. Also needed is a scenario of what effects he imagines, related to employees, customers, family if applicable, friends, suppliers, and other stakeholders. The question arises whether a stress-generating strategy is really promising and whether a collaborative strategy (cooperation among enemies) could possibly be an alternative.

Carla Albrecht

For the coach, the situation described is difficult because, in his opinion, it involves an ethical dimension: Am I helping my coachee take someone else down or put them under increased stress? The coachee's choice of strong war metaphors and martial imagery reinforces the coach's deterrence. In terms of his understanding of his role, he sees himself more as a helper and personality developer and seems to be influenced by a humanistic view of man.

For me, the ethical dimension would be less in the foreground at first. The client makes me curious above all and I would take time to explore how he comes to these strong metaphors. The coachee would have to seem very trapped and sadistic—torturing for the sake of torturing—to me that I would turn down the assignment. What happened in the backstory with his colleague that would make him want to throw him into the abyss? Where does the coachee come from, what does he bring with him, what experiences has he had with wars? Metaphors are expressions of very strong emotions. I would work with these in two ways. On the one hand, I would try to *contain* the coachee. In other words, I would try to understand not only conscious content but also unconscious material through emotional reflection and return it to the client in an appropriate form (cf. on containment also Bion, 1990; Giernalczyk et al., 2012; Giernalczyk & Möller, 2018). In a containment process, the coach needs to provide negative capacity, i.e. internally provide space for associations, emotions, and emotional digestion (cf. Giernalczyk et al., 2012). In the best case, this can generate new ideas and thoughts that help the coachee to better understand his or her own affect. On the other hand, strong negative affect is often an expression of helplessness and a sense of loss of control: "I can't do anything about the other person. He has me in the palm of his hand." Then it helps to gather ideas and imagine what you could do to the other person or what you could do to him in order to regulate your own emotions (cf. Storch & Tschacher, 2016). Humor and exaggerated images also help, if they are used appropriately and fit the relationship between coach and coachee, to take the pressure off the statements: "When you describe it like this, I imagine you standing on the battlefield with your sword dripping blood, shouting 'Victory' and then collapsing in exhaustion. That feels pretty exhausting and draining."

Only after a thorough exploration would I position myself on the, now honed, assignment. When it comes to a clever strategic positioning towards the colleague, I would support the client. Also with the help of perspective taking: Why does the colleague behave the way he does? What are his motives and goals, etc.? This takes the pressure off and helps the coachee out of his feeling of loss of control.

Mathias Lohmer

In such a clear case as this, one is of course immediately tempted to say: "That's not possible at all!" The assessment and the behavior of the colleague, as well as the subsequent termination of the coaching, seem logical, even ethically required.

If we take a slightly less blatant case, however, we find: Wait a minute, that is what we often do—that we also support a coachee in a power struggle against a colleague, competitor, or superior. We help him strategically position himself wisely, and claim to selectively engage in conflict—following the motto: Only fight battles you can win and seek powerful allies. Most coaches would probably have an inhibition against dirty warfare, in this case of deliberate under-stressing. But we certainly work as spin doctors, supporting a coachee's campaign and working with them to figure out how they can come across better than their competitor. So it strikes me that I definitely speak in war metaphors in my work with coachees as well. And as coaches, we are indeed mercenaries in such power struggles from time to time: it is a matter of chance which of the opponents chooses us and which party we support!

Perhaps the coachee's desire to fight is indeed so pressing that reflection and adopting a meta-level are not possible. Nevertheless, it would be worth a try: "Let's reflect for a moment on how the collaboration with your managing director colleague came about, what about it was perhaps successful, what was frustrating. What is it about sharing power?" In this intervention, the coach would not be overly impressed by the coachee's direct brief, but would seek to expand the thinking space around that brief, testing the coachee's appropriate reflective capacity and willingness.

Thomas Giernalczyk

The coachee is obviously in a dispute with his management colleague, is suffering due to him, and wants support from his coach. The vocabulary he uses to formulate his request is chosen in a bellicose manner.

Analysis of my countertransference reactions leads to the following consideration: The coachee chooses fighting metaphors, which indicates his interpretation of the interaction. I suspect that it is an escalated conflict in which the coachee only has the idea of "him or me" in his head. Glasl's (2017) staircase of conflict comes to mind and I can imagine that the coachee is afraid of a "lose-lose" outcome and therefore fantasizes "win-lose" for himself. The martial language piques my interest and makes me wary. Does he tend to exaggerate conflicts? Or is this really a tricky situation? What makes him want to inflict more suffering on his colleagues?

Internally, I refer to the concept of micropolitics (cf. Neuberger, 2002). Pursuing one's own interests in the context of role action is commonplace and is more or less limited by rules and structures. In addition, it is perfectly normal for managers in the hierarchy to devote some of their energy to maintaining and expanding their power base, otherwise they will not be able to hold their ground against similarly acting colleagues. Against this background, I can then examine how functional the campaign against the colleague is in terms of maintaining and expanding one's own position and wider interests.

I would be interested in the account of the situation and clarify the following questions: How did the conflict develop? Is there a history to this? What were important milestones along the way? What has the coachee already done to calm down the situation and what would he describe as the best and worst case scenarios? In addition, I would work intensively with him on mentalizing issues: Why does he think his colleague acts exactly the same way? What are his motives and how does he feel about it? For this analysis I would refer to individual situations described and evaluate them.

In addition to conflict analysis and mentalization, I would be interested in the organizational dimension of the conflict: What institutionalized conflicts are inherent in the division of managing director responsibilities and how have they been dealt with so far? Are there signs that we have a "moving conflict" here that originated elsewhere? For example, is a conflict from the supervisory board being carried into the interaction?

I would also talk about the benefits and risks of his plans: What would he gain and how would he endanger himself if the colleague came under increased stress? In this context, I find the saying from Asian martial arts interesting that it is dangerous to get involved in a long fight because it ties up too much energy and makes you vulnerable. So overall, I recommend a neutral and exploratory stance. If the coach is not too quick to occupy the ethical side, sooner or later it will surface again in the coachee.

For me, the role of the coach is to take a neutral and emphatic perspective, which is suitable for thinking about the advantages and disadvantages of strategies, taking into account feelings and values.

Heidi Möller

If I take the foreground of the case description, the coachee could be a person with Machiavellian tendencies. These strive for power first and foremost. Machiavellianism is part of the dark triad consisting of narcissism, Machiavellianism, and psychopathy. Recent research may have shown that individuals with high tendencies toward the dark triad more easily attain leadership positions (see Schiemann & Jonas, 2020). Their manipulative and often unethical strategies help them make a big impression and get the position they seek. The motivational structure aims at ever higher, more powerful, and prestigious functions. However, in the long run, these personality dispositions have numerous negative consequences for the organization. Power-oriented, ruthless, and egoistic behavior, the pursuit of one's own advantage—even going over dead bodies—brings difficulties in interpersonal relationships, Machiavellians are not very compatible. The overestimation of one's own competences and the orientation towards the criterion of always leaving the most effective impression in the company lead to less success of the organization in the long run.

Coaching has different focuses at different levels of the hierarchy. In middle management, questions of power and micropolitics are less important than in the executive suite, where strategic positioning and maintaining power are always at stake.

Interestingly, in the group discussion initially only the men participated in the case discussion. The gender issue is thus obvious. Rastetter and Jüngling (2018) describe the blind spot of female managers in questions of micropolitics. Women definitely have some catching up to do in this regard. It is more difficult for them to perceive micropolitical phenomena. However, it is even more difficult for women to position themselves meaningfully in terms of micropolitics. One dilemma faced by female managers (cf. Möller, 2012; Möller & Müller-Kalkstein, 2014) can be described as the inhibition to engage offensively in power politics.

4.3 Practical Example 17

Case Description

I found a situation difficult and challenging in which a coachee kept asking what he should do in his situation, what would be the right thing to do. He found the communication with the company owner (he himself had a share in the company) and the superiors (he was also a manager) very difficult and exhausting. The coachee felt great distress and expressed that the way his boss was acting was negative for everyone, including the good of the company. It was his task to change this, to change the boss and to develop strategies within the framework of coaching as to how this could be achieved. Within the framework of several sessions over a period of about 3 months, it was possible to support the coachee in determining for himself what he needed in order to be able to work well and productively and what strategies he could use to implement this. His changed behavior also led to changes in the boss's behavior. It was very stressful for me *not* to comply with the demands for advice, solution techniques, and correct behavior, but not to do so too offensively so that the coachee still felt he could take something away from each session. I sometimes felt like I was tricking the coachee and do not think this is ethically correct. But at the same time, I felt like I could be helpful that way and still be on the side of the good guys.

How Did the Coach Go About It?

I have put a lot of statements into perspective and tried to show a wider range of possibilities. I put *wrong* and *right* into perspective. I asked many questions and supported the coachee in remembering satisfactory and successful situations, analyzing them and thus discovering successful strategies for himself. I approached the coachee with great empathy for his suffering and concerns and also showed empathy towards his boss or towards his description of the boss.

Ursula Hermann

Already in the introduction a pronounced dichotomy is described. The coachee conveys a strong black-and-white thinking, expressed among other things about *what would be the right thing to do*. The pressure associated with this dichotomy is quickly transferred to the coach. It manifests itself in her resistance to presenting advice and solutions. Because this crucial dynamic remains hidden, the coach feels that she is being tricked. This trickery finds expression in a debate of its own—conducted internally by the coach regarding right/wrong, ethically correct/not correct—which remains unused for the counseling process.

These countertransference feelings are an important tool and helpful diagnostic instrument here (cf. Oberhoff, 2009), which the coach holds in her hands but does not use. Thus the process remains on the surface, empathy is conveyed, the situation is put into perspective, and the coachee's needs are not addressed. It does not come to a getting-to-the-bottom-of and laying-on-the-table.

The basis of my approach would be to get to the bottom of the feeling due to the countertransference, to make it discussable and subsequently also understandable.

It is crucial to reflect and to get out of being driven: Reflection is becoming aware of what we speak, do, feel, or perceive.

This means that it would be important for me to inquire and trace: How did this company constellation and participation come about? What role did and does the coachee have in the company? How is he or she doing with it? Which other people have an important position in the company and how does he assess their view of the current situation? Through whom and how does he experience support and recognition? Does he experience devaluation? etc.

It is important to reflect and to address the emotional dimensions of the experiences. In other words, not only to ask for facts, but also for feelings that go along with them. For the counseling setting, this means that the coach functions as an object, place, or container that takes in something from the coachee, holds it ("contained"), whereby a third thing can emerge (cf. Lazar, 1994). Therefore, it is crucial as a coach to make transference feelings such as pressure or trickery available and relate them to the coachee's work context. It is not a matter of following the pressure for prescriptions, but of making what is actually conflictual discussable in order to understand the emotional dynamics that are hidden behind the pressure. If this third thing is on the table, it is possible to think about options for action and strategies that open up other shades of color besides black and white.

Kornelia Steinhardt

Here a coaching process is described in which the coachee is taken by the coach's hand, so to speak, and wants to find out how he can change his superior. The analysis of the countertransference shows that the coachee sees himself in the role of the better leader, whose task it is to save the company. Behind the coachee's great pressure of suffering, there also seems to be unconscious competition with or envy of the company owner and superior. At the same time, the coachee presents himself as the sole savior and redeemer of the company—he is supposed to succeed in turning everything around for the good of the company if he can only find the right strategies and techniques to change the boss. In my opinion, this latently reveals his ideas of grandiosity and thus his narcissistic personality accentuation, which can be easily concealed behind the mask of concern for the company.

This narcissistic attitude is unconsciously re-staged in the relationship between coachee and coach. Because the coachee conveys that he only needs help from the coach to change the boss's mind. This also degrades the coach to a subordinate service provider who is supposed to work for him. It can be assumed that this scenic reenactment can be understood as an indication that the coachee is not very willing to cooperate with his superior in everyday work, but rather presents himself latently as a better boss.

The narcissistic component, however, does not seem to be so pronounced, because the coachee—at least partially—engages in a process with the coach. Especially in coaching work with professionals with narcissistic personality accentuation, it is important to accommodate them to some extent and at the same time open up other approaches for them. It is a great challenge for the coach to maintain this balance.

When planning the intervention, it is important to clarify in advance—if this has not already been done—why the coachee is coming to coaching at this particular time. Does he come on his own initiative or is he motivated by his superior? It is also necessary to reflect on the function and role of the coachee in the organization, what the primary task of the company is and what the specific tasks of the coachee are. In which structures and processes within the organization are the coachee's fields of work integrated? To what extent does he have to cooperate with the company owner and boss or is he directly subordinate to him? Against this background, the coaching assignment can be clarified and sharpened once again, which can lead to the assignment focusing not on changing the boss, but on the (further) development of the coachee's ability to work. However, this must be formulated in such a way that the coachee does not feel narcissistically offended and break off the coaching.

The relationship to the boss and company owner seems to be of particular importance for the coachee, which can be partially investigated in the scenic understanding of the unconscious reenactment in the here-and-now of coaching. This could open up affective access to the coachee's latent transference feelings towards the supervisor. However, work on scenic understanding can only take place when the working relationship between coach and coachee is sufficiently sustainable. Parallel to this, the coachee can be supported in questioning the work processes in his/her sphere of influence and possibly developing new patterns of action and strategies.

Wolfgang Knopf

The desire to gain clarity about what might be right and what might be wrong stands out at first glance. Likewise, it becomes clear that it is about the good of the company. Interesting is all that is unclear in this described situation, what is not told.

It can be assumed that the situation has a communicative aspect, embedded in an organizational structure. However, the actors remain unclear here: In which function, with which role design is the coachee sitting here in the coaching? As an executive, as a participant in the company? From which position—and I find this particularly important—does he derive the task of changing the boss? In principle: It can be assumed that the legal form of the organization, which is not known here, the core business, which is not mentioned here, and the unknown organizational culture, which depends on it, play significant roles.

In the coaching described, it was possible to develop strategies for the coachee that also brought about changes in the boss. Despite this success, the coach had the impression that she was tricking the coachee. Where does her feeling come from?

Let us assume that the coachee is concerned with the well-being of the company. From which perspective, from which angle, from which position? And with what intention? From the perspective of the coachee? If so, what co-determination, design bodies, etc., are there in this company and how can these be used?

Wanting to change the boss, to develop strategies for this, is an announcement to deal with authority and thus with power. Since, according to the description, the boss has also changed through the coaching of the senior employee, this has been achieved here without having to use structural bodies. It is understandable that a feeling of being tricked can arise. Only: the tricking took place together: Coach and coachee against the boss. And so the question arises: Are aspects of the organizational culture reflected here?

To put it bluntly: The coach can be empathically seduced! Of course it is important to perceive the pressure of suffering, to absorb it, to *contain* it. However, the solution described here remains limited, even stuck, at the personal level of the coachee. The coachee is not perceived as a structural member of the organization who, due to his or her position, be it as an executive or as a company employee, also has structural options for shaping the organization. Too much empathy prevents effectiveness here! For me, an important first step would be to clarify the above questions.

Heidi Möller

A dilemma in coaching is the fact that—if there are no triangular or quadrangular contracts—we only have the narratives of the coachees at our disposal: Meaning subjective constructions in social perception. I still notice that the account of significant "coworkers" (here company owners) is not broken. Apparently the account is taken one on one and not questioned. Good coaching, in my view, needs to be depth hermeneutic here: Why is a person described in this way? What is the function of this perception? Which transference processes are possibly at work? What would happen if a different perspective were adopted? As a coach, adopting a view: "My boss is such a terrible person" and not putting a question mark behind it may be understood as an expression of the experienced powerlessness and loneliness of the coaching client, but not as a statement about a real person. This person may be a very wonderful person, but unfortunately the client cannot get on with him. As a coach, I can only state: The interaction partner is portrayed in the following way and this narrative is in need of interpretation. Showing maximum empathy at this point is, in my view, only half the battle. However, empathy—according to the mental model of effectiveness in coaching—is not always helpful, especially if it no longer opens up the possibility space of "It could also be completely different."

4.4 Practical Example 18

Case Description

The client reports that his colleague on the board has initiated a project on the topic of organizational culture. He is skeptical about this because he is skeptical about his colleague anyway, but also because he has the feeling that this would be to his disadvantage, that facts would be created, that a process would be initiated which he could no longer control or whose results might not suit him. His idea is to develop his own paper and to oppose it in the board circle. This would allow him to reclaim territory and keep his fingers in the pie.

And he already has an idea how to implement it: "You [he means me as a coach] know a lot about organizational culture. Can't you create such a paper for me? I'll pay for it, of course."

What Was the Coach's Approach?
I replied that I could not see what the point of this action was. After all, you cannot prescribe culture. He wiped the objection off the table: "It doesn't matter, it's tactically helpful." I replied that I could not draw up the paper for him, as that would turn me into his assistant. As a coach, however, I could not and would not be his assistant, but would work with him as equals. The answer did not sit well with him and he broke off the coaching a short time later and with a little power struggle over a very short notice and unfounded cancellation of an appointment, which I would not let him get away with.

Regina Gibhardt
The first thing I would clarify is: Is this a consulting or coaching engagement? In the case of consulting, the matter is relatively clear. Here, there is a desire to purchase an external service for a concrete product: A concept for the realignment of the organizational culture.

But when it comes to a possible coaching assignment, the first thing that strikes me is the bellicose language in the case description. Language is always an expression of attitude, of values, of culture. What does it mean to a company when one board member makes war on another board member? Here, trenches are created at the top level that, in my experience, run through the entire company. This creates fronts at the department and employee level that fight against each other. It does not take much imagination to come to the conclusion that this consumes unnecessary resources that are then missing from the actual purpose of the company.

So underlying this symptom, the *desire for an appropriate text as a counter-design for a new organizational culture*, are much larger challenges. Ideally, the entire board is willing to look at this dynamic and address it in order to better serve the company's purpose. This can succeed if there is a driving force at a critical juncture to drive this reconciliation or peace process.

In the case of a coaching assignment, I would make my considerations transparent in the first meeting and explain the model BEING + DOING = HAVING (see also my comment in Sect. 5.1). If the coachee is open to work on the BEING level, the coaching could start with him alone and without the whole board. If there is no willingness to do so, it would be a consulting case that could be assigned to appropriate experts.

If there is a willingness for coaching, I would first find out what the client's need behind his coaching assignment is. Not infrequently I discover behind similar constellations a deeply hidden lack of self-esteem and a younger part in the coachee who still wants to show one or both parents that he can also do something, also has a right to exist, is also lovable.

In the case described, this younger-child part may therefore jump onto the stage of the adult client in his role as a board member. The belligerent language in the case description could also be an indication of an old, unresolved sibling conflict, which is once again visible here in the professional context. The sister—represented here by the colleague—seems to have always had it better.

If the coachee is open to it, I would in any case first make the basic dynamics, the original root of the current professional challenge, visible through a systemic family constellation and ideally pacify it. This would give the client the chance for a new view of his coaching concerns and a deeper understanding of the overall situation. Only then would I think about possible next steps together with the coachee:

- Who am I as a board member without my old pattern of having to prove to someone how good I am? What can I do better then?
- What might happen if I could switch from confrontation to collaboration?
- What impact would this have on me, my fellow board members, our managers and employees, our customers and business partners?
- What am I willing to do for it? What am I willing to give up for it?
- What might concrete steps toward board-level collaboration look like if I were to initiate them?

A new behavior of a system member can lead to a change of the whole system. Thus, after a successful coaching process with even one board member, there would at least be a chance that something could change in the board as a whole: Away from fighting against each other towards constructive cooperation.

Jannik Zimmermann

In the course of a coaching process, coachees also formulate assignments that do not belong to the coach's area of responsibility. This becomes clear in the case described: During a session, the coach is asked to prepare a written paper on the topic of organizational culture. Dealing with such a request in coaching is sometimes experienced as difficult, as both acceptance and rejection can be momentous. I will briefly discuss some of the reasons for this below.

The relationship between coach and coachee differs from relationships in many other work contexts. It can usually be described as a partnership and equal, i.e. as a relationship at eye level. This eye level does not exist when providing a variety of other services. Therefore, if the cooperation with the coachee is extended to another work context, the relationship with the coachee may change.

Also, in coaching one acts out of the role of the coach. This role is associated with certain demands and expectations of one's own person and one's own behavior. The situation is similar on the side of the coachee. If other contexts of cooperation arise parallel to the coaching, the different roles may become blurred. In the case described, acceptance of the additional assignment could, for example, lead to the coachee seeing his counterpart less as a coach and more as a technical expert who provides assistance.

The previous explanations about coach–coachee relationship and different roles make clear: Accepting such a request potentially negatively influences the coaching collaboration. But a coachee can also react negatively to a refusal, as his expectations remain unfulfilled.

If I as a coach am confronted with such a request in coaching, it is helpful to consider and reflect on these different points. Such a reflection can take place in an appreciative dialog with the coachee. It is also helpful to look more closely at why the coachee is approaching you with the particular request at the particular time in the coaching. It is possible that the coachee in the case described does not want to get involved in a more in-depth management of the conflict between him and the board colleague and that the request represents a point at which this once again becomes particularly clear. In this case, it would be a good idea to explore the background of the request further by asking specific questions and to work on these if necessary.

Andreas Knierim

I ask myself: What is there? What happened in the initial conversation between the coach and the coachee? What is the original assignment? My guess: There might be a larger assignment behind it, where the topic of organizational culture is just the beginning. What personal issues does the client bring to the table? What relationship-level issues are being left out? The client's behavior suggests a lack of eye level between coachee and coach. The coachee makes an offer to play—at the beginning of this top executive coaching, the client first seems to check whether the coach is up to the situations at all. If the coach gets involved in writing a paper, he is a kind of executive. The coachee guides and controls him, stays in his role as a leader, does not reflect on his behavior. An order is given to the coach, a typical non-eye-to-eye behavior.

The systemic context shines through concretely at the beginning, in coaching I would get a detailed picture of the roles and working relationships in the board by asking questions and offer this to the coachee for structure. The format of *constellation in a single setting* is conceivable here for the coachee to gain systemic insights: With the help of chairs we can create a picture in the room, the coachee stands at the different positions, sees the roles and working relationships from different angles. Then he steps out of the picture again. We mark out a meta-position from which we can repeatedly talk about the people, form working hypotheses and develop alternative behaviors.

The coachee has high control needs. I would ask him questions about his self-worth, for example: When does he need this control? How does he rate his successes in doing so? What does he suppress?

I would mirror the coachee game offer to test eye level to him early on in order to stay at eye level. In the intervention I would offer him the interpretation "Now you're doing what you always do but with me now." In the best case the coachee stops, gets involved and thinks: "What is he saying? Nobody else tells me that." This holds a chance for him to give up his need for protection and control for a while, he sits alone with me in the session, he does not feel under observation or put on the spot. If he does not come next time after this intervention, that is OK too. However, my experience tends to be positive: I set the intervention, mirror what is happening there, and the coachee realizes that this is a chance to pause and reflect—maybe for the first time: Gee, that might be true. As a provocation and more in jest, I might also say, "Oh, so you want me to be your assistant. But that will cost double the hourly rate." Humor always helps.

Peter Döring

Seemingly out of nowhere, a question is asked about writing a paper on the topic of organizational culture. This request calls into question the consulting relationship. In parallel to the coaching assignment, the coachee wants to award a contract for work. Thus the coach becomes an assistant and/or ally in the fight against the board colleague.

In my perception of the coachee, destructive envy plays a significant role in the relationship with the board colleague. Envy arises when someone else has something that I lack. The most diverse things can trigger envy. Constructively, envy leads to personal effort and competition—I make an effort and achieve something in order to catch up, to be successful, or to attain the coveted good, the coveted characteristic myself. Destructive envy, however, aims to destroy what is coveted in the other. Part of the development of destructive envy is a negative self-image of the envious person. The prospect of developing oneself through one's own activity, of succeeding for oneself and achieving one's own goals is not seen. Envy can only be reduced by bringing the other down to one's own level. People who tend towards destructive envy often live in the idea that there is only above and below in relationships. A secure position can then only be on top and the person does everything to occupy this position.

However, coaching starts from a relationship at eye level. The coach provides a space for reflection and feedback that enables the coachee to question himself and his view of his professional role and his relationships and thus to develop them further. From the brief description of the relationship with the board colleague and the way the coachee expresses his offer of an assignment, I suspect that there has not been a coaching relationship in this sense here before. My role as a coach here would rather be that of a specialist advisor who gives useful communicative tips that the coachee can use to strengthen his position in the battle for the top position.

For me it is a central question whether I am in agreement with my personal values in an assignment—supporting a destructive envy would not fit to this. Furthermore, it is important for me to consider the overall interest of the organization when advising a (senior) member of an organization—after all, the organization is paying for the coaching. This would not apply here if I unilaterally supported the coachee in his fight against his colleague. All this would be important for me to clarify at the beginning in the coordination of the assignment and to agree with the coachee.

When the coachee makes a request regarding the preparation of the paper, I would first ask myself what relationship we have had so far, how it comes to this request. I would probably be surprised and, together with the coachee, would want to understand his motives. Whether I accept the assignment or not, I would initially leave open in order to better understand what the background is on the part of the coachee.

Claudia Bredt

It sounds as if the client wants to instrumentalize the coach for his own power-political interests in a struggle for position. It is no longer about the expansion of options for action, since these are already fixed for the client. The service would be more than that of a ghostwriter, almost a second, who supports the client in ensuring that he suffers no disadvantage, that he can reclaim territory and keep his pieces in the game.

It could be an intervention to offer him coaching to expand his scope of action from tactics to the strategic perception of interests, to examine the extent to which his chosen strategy would serve his own long-term goals and what alternative strategies would be possible: Reframing and changing perspective would be indicated. The issue behind his primary concern would then be illuminated. On this basis, a contract would be conceivable for me.

Heidi Möller

I would focus on the coachee's mental model. His anthropological premise seems to be that the world can be structured by relations of superiority and inferiority. So either I am on top or I am at the bottom and that is why I always have to try very hard to stay on top. Cooperative modes do not seem to be represented. In the coaching relationship, the client might experience a corrective emotional relationship: How does it feel when no one wants to empower the other? What affects would the coachee come into contact with and how unsettling is the experiment of a worldview that we do not live in the shark tank, we do not always have to keep the other threatening people at bay with hypervigilance? Not every moment is a matter of life and death.

4.5 Practical Example 19

Case Description

A chairwoman of the Board of Management suffered a severe verbal attack from an internal source. The works council wrote an open letter to the supervisory board. The chairwoman of the board wanted coaching from me, which the supervisory board refused. The reason given: The coaching had to be done by a woman and not a man. After the rejection, however, she and her colleague on the board commissioned me with an organizational development project; I was to develop a new understanding of second-level leadership. This would allow her more role clarity. I felt this was appropriate and the right thing to do, and I worked with her second-level leadership in a trusting manner. This has had the desired effect in that she has had less immediate conflict with staff and has experienced real support from the divisional managers. However, the company has experienced increased turnover since the time with the open letter. Of course, the top performers leave first. When colleagues leave, people still blame her for it. Now I experience her in conversations as reproachful, that she is still considered the bad one.

What Was the Coach's Approach?

I discuss the different levels with her: Her own behavior, which is still often based on a lack of appreciation; the management level, which has improved, but also does not show the necessary loyalty at all points and does not demand this clearly enough from the female employees; the employee level, which cultivates a decidedly resentful social culture, always spreads professional issues throughout the entire organization and regards contribution margin accounting as unethical.

Jannik Zimmermann

Coachees approach coaches with certain expectations that are not always met. Failure to meet these expectations can lead to resentment on the part of the coachees, which is then directed against the coach. If we look at the case described from this point of view, the following reading emerges: A chairwoman of the board is confronted with massive criticism in her organization. She sees the way out in being coached by a certain person. However, a corresponding assignment by the organization is officially rejected. Despite the rejection of coaching, she is able to commission this very person to carry out an organizational development project. However, the prevailing problem is not completely solved by this measure: Sporadically, she still encounters criticism and recriminations. She holds the coach partly responsible for this.

Now it has to be taken into account that in the case described no coaching took place. It remained only with the desire to initiate such a coaching. Instead, the coach carried out a different consulting format in the organization. Thus, strictly speaking, he was not acting in his function as a coach, but rather as an organizational developer. Nevertheless, it seems that the CEO expected the coach to solve the existing problem completely even without coaching, regardless of whether this was even possible with the implemented measure and intervention.

In such a case, I think it is a good idea to talk directly with the other person and to openly discuss the expectations. In the first step, it can be helpful to explore in more detail what the other person expects. In the second step, it is then possible to relate the concrete expectations to the possibilities and limits of the planned or implemented measures and interventions. In the case described, for example, an organizational development measure is hardly suitable for dealing with the board chairperson's own possible contribution to the problem. In a direct conversation, there is also the possibility of showing his counterpart further options for action. For example, the chairperson could commission coaching privately.

Andreas Knierim

When open letters are formulated, the trust between the parties involved is often disturbed in the long term. What are the intentions of the works council when it communicates with the supervisory board in this way? Who else should be listening in? Direct communication between the chairwoman of the board and the works council seems to be long gone.

The coach decides in favor of the organizational development project in the second level without questioning the choice of gender for coaching, or even without being able to question it. He is also effective in this project, but he cannot solve the problem of increased fluctuation there. Why does the coach continue to experience the chairwoman of the board in conversations as reproachful, towards whom is that meant?

Another thought: I suspect the potential coachee is the only woman at the top of an organization in a possibly male-dominated industry. Maybe in this situation she gets a man as a coach who tells her what is common in this communication and works with her on strategies for coping. I know this from other contexts when women say, "I just want to do coaching with a man so I can better understand what's going on in this male-dominated boardroom work in the first place." Then the coach would be kind of a traitor to the other men in that climate. This is possibly the reason for the rejection of coaching.

When I work with companies, I decide on level and formats. It is not possible to jump up or down in level, the conflicts of interest become too great. So I would not have accepted the assignment for the second level, but in the discussion with the works council and supervisory board I would have taken the opportunity to ask questions about the course of the conflict so far (while I am there): How does such a strong signal of an open letter come about?

It would be a gamble to propose a tool that I have been using for two years: live coaching in a closed group, led by a colleague and myself. The process is as follows: Before the live coaching day, we ask for the participants' concerns in writing. Each live coaching session in the group starts with the client asking for a good outcome. Then the situation is outlined, we contribute interpretations and working hypotheses, exercises are mutually agreed upon, and the results are recorded on the flip chart. After each coaching session the whole group is asked for feedback on what they have heard. Everyone can contribute experiences and give hints. We work with clear rules so as not to hurt or teach others. At the end of each live coaching session there is an exercise for the whole group.

Peter Döring

There is a problem in this company. In my experience, open letters are not just written, but usually have a long history. Also, the high turnover of qualified employees and the refusal to provide requested coaching support are clear indications that something is fundamentally wrong here. And this seems to be related—rightly or wrongly—to the CEO: Either by not being clear about her role, by making mistakes in dealing with employees, or by projecting grievances onto her that may be older.

Instead of insisting on focusing on this issue and analyzing reasons and backgrounds, the consultant gets involved in an organizational development project and should develop a new second-level understanding of leadership. It remains unclear how the coach comes to think this is "appropriate and the right thing to do." Although the project may have improved some things—turnover remains as a problem. The medicine that the CEO and her colleague came up with and that the coach got involved in does not work—and the coach gets reproaches from the CEO, who hoped to stabilize her position and the situation with this measure. In my view, he did not insist on an analysis and clarification of the initial situation and allowed himself to be seduced into a (presumably lucrative) alternative project, which, however, could not solve the underlying problem because it was not understood at all.

As indicated above, I would not have gotten involved in this organizational development project as a (bogus) solution. Instead, I would have conducted an analysis of the development that had occurred with the CEO and her colleagues on the board. For me, it would have been a matter of understanding the background in detail, including the role of the works council and the supervisory board. What are the respective interests here? What attempts were made to reach an understanding? Why did they fail? I would have been particularly interested in the supervisory board's ideas for solutions and implicit or explicit mandates. The next step for me would be to talk to the works council to understand what went wrong from their point of view. Against the background of the results of this analysis, I would then make a proposal on how to proceed.

Regina Gibhardt

The case description is missing essential information: Why was the CEO "attacked" by the works council? What is the content of the open letter to the supervisory board? A works council does not just write a letter to the supervisory board. It needs a corresponding history. What did the chairwoman of the management board contribute to this story?

Due to this lack of information, I try to exemplify possible different background scenarios with the following five hypotheses. None of these necessarily corresponds to reality. But it makes clear that a different approach is needed in each case.

- As a woman, she does not know how to recognize the unspoken rules of the game of men (insider relationships) in the company and how to deal with them wisely.
- It endangers the company by, for example, preventing innovation, dragging it into dubious business, not pursuing a clear direction for the future, etc.
- There is a personal conflict between her and the works council chairman, which is now being taken to the company level.
- The communication culture in the company prevents open, trusting, and goal-oriented interaction with each other.
- She is letting herself be used as a scapegoat for something she is not responsible for.

On the other hand, it is obvious that the second-level managers and presumably also the other levels do not have any lived role clarity. The organization appears to be unclearly structured and does not offer top performers the space to contribute their full potential. The result: Fluctuation. The second level of management does not have the status that the organization needs: Employees go into direct communication with the board chair. This points to a patriarchal, Tayloristic[1] management culture in the past that did not initiate in good time the change to the dynamic market rules of play that exist now.

In a possible coaching process with the CEO, I would keep the following guiding questions/thoughts in mind:

1. In terms of the person who holds the role of CEO, at the BEING level, my focus would be on issues such as victimhood (this is clearly evident in the accusations) and meeting other people's expectations (Is she even in the right place? What is really her thing?) On the DOING level, I would look at which skills she has lacked so far for her function (communication know-how, systemic understanding of the organization, decision-making, agile goal management).
2. What does the organization need in order to continue to fulfill the company's purpose in the future and to adapt as best as possible to the changed conditions on the market? In the case described, this would result in a prolonged change process throughout the entire company.

Heidi Möller

The gender perspective appeals to me most: "Equality is still not equal in organizations" (cf. Möller & Müller-Kalkstein, 2014). Women in leadership positions tend to attribute difficulties internally, asking themselves what they have done wrong. Men attribute more externally, citing environmental factors for complications (cf. Möller & West-Leuer, 2018). Female leaders are quick to blame themselves due to greater self-esteem instability. This mechanism relieves pressure on the system but prevents shared organizational learning. When push comes to shove, the quota debate is waged. Even when large corporations currently appoint female board members, the daily press gives us plenty of reason to marvel at how quickly the women disappear again. Unlike men, they often have less stable internal and external networks. For many companies, it lends itself to blaming difficulties on women's lack of leadership skills. Unfortunately, women are only too happy to adopt this view of things. So, positively *reframed,* coaching by a female coach could make sense here, if she is sufficiently gender sensitive and familiar with these dynamics. Negatively interpreted, the suggestion for coaching by a female coach represents a secondary stigmatization, as a women's self-help group.

Developing the second level further may have made a lot of sense: A leeway that the board member used sensibly. Here, role clarity emerged and this can—from a systemic point of view—also have an impact on the entire company. A changed subsystem changes the overall structure.

It is a real challenge in coaching to support a high performer in a high hierarchical position, who has been attacked, in successful, even micropolitical action (cf. Rastetter &

[1] Taylorism emerged at the time of industrialization. Characteristics include: Clearly prescribed work processes that leave no room for individuality; separation of mental and physical work; top-down.

Jüngling, 2018). The scapegoating of a female leader is enormously relieving for the organization and is thus quite stable. Breaking the labeling as an underperformer needs a lot of surprising and successful visible behaviors to regain the internal standing. This is no small thing.

References

Bion, W. R. (1990). *Lernen durch Erfahrung*. Suhrkamp.

Erdheim, M. (2002). Die Veränderung der bedeutungsgebenden Struktur durch Adoleszenz und Therapie. *Psychotherapie in Psychiatrie, Psychotherapeutischer Medizin und Klinischer Psychologie, 7*(1), 88–90.

Fürstenau, P. (2001). *Psychoanalytisch verstehen, systemisch denken, suggestiv intervenieren*. Pfeiffer.

Giernalczyk, T., & Möller, H. (2018). *Entwicklungsraum. Psychodynamische Beratung in Organisationen*. Vandenhoeck & Ruprecht.

Giernalczyk, T., Lazar, R. A., & Albrecht, C. (2012). Die Rolle der Führungskraft und des Beraters als Container. In T. Giernalczyk & M. Lohmer (Eds.), *Das Unbewusste im Unternehmen. Psychodynamik von Führung, Beratung und Change Management* (pp. 25–37). Schäffer-Poeschel.

Glasl, F. (2017). *Konfliktmanagement: Ein Handbuch für Führungskräfte, Beraterinnen und Berater*. Haupt.

Lazar, R. A. (1994). W. R. Bions Modell "container-contained" als eine psychoanalytische Leitidee in der supervision. In H. Pühl (Ed.), *Handbuch der Supervision 2* (pp. 380–402). Edition Marold.

Lohmer, M., & Möller, H. (2014). *Psychoanalyse in Organisationen. Einführung in die psychodynamische Organisationsberatung*. Kohlhammer.

Möller, H. (2012). Sie kamen, sahen und siegten – der lange Marsch der Frauen in Organisationen. In T. Giernalczyk & M. Lohmer (Eds.), *Das Unbewusste im Unternehmen* (S. 91–110). Schaeffer-Poeschel.

Möller, H., & Müller-Kalkstein, R. (Eds.). (2014). *Gender und Beratung*. Vandenhoeck & Ruprecht.

Möller, H., & West-Leuer, B. (2018). Stolpersteine weiblicher Karrieren – and what about Sex? *Zeitschrift Psychodynamische Psychotherapie (PDP), 2*, 97–105.

Neuberger, O. (2002). *Führen und führen lassen. Ansätze, Ergebnisse und Kritik der Führungsforschung*. UTB.

Oberhoff, B. (2009). *Übertragung und Gegenübertragung in der Supervision*. Deadalus.

Rastetter, D., & Jüngling, C. (2018). *Frauen, Männer, Mikropolitik: Geschlecht und Macht in Organisationen*. Vandenhoeck & Ruprecht.

Schiemann, S. J., & Jonas, E. (2020). Streben nach Macht fern von Ethik: Die "dunkle Triade" bei Führungskräften und die Folgen für Organisationen. *Organisationsberatung, Supervision, Coaching, 27*(2), 251–263.

Schlippe, A. v., & Schweitzer, J. (2016). *Lehrbuch der systemischen Therapie und Beratung I*. Vanderhoeck & Ruprecht.

Schreyögg, A. (2011). *Konfliktcoaching: Anleitung für den Coach*. Campus.

Storch, M., & Tschacher, W. (2016). *Embodied Communication. Kommunikation beginnt im Körper, nicht im Kopf*. Hogrefe.

Demanding Working or Living Conditions of the Coachees

5

5.1 Practical Example 20

Case Description

The assignment was made by the company: A long-time manager is to be qualified for the internal application procedure. The previous department is dissolved; The employees are distributed to other departments. This employee was left behind. In the first contact, the employee was very reserved, completely frustrated because of his application status and the way the company management dealt with him. We clarified our work assignment for him again well and then worked very strongly and in a continuously resource-oriented way. The employee's last application was more than 30 years ago and at that time consisted of a colleague recommendation and a 10-minute interview. So we had to work intensively on content. In doing so, it was helpful for him to get to know the thoughts of a personnel manager in the application process and to repeatedly compare them with his aspects. According to his statement, after three coaching sessions, the employee went into the new application process self-confident and well equipped in terms of content. Two days later, a call came from a happy coachee: It worked with the application and at a better location, too.

How Did the Coach Go About It?

The coachee's emotional state of anger and disappointment due to a lack of self-competence coupled with anger at the company is not unknown to me in my work as a coach. It was helpful that at the beginning, I focused on the coachee's interests and was able to make him believe that I was working exclusively with him—even if commissioned by the company—to strengthen him. Gradually, we then added the company's perspective. This was especially possible after the coachee had done a good job of clarifying his competencies. I kept encouraging him and confronting him with his skills and

H. Möller, J. Zimmermann, *Difficult Situations in Business Coaching*,
https://doi.org/10.1007/978-3-658-35087-1_5

competencies. Another helpful aspect was acknowledging and naming negative feelings in the first contact. The company's HR department had sent the employee to internal coaching sessions several times and repeatedly told him that he should not behave so negatively. I acknowledged him—as a neutral authority—in his pain about the situation by actively listening and verbalizing emotional experience content. And then worked with him again and again in a resource-oriented and goal-oriented way.

Claudia Bredt

It is like a miracle that the coachee in the case described is "self-confident and well equipped in terms of content" after three sessions. At first, it is astonishing that the coach brings in the case as a difficult situation at all. Where is the difficulty in the coach presenting this success story? Possibly the coach experiences the coachee's initial situation and the associated assignment as difficult. Or the coach knows from her own experience the effects associated with the coachee's description of *not being noticed, left behind* and *being aggrieved.*

It is unclear how the coach worked. The statement: "We clarified our work assignment for him again well and then worked very strongly and in a continuously resource-oriented way" seems to me like an exaggeration. Possibly the exaggeration in the sense of a formation of opposites in the consulting process is the miracle-working means for the quick success of the coachee: From *not being perceived to* the desire to be perceived and taken seriously by the external coach to a special degree. From *being left behind* to being all there and being seen in the coaching. From being *aggrieved* to being valued.

Regina Gibhardt

There is no specific question from the case description. It sounds more like a hero's story. No obvious difficulty is described because everything seems to be done in three settings. This can work if the settings have a sufficient number of hours and if the focus is only on the increase in methodological competence.

When I am in the initial conversation with my coaching clients, I like to offer them the image of BEING + DOING = HAVING. BEING stands for inner development, values, attitudes, beliefs, etc. DOING, on the other hand, has to do with concrete skills—in this case, communication skills for job interviews. There are clients who do not want to work on the BEING level. For them, it is completely sufficient to look at the DOING level and to become active there. Just like the motto: "Give me a few tools, a few models and methods with which I can work differently, and then that is completely enough for me." If this has been the primary concern of the coachee, then it is really all about behavioral competence. And of course, as a coach, you have to accept this and align the process to it.

What remains unresolved, however, is the BEING level, on which a presumable grievance may exist on the part of the company as a result of its treatment of a long-time employee.

Since I do not have sufficient expertise in job application training myself, I would recommend this request to my network.

Jannik Zimmermann

Coachees bring extremely diverse issues into a coaching process, which are sometimes negatively colored. Therefore, coaches regularly come into contact with negative emotions and descriptions of quite destructive, stressful circumstances in the coachees' environment. It stands to reason that quite a few coaches experience this as difficult. The case described can be seen as a good example in this context: For the coach, the difficult situation does not lie in the fact that the issue is difficult to solve, but in having to work with and endure the coachee's frustration and the circumstances described.

The way in which a coach can work with a coachee in such a situation has already been indicated in the case described. In order to relieve the coachee, one starting point is to have the coachee's emotions and situational circumstances reported. Both the emotions and the described circumstances should not be banished from the coaching but should be given space and consideration. In order to support the coachee, it can help to convey to him that his emotions are appropriate as a reaction to the circumstances. I also see a starting point for supporting desired changes in working with the coachee in a resource-oriented way. For this purpose, the Zurich Resource Model can be used; a detailed description of this self-management training can be found in Storch and Krause (2017).

In addition, it can be helpful to specifically address the following question: Why is it difficult for me as a coach to endure the coachee's emotions and circumstances? Indeed, it can be assumed that one's reaction to the coachee's emotions and circumstances offers information about the counterpart, but also about one's unresolved issues. In this context, I would like to refer to the concept of countertransference from psychoanalysis (see Körner, 2018). If one follows these thoughts, it can help to take a closer look at one's unresolved issues. This is illustrated by a fictional example: The coach is conducting the coaching in the case described. She has the tendency to feel highly responsible for any grievances, regardless of her actions. It will almost certainly be difficult for the coach to work with the coachee because she feels responsible for the coachee's emotions. A confrontation with one's issue of responsibility could possibly help to achieve more acceptance, confidence, and serenity here. Coaching supervision can provide the framework for tracing unresolved issues.

Andreas Knierim

"Everything's fine" pops into my head. When I have this thought in coaching, it is very likely that I have missed something. My guess in the case described is that the company is hiring: For what internal application process should this long-time professional be qualified? There is simply no more room for this employee at the site—does the coaching serve as a bonus, an emotional compensation for the sober, rational, organizational change measures? Who is soothing his conscience here, who is disguising his behavior here?

Besides these systemic thoughts, I get stuck on "clarified [. . .] well" and "very strongly and in a continuously resource-oriented way" and especially on the call "from the happy coachee." These are exaggerations and evaluations—by whom were they made, by the coach or by the coachee? How will the employee prove himself at a better location if he has not sufficiently reflected on his situation at the old location? Because the choice of words suggests moderate reflection, precisely in the sense of "everything is fine."

The case reminds me of a new placement coaching: The coachee and I were in a similar situation. It was not the application process that was the topic at the beginning, but the initial situation. For this reflection, I, as the coach, had taken the precaution of agreeing on a safety cushion of eight sessions to be able to go into depth.

The first three sessions can be about working through the initial situation and, above all, about the question of how it came about that the manager remained. What behavior, what patterns have led to the coachee looking so little for a new job and now, practically at the last minute, needing coaching? This pattern reflection, in particular, can lead to the executive behaving differently in the new location and seizing the opportunity to start anew and present himself differently.

After that, there is time to look at the person in the context of the application procedure—in my new placement format, I always work together with a personnel consultant, who in parallel works out the formalities with the coachee and trains application situations.

It is also helpful to schedule the coaching so that there are still sessions left when the coachee is already in the new job to deepen the insights gained from reflecting on the old behavior patterns and to practice them in current situations.

Peter Döring

The first question for me here is what the difficult situation is for the coach—this is the aspect from which the situation is described. In my estimation, it is the coachee's intense, partly suppressed negative emotions. My guess is that the coachee is dependent on receiving impulses and suggestions from outside in order to then become active himself. One could call this a well-compensated depressive structure over decades. As long as the work environment is stable, the daily demands in terms of tasks and collegial interaction are clear, and the underlying structural feature does not become visible. However, the coachee himself finds it more difficult than his colleagues to take the necessary initiative in the restructuring situation to look for a new field of activity within the group and to apply for a job that suits him—an element of the depressive inhibition of initiative could also be not knowing what suits him and what would suit him as a new field.

Against the background of this structural assumption, the process of spontaneous healing in three sessions becomes understandable: In personal contact with the counselor, he can find access to his resources and develop new initiatives. After he has gained trust, he can get to know the thoughts of a personnel officer in the application process, absorb new ideas and suggestions. He manages to overcome his depressive inhibition of initiative within the framework of this trusting counseling relationship and successfully applies for a job. If he finds a good connection in the new position, he will probably be able to continue working there without a renewed symptomatology.

In retrospect, a failure of leadership in the run-up to the development shown becomes clear here. Presumably, the coachee's manager did not engage enough with him and his coping options in the change process. Again, no special effort by the manager would have been required to support the employee in the change. The manager could have found out what he is good at and what qualifications he has—as I understand it, being informed about this is one of the basic tasks of a manager. She could then have asked around in the company and given the employee an impulse to apply for a job—as she did 30 years ago. However, it can be observed that managers today have less and less time and resources available for their core tasks. One background to this is that they are entrusted with additional tasks by their managers so that the importance of personal management relationships recedes into the background.

The consultant has implemented the order competently from my point of view. Personally, I have no experience with such application coaching. If the company had approached me, I would have wanted to deal more with the question of leadership in the sense described above and the design of the change process. For this, it would certainly have made sense to be involved in the process earlier.

References

Körner, J. (2018). *Die Psychodynamik von Übertragung und Gegenübertragung*. Vandenhoeck & Ruprecht.

Storch, M., & Krause, F. (2017). *Selbstmanagement - ressourcenorientiert: Grundlagen und Trainingsmanual für die Arbeit mit dem Zürcher Ressourcen Modell (ZRM)*. Hogrefe.

6 Own Delimitation of the Coaches

6.1 Practical Example 21

Case Description
As an industrial and organizational psychologist, I carry out several individual coaching assignments in a state theater on a fee basis. A problematic situation arose because I had taken over two individual coaching sessions on the hierarchical level and was also invited to a management meeting with the theater's dual leadership. In the house, there is always a discussion about the lack of understanding of leadership and the necessary leadership qualifications. In this situation, it was quite difficult for me to stay in the neutral coaching role. The conflicts between the management levels have come to such a head that it pretty much requires a decision from the highest management level to resolve the conflict. When I was asked to provide decisions, I did not allow myself to be taken out of my neutral position, but in the next leadership coaching session, it was difficult for me to remain impartial and authentic between the necessary neutrality and my information and knowledge. The role confusion noticeably carried over to my role as well.

What Was the Coach's Approach?
I was able to weaken my expectations and superego demands for authenticity and thus found an inner attitude that made it possible for the moment to continue working with the manager concerned. It remains for me to reflect and question to what extent I can again resolve and clarify my role overlaps and confusions.

Tom Levold
Obviously, this is about the understanding of leadership in the company and the conflicts between different management levels, which he advises in parallel, which understandably puts him in a dilemma. Apparently, he is expected to take a stand on necessary decisions,

H. Möller, J. Zimmermann, *Difficult Situations in Business Coaching*,
https://doi.org/10.1007/978-3-658-35087-1_6

which he can avoid due to his claim to neutrality, but apparently at the price of his role confusion. It remains unclear what neutrality means in this context. Is its neutrality with regard to necessary decisions or neutrality with regard to persons or different hierarchical levels?

Leadership and decision-making conflicts in organizations in the cultural sector often arise from the tension between the organizational form as a company on the one hand and the demand and necessity to offer an audience top artistic performances on the other. A theater is, first of all, a state, municipal or private enterprise with personnel responsible for a relatively large apparatus of people who are permanently employed and then an artistic ensemble whose members are each engaged for a limited time or only for a specific project. Leadership issues are handled differently in both areas, which results in a specific field dynamic that, in my view, is clearly different from other organizations. This tension is already structurally inherent in the dual leadership of management and artistic directorship and is prone to role confusion.

In my experience, on the one hand, the use of power in such contexts is readily denied, but at the same time, it is often very ruthlessly enforced, both in terms of artistic autonomy and organizational constraints.

In the case described, it seems as if the problem of the lack of leadership understanding or qualification is presented in the system as a personal rather than an organizational problem: The organization as a whole does not come into focus, but only the conflict between persons with different aptitudes on different hierarchical levels. The coach has allowed himself to be drawn into this conflict by accepting a seductive assignment from the top management, with the request to prescribe decisions, i.e., to take on executive functions himself, which should be reserved for the decision-makers in the system. Even though he recognizes that a decision is needed at the highest level of management, he sees the problem primarily as how to maintain his impartiality and authenticity.

Consistently, the author works to mitigate his expectations and superego demands for authenticity, the severity of which would otherwise have made his continued work as a coach with the executive, who was apparently affected by a necessary top-level decision, difficult. In doing so, he makes his confusion the fulcrum of his attempted solution, leaving the system on the outside.

What would change if one were to view the described confusion regarding conflicts over leadership behavior and competence not only as a personal dilemma, but as an indication of the system's possible lack of ability to clarify and constructively handle issues of leadership, hierarchy, responsibility, and decision-making? In this case, the focus would shift from advising an individual manager to dealing with organizational problems and would require a new assignment—be it organizational consulting or coaching of top management. If such a change in work assignment seems too complex or a breach of pre-existing working alliances and associated loyalties, a friendly refusal pointing out the obvious need for such clarification would be advisable.

Ulrich Beumer

In terms of role analysis (see Beumer & Sievers, 2000), this is a complex situation that cannot be adequately understood either by an individualistically truncated view of the professionalism of the counselor or by focusing solely on the manifest issues. The focus of understanding must be on the complex interplay and interweaving of the personal dynamics of the individual and the psychosocial dynamics of the organization.

The starting point is the symptom, in this case, the confusion of the coachee, whose meaning is to be asked and whose sense and emotionality must be taken into consideration. The coachee assumes—certainly rightly—that this confusion is not personally fed alone, but is transferred to him and delegated for processing and resolution. One hypothesis is that the institutional contribution to the confusion of the counselor and the coachee lies in an unresolved leadership issue that is doubly fed, firstly by an overall lack of a leadership concept and secondly by divergent leadership perceptions between the two leadership figures. The fantasy that this can be solved by a leadership decision, i.e., by power, falls short in my view.

Psychodynamic coaching is about a more comprehensive understanding of the scene in its conscious and unconscious parts. There is probably a latent assumption that the establishment of a clear hierarchical structure would mean the solution to all problems. However, given the specific culture of a theater with a fundamental tension between economic necessity and artistic freedom, or between a culture of order and emotional culture, this is unrealistic and possibly rather harmful for a good theater.

In addition to the institutional dynamics, the emphasis on confusion regarding one's role or the contradiction between experience and professional aspirations is striking.

The focus here is on a neutral coaching role. Presumably, the involvement at the top management level is unsettling and calls into question the coach's understanding of his or her role. Traditionally, especially supervisors tend to be critical of leadership and find it rather difficult to identify with this role or the task of leadership. Furthermore, the claim to neutrality is prevalent, on the one hand, in the sense of an all-partiality, as it prevails in mediative concepts, and on the other hand, in the sense of a distance to emotional identification or too much closeness.

If this coach came to me for supervision, I would first try to better understand the history of the consultation in order to understand together with him how the role confusion came about. Then, it would make sense to work on this experience of role confusion in the sense of a clarification and to work in the sense of a role-analytical understanding on which parts of the confusion are a reflection and delegation of the organization and which parts are rather conditioned by the professional biography and the professional self-image as a consultant.

In principle, from a psychodynamic perspective, it is not harmful to work across several hierarchical levels in an organization, but this requires above all self-management in roles (see Lawrence, 1998), i.e., role clarity, and the skillful handling of boundaries. It is precisely the work with different levels that then offers an opportunity for a more comprehensive view of the psychosocial dynamics of the organization. The coach can become a kind of "sounding board" for the leadership to support them in their decisions.

With regard to the problem of leadership, this means, for example, finding out where the pressure to make decisions described above comes from, or to what extent the fruitful tension between economics and artistic leadership is not part of the fundamental constitution of a good theater.

Furthermore, the case described would be a good opportunity to work with the coachee on the questions of professional self-concept. On the one hand, I would ask what the assertion of emotional neutrality actually achieves and whether it is not also a sign of a form of fear defense (see Menzies-Lyth, 1974). Especially in the field of coaching, I often experience this form of distancing in order to ward off one's insecurity and fear of making mistakes. Coaching, however, has to unfold fruitfully between the poles of willingness to be entangled and the ability to step out of identification and emotionality again.

Conceptually, it would also be necessary to work on whether working across different hierarchical levels is not proof of competence and less an expression of unsuccessful role clarity. Larger institutions, in particular, work with coaches who are deployed in different roles (in relation to hierarchy and activity), and the competence to be able to take both the management and the employee perspective is expected and expressly desired. A constant willingness to self-reflect, to endure conflict tensions and emotional entanglements, even confusions, is indispensable in order to be able to use these constructively for the further development of the organization.

Agnes Büchele

The coaching assignment seems interesting and challenging at the same time, but the presentation remains nebulous. The coach struggles to remain neutral and impartial—one wonders: What specifically? Towards whom? In general, the demand for neutrality carries the risk of getting caught in a straightjacket in emotionally charged conflicts, and as a coach, of being restricted in one's ability to act. Neutrality also stands in contradiction to authenticity.

By registering a conflict in himself and reflecting on it, the coach creates a favorable condition for distancing himself from the team conflicts of his clients, and in this way, he can also loosen the constriction of rigid demands on himself. It is a constant and general theme of coaching and counseling to reflect on one's resonances in the countertransference—with regard to neutrality, partiality, authenticity, and to figure out for oneself where and to whom the partiality wanders, in order to understand the personal and organizational systems.

Wanting to maintain neutrality could indicate that the coach is stuck in unrealistic demands that *overwhelm* him or her. This could be an indication for the coaching to clarify which concrete demands the individual participants and the whole team currently have to cope with. For this, it would be important to know which levels and areas of the theater are involved in the coaching assignment.

If this coach came to me for supervision, it would be a matter for me—as is so often the case—of clarifying the roles and positions of those involved and discussing which ideas on the part of the theater are associated with the coaching assignment. It is conceivable that conflicts at the theater often consist of entanglements between complex operational necessities and demands for artistic freedom. So, it would now be a matter of sorting out the levels between the structures of the organization, the personal understanding of those involved in the conflict and possibly—being a state theater—also cultural policy. This initial reflection on oneself in the coach position, one's distresses with role confusion could thus lead to an analytical perspective in which the structural conditions of the theater business are seen in relation to the demands of leadership and personal entanglements (see Lohmer & Möller, 2014). The coach's further approach could then be understanding—both emotionally and professionally knowledgeable—rather than neutrally detached.

The coach's problems with this assignment also seem to me to be exemplary for the importance and understanding of organizational culture (see Schein, 2003) and, derived from this, for the conditions for leading a particular organization. For the theater as an organization, knowledge of the peculiarities of acting, directing, organizing, and many other things, also in connection with cultural politics, would have to be known or deepened accordingly. The function of roles in the literal sense is at the core of existence at the theater and a constant source of personal, social, artistic, and organizational confusion and contradiction. Everyone wants to be a star and yet is dependent on the ensemble and the director, and is only part of a complex and inherently contradictory cultural organizational whole. The (also theoretical) study of these areas can strengthen the coach on the axis "professional knowledge—emotional experience" in the sense of field competence (see on this topic also Klein, 2009). Increased prior knowledge makes it possible to make preliminary assumptions about manifest and unconscious conflict situations of the organization as well as of the persons and is suitable for adjusting to the coaching in a more coherent way.

It would be necessary to clarify with the coach what demands he imposes on himself in his efforts to remain neutral, and he could be encouraged to explore resonating feelings and emotions in himself; from the perspective of countertransference, reflections on the coachee's problems could be derived. On the other hand, biographical experiences with theater and acting, with hierarchies and social prestige could also be significant in the sense of the coach's transferences. Which obstacles and which competencies could be included in his own experiences?

Achim Mollbach

The case maker's comments suggest that, firstly, at the beginning of his mandate he did not have a useful picture of the organization as an orientation for him and, secondly, that he may not be aware of the necessity of such a picture for successfully acting as a consultant and as a coach in an organization. This necessity, however, exists especially when there are several poorly defined mandates that are realized in one and the same client system.

If the "several individual coaching assignments" he refers to came more or less in parallel and isolation as initial assignments, there is indeed a great risk that the coach will be drawn into the conflicts, power and influence relationships, etc., even if he has the awareness of such potential dynamics. The confusion arises because the consultant (as well as the client) derives his role from the individual, isolated consulting assignments and has no consulting or coaching format or role or role model ready for the fact that the consulting processes take place in the same client system and the clients interact in the client system. The present case shows that the coach working in an organization, who may receive multiple consulting or coaching assignments, needs models, competencies, and techniques that go beyond immediate coaching knowledge. In terms of coaching knowledge, these are meta-models and organizational diagnostic and systemic competencies that are superior to coaching. What is needed here is the availability not of a coaching model but of a more comprehensive organizational model as an orientation to how the individual coaching processes and the clients themselves are embedded in the formal and informal organization of the client, what expectations, conflicts, etc. arise from this within the organization and for the coach and consultant. Particularly in cultures characterized by weak formalization, it is especially necessary for a consultant to have an awareness of these dynamics since the ordering and delimiting function of formal processes is missing in both the consulting and client systems. For counseling and coaching in a rather weakly formalized organization, it is even more necessary for the counselor and coach to have an awareness of the informal organization, i.e., culture, rituals, relationship networks, power and influence mechanisms of the organization, and to be able to move confidently in this context.

In the short term, I think it would make sense for the coach to first clarify the entire landscape, e.g., in a supervision session. This should not start with the coach's expectations, but first of all, reconstruct the organization or the system of the state theater in the formal and above all informal dimension. This also includes the reconstruction of conflicts and conflict contexts. It is, therefore, a matter of adopting a decidedly organizational or systemic perspective. The next step in supervision would be to reconstruct the formulated, but also implicit, expectations which the various players in the organization have of the coach from the coach's point of view, and how these expectations relate to each other from the coach's point of view. It is, therefore, important to oscillate between reflection on the organization and self-reflection in supervision, so that a position develops in the coach that provides answers to two questions: What is possible in this organization and what is not? What do I need as a coach in terms of clarity and unambiguity so that I can work well? In the supervision, a strategy for action would then also be developed for him as a consultant and coach.

In the long term, it would certainly make sense in the sense of learning from experience if the coach learns that coaching is always embedded in an organizational context—and this also means that the coach clarifies and, if necessary, expands his or her understanding of the organization. In addition, it would be useful for the coach to pay more attention to exploring the formal and informal organization at a practical level as part of the clarification of the assignment. Furthermore, it also makes sense for certain individuals to establish principles for themselves as to where the boundaries of accepting an assignment or mandate lie.

Edeltrud Freitag-Becker

Without role diversity there is no theater, without role confusion there is no drama. The theater lives from confusion, intertwined casting, the simultaneous in the non-simultaneous, from longings and other feelings, from resolutions and the search for the real in the unreal.

The State Theatre as an organization organizes the processes, bears the responsibility for all structural and economic matters of the house as well as for the appropriate casting of all the roles necessary for the interaction—and must also be in the service of the public interest.

If we use the metaphor-analytical approach, it becomes clear that the notion of roles and role occupations, of stagings and dramas, etc. have different meanings in the two structural forms and consequently shape the working relationships.

The coach gets caught up in this dazzling world and gets caught up in the complexity. He moves from the backstage to the frontstage—and stands in the spotlight. He is supposed to bring the solution, resolve the tensions—and does not know his role. His brooding points to an individualistic understanding of consulting; his view of the organization remains clouded.

It seems as if the coach has not yet embraced this organization. He does not develop an overall picture but sticks to current requirements and moods, to scenes, so to speak.

Fathoming and understanding the scenes might provide a different view of organizational dynamics and allow him to more clearly define his role and task. He strives to remain neutral—neutrality in an organizational culture where the lifeblood is identification and engagement with the role at hand is the primary requirement. The fear of partisanship confronts him with the need to admit to himself: Who am I in this place and how powerful do I want to be?

If we turn to the implied conflict, we might be dealing with an institutionalized fear defense: What is really happening backstage? What dramas are simmering in the background? What are the scenes meant to distract from?

This brings the entire organization of the theater into view and into the focus of consulting. For this, the coach would need more than an individual-oriented approach to consulting. If the coach's fear of losing himself keeps the upper hand, he will remain an uncertain seeker.

If we stay with the theater metaphor, we are dealing with an as-if or what-if situation in every play. What would happen if the theater as an organization was put on stage in coaching? What might become clear, what images emerge, what roles become visible, what role might the coach take? Scenic understanding as an invitation to the participants to enter into the analysis of the situation together could enable the following topics:

- Get involved and understand the culture
- Figure out the dual leadership and let the conflicts become clear
- Identify and track leadership roles
- Understand the fear of the dramas of the organization

If we apply this scenic description to the theater within the theater, it becomes clear that there the true characters and the true story often only emerge over time. The play must develop, unroll, be brought to its climax. Only when you look back, only after the performance do you know what you have seen and how it is possible to be interpreted and understood. It takes patience and the willingness to let oneself be drawn into the depths of irritation and incomprehension until an overall picture emerges and the development of one's role becomes possible.

In my opinion, an organizational and cultural analytical approach is essential for this coaching assignment. The seductions and confusions that organizational theater exudes and invites require both understanding and empathy as well as detachment. Executive coaching is also not detached from this dynamic.

It would be wonderful if the coach felt like working with metaphors and scenes and inviting the coachees to make associations and resonate. The playful approach could bring lightness into the heaviness of the suggested scenes and offer the protagonists involved the chance to allow multiple perspectives on the conflicts.

Heidi Möller

When I identify with the coach, I immediately feel my fascination. There is this dazzling field: The state theater! I immediately shout "Hooray!" At last, an interesting field! In me, there would be the danger of suspending rational analysis out of sheer enthusiasm for the field. A cool field: Everyone is on first-name terms, superficially "easy-going." At this point, I would be in danger of getting caught up in the excitement of being involved. The exciting question is, how is leadership meaningfully realized in the theater? How do you manage actors? Do you need other concepts than the typical leadership concepts we all know? Do you need different approaches for the creative sector? It would also be very charming for me to be a court or theater psychologist who is always present when needed, like a consultant, especially because I have great admiration for the world of theater. Knowing its seductiveness, I would work with colleagues, crafting a counseling architecture that I am not alone in. Systems need systems to mirror each other. I would create resonating spaces for myself together with others.

One last remark: What is authenticity in counseling? By this I mean not always saying everything, but specifically releasing my countertransferences, perceptions, and evaluations.

6.2 Practical Example 22

Case Description

It is about a situation where the coachee told me about a lawyer she dealt with professionally and spoke about in an infinitely foul and discriminatory manner. In the course of the conversation, it turned out that I knew this lawyer and had hired him twice before for our family a few years earlier. We found him to be good and constructive. I had resolved not to tell the client this. However, when we did a little breakdown on the professional relationship of the two parties and she told me she would call the lawyer by his first name was on a first-name basis with a certain attorney, I stupidly let slip his first name. To which the client said, "How do you know his name?" After that hour, the client dropped out of coaching. I wrote her again that I would like to know the reasons for her absence, but she did not reply.

How Did the Coach Go About It?
I found myself being unprofessional. I should have said right away that I know this lawyer and therefore might be biased if we continue to talk about him.

Mathias Lohmer
The difficulty begins with the coach treating a *shared* dilemma of the coach-coachee relationship (the shared knowledge of the lawyer as the client's adversary) as a dilemma of *her own*. She wants to resolve it without involving the coachee. In the short term, the coach thus avoids risking termination of the coaching process—in the long term, however, she risks her client finding out about her, which then promptly happens, trust is damaged and the coaching process ends all the more conflictually.

Here again, a countertransference analysis in the sense of a "containment" (a holding, understanding, and processing; see Giernalczyk et al., 2012) of the momentary tension is recommended:

1. I *notice* irritation, inhibition, anxiety (about knowing the lawyer) and take it seriously.
2. I pause and *analyze* this irritation for myself: What do I fear when I bring up this complication? Am I annoyed by the client's invalidating manner? Why might I feel guilty about my knowledge of the lawyer? Do I feel pushed into an either-or (I take sides with the client or the lawyer)? Would I have the option for me to continue working with the client, or is this an issue of partiality and abstinence that suggests ending the coaching?
3. I *use* my inner process as a starting point for an intervention to the client, e.g.: "I would like to pause with you for a moment. I just realized that I know your adversary personally from a previous professional experience. Since I am not in a counseling relationship with him, I could imagine continuing to work with you about this relationship that is problematic for you. However, I could also understand if at this point you would first like to examine more closely whether the coaching process continues to make sense for you. What do you think?"

Klaus Eidenschink
Triangular constellations are fundamentally difficult to handle and often cannot be avoided. Triangulations—that is, relationship situations in which there is a first, second and third party—stimulate in every person fundamental, existential questions such as: Might I become the excluded one (of the three)? Am I in danger of becoming the excluded third?

Am I being appropriated or abused as the second? Do I pay a price towards the third if I come close to the first as the second?

The case description raises the question of who is loyal to whom and for what reasons, and who is in pact with whom. Such constellations are frequent, if not the rule, in coaching, since the coach, for example, is always committed to both the coachee and the company. The artful handling of this phenomenon—in the industry this is called a triangular contract—is part of the professional competence of every coach. It should be noted that there is no way in this terrain in which the hands of the coach, the coachee and the absent third party can remain entirely clean. Situations will always arise in which one party tries to functionalize another in its favor. Companies give (covert) assignments to the coach, the coachee does his coaching in pseudo-compliance to appease the company, or the coach tries to gain access to other principals in the company through the coachee. Full transparency or honesty is often as dysfunctional as opportunism or covert interest manipulation. This is the overarching framework of the situation described here.

The case giver here ostensibly becomes the victim of a slip of the tongue, which—understandably—completely destroys the client's trust in her. On the surface, it could be assumed that the coach, for her part, was incensed by what she saw as a derogatory speech about a person she values and who has already been helpful to her.

The idea of a solution expressed by the coach is obvious and of course possible, but not absolutely necessary or helpful in every case. The client would in all likelihood have been very overwhelmed with tolerating the coach's double loyalty, otherwise, she would have no such need for pejoratives against this lawyer. Her knowledge of the lawyer's person could, in my view, just as easily have been used by the coach in the background to better assess the client's biases in this conflict. This would have given her ideal conditions to be able to recognize well the client's parts in the conflict.

In any case, the outcome of the counseling session is an instructive example of how contact between people cannot really occur if what is going on inside is not expressed in a way that is appropriate to the role and situation. The coach's mistake was not so much a failure to inform the client of the lawyer's knowledge, but clumsy handling of her rebuttal of the client's "foul and discriminatory" speech.

Thomas Giernalczyk

The coach describes a critical scene in a session and assumes that she acted incorrectly. This is expressed most clearly in the phrase "stupidly let slip his first name." In her countertransference, she comes across as feeling guilty and ashamed of her actions. I have the impression that this is related to the enormous discrepancy with which they both assess the lawyer.

In the event that a noticeable irritation occurs in the coachee during the interaction, it is a good idea to pick up on this with the following formulation, for example: "Could it be that I have irritated/annoyed you? I would be interested to know how I triggered the affect." If we would like to describe this approach as a method, we use the stop-button technique and introduce it, for example, as follows: "I would like to interrupt our conversation and press the stop button. Afterwards, I'd like to explore with you how we experienced our conversation and what switch points were critical for you and me."

Such an approach, however, presupposes that the coach is not herself too preoccupied with her affect regulation. Again, following on from the vignette, before applying the stop-button technique, it is a matter of evaluating and using one's countertransference: I feel caught and ashamed, I think I made a big mistake. What could this have to do with? Perhaps I have been angry for some time about the disparagement of the lawyer I valued and also felt caught in my anger at the coachee. Presumably, my embarrassment mirrors my coachee's shame, as she surely feels equally exposed, since I knew the person being berated and was able to form my own opinion. Through thoughts of this nature, the coachee can perceive the situation more as an intense emotional encounter and move away from the one-sided attribution of the fault and experience the moment more as the revelation of an entanglement. The following intervention could be derived from this counter-meeting analysis: "Now we are probably both startled because you noticed that I know the lawyer and I am embarrassed that I did not tell you right at the beginning. Shall we examine this difficult situation together and see what we can learn from it?"

The vignette generally raises the question of what information a coach should share or keep private. The vignette-giver seems to assume a model oriented towards transparency. I would counter that a coach has to exercise a filtering function similar to a manager (see Giernalczyk & Möller, 2018). She decides on the basis of her professionalism which information she puts in and which she withholds. If we imagine that the lawyer was also a coachee of the coach, it would be obvious that she would not have said so. In the culture of many organizations, it is still a stigma to be coached, so the question of who is in coaching is subject to the filtering function of the coach. In the parlance of psychoanalysis, the filter function is introduced much more strictly than abstinence. According to this, the coach should not burden his coachee with material that engages the coach (conflictually) but should focus on the coachee's perspective.

6.3 Practical Example 23

Case Description

I receive a call from a coachee whom I supported 8 years ago in her attempt to change companies. At that time, the change did not succeed. Now, she is keen to leave the company again and apply for a new job with more customer contact. She currently works in a city administration and is responsible for the financial area. According to her statement, she is increasingly being pushed into the controlling department there. My difficulty is that I have my ideas about what area she fits into and what area she does not fit into. I clearly do not see her in the position she is aiming for. She barely responds facially, exudes no dynamism, and always seems unfriendly even when she is just thinking. So, I fall into a trap of my own making: My own longstanding HR experience.

What Was the Coach's Approach?
First, we analyzed the requirements profile of the desired job and looked at the personnel perspective. Then, we worked out concrete situations in which she could properly show her professional abilities and especially "softer" skills. Here an increasing development of the own self-awareness took place. In the second appointment, we worked again on the aspects of behavior and effect and addressed aspects that could be tricky for her. Now, my personnel experience was allowed to take up space and through a very careful description of her behavior and her effect on me, she was able to develop self-descriptions with which she could go into the application process in an equally authentic, honest, and positive way. I was still skeptical that she could adequately represent that in the interview. She claimed she could! What was helpful here: Before starting the second collaboration, I made it clear to myself what was irritating me about the situation at the moment. In this way, I was able to develop a procedure that allowed us both to perceive her positively at the beginning factually and increasingly also with her soft competencies.

Brigitte Fritschle
In this case vignette, a coaching task is to be addressed which may be overlaid by a previous experience between coach and coaching partner. An experience that may not have ended positively for both. The client has said at the very beginning that the move to another company was not successful at the time. However, it is not clarified why. This is an important initial question: What did not work? Was she too old, too young, too expensive? And now she desperately wants to leave (again), but there is no rationale, no explanation as to why this time.

My impression is that the coach is getting in his way. He talks about his many years of personal experience, which may influence him mentally. The danger that can arise here is that he tries to locate the coaching client differently than she wants to locate herself or might want to locate herself in the future. This could mean a very strong role confusion for the coach. He may, therefore, find it difficult to establish the necessary distance between himself and his coaching client.

I wonder if, in the case described, there is not also a carryover from the scene of 8 years ago. The coach will not be able to simply brush this off. What exactly was it like 8 years ago? Today, at the time of the call, we have a new situation, a new question. As a coach, I would look at the new situation with great equanimity. There is a new entry point, even though I think I know the person with their possibilities and shortcomings. Before I get into transference problems, I look at the situation for a while. I may need two sessions to do this. I take the diagnosis very, very seriously.

My recommendation: Let the client talk, listening is the first commandment! If necessary, ask accompanying questions that not only meet the coach's needs but primarily mean clarification and development for the client. Inquire and elaborate: How did she get the idea? What is her motivation? Never interrupt. That someone opens up is the most important thing about the whole measure. And then at some point, you can get around to giving explanations or sharing what is on your mind. Moving from finance to a client-facing area seems to me to be a huge leap that might be too big for the client. As a coach, I might discuss with her what that leap would mean for her. What might it mean if the leap succeeds, and what if the leap does not succeed? I would try to reflect on her desires or her goal setting: How does this fit together?

The coach could ask the client for her agreement to use a test to reinforce the diagnostic that shows her competencies. If she would agree to this, the coach would have stabilizing material. The impression created by her facial expressions could lead to a wrong conclusion. Here it is important as a coach to be very careful and cautious with attributions. The coaching client's wish is absolutely legitimate at first. Only in the course of the process can both—coach and coaching partner—jointly examine whether and how the request becomes meaningful and achievable. Depending on the decision, work can be done on the development of a future employee "with more customer contact," her attitude, expression, etc. Based on a growing trust, the coach can make recommendations and weigh the pros and cons. Perhaps because she has not received feedback, she has never learned what impact she leaves. These are things that can be learned: Through description, paraphrase, and feedback.

I expect myself as a coach to have a confident distance from my coaching partner and his problem. I have the time and the patience to look at the behavior of the coaching partner without imposing or suggesting my associations and images to someone. I look at making contact with me with great patience. In my understanding, the coach is responsible for the process, not the movement or content. For me and my understanding of coaching, non-judgmental communication is paramount, especially at the beginning of the process.

I hold back as much as possible in the beginning, but can then become very clear in the course of the process and can then also confront: This is the desire. With what justification? What are the reasons why this wish could come true, or does she want to experience the next Waterloo like 8 years ago? So that I then become very clear. But I do not go in with hypotheticals. For me, hypotheses are always a dangerous tool. Before I could test my hypotheses, the process would continue.

Silja Kotte

In this case, the coach is confronted with a conflict that could well have arisen without his personal experience. At this point, the reference to his many years of personal experience also seems to me to be a rationalized explanation of why the experienced difficulty has arisen. That I as a coach think that certain tasks would be suitable for my coachee, while others would be unsuitable, that I see her in a certain role, but not in another, is nothing unusual and first of all independent of my professional background (as a personnel manager, as a freelancer, etc.). It, therefore, becomes exciting to ask the question: To what extent do I then explore as a coach? To what extent do I pursue the question of why a certain impression arises in me?

As a coach, I would start with my experience, specifically here that I do not trust the coachee with a task area with intensive customer contact. Freely according to Kernberg: Enjoy your countertransference, also the negative ones or especially the negative ones! In my opinion, it is important to perceive, allow and follow your impression, especially at the beginning.

One's own experience always contains information that can be (better) utilized for the coaching process through reflection. If, for example, I react strongly in the sense of "I do not see that my client can do it," this may indicate that there are other people in her professional environment who share this impression (in the sense of complementary countertransference; see Racker, 1978; Möller, 1996). However, it may also indicate that the client herself does not even know whether she can manage a change, thus my critical assessment gives me access to her uncertainty and ambivalence, which I would otherwise pass over (in the sense of concordant countertransference; see Racker, 1978; Möller, 1996). Negative countertransference can also be understood as something positive, as an added bonus for understanding!

I would not verbalize and address my experience straight away, but first, use it behind the scenes as an option for understanding and then examine and, if necessary, explore it in the further course of the coaching. In this way, in the further course of the coaching, I would give room for the coachee to process her ambivalence regarding the changes associated with the job change, as well as encourage her to deal with the image that professional interaction partners have of her, to possibly obtain feedback on this, and to examine the extent to which she would like to use the coaching to change things.

In the case described, it seems to me that the coach remains stuck in a somewhat technical and customary way of working for the actions of a recruiter. This can be understood as moving on safe terrain. This seems understandable to me, but it also carries the risk of limiting one's possibilities for intervention. Engaging with one's own experience and the associated countertransference and reflecting on where one's own (HR) experience is helpful but also obstructive and can be a helpful extension here.

Uwe Böning

As a first impression of the coaching situation vignette arises: The coach apparently reacts spontaneously with an evaluation of the situation without having analyzed it sufficiently and understood it neutrally. An old pattern jumps out at him without having neutrally examined possible developments of the coaching partner in the past 8 years and without a current situation view. It seems as if he moves quickly, perhaps too quickly, into a specialized role. A diagnostic slowdown in the assessment of the person as well as the situation and appropriate motivation and goal analysis seems to me to be appropriate here.

From my coaching understanding, the case presented lacks the redundancies of a clean, i.e., a relatively neutral data collection, in order to arrive at a serious, secured assessment. Too-early assumptions and also their too-early feedback or interactional examination trigger, in my understanding, the danger of an accidental thematic reinforcement of aspects that take on a direction of their own and perhaps not intended by the coaching partner. So, they can also bring about unintended interpretations and dynamics. The combination of a strongly behavioral and a systemic approach, as practiced by me, does not intend a so-called scenic understanding, which could arise from the too-early dialogical introduction of one's fantasies, assumptions, interpretations, and hypotheses[1] into the initial process. A possible consequence of this would be a narrowing or distortion of perception by the coach. The essential goal of this part of the initial diagnostics should rather be the search for relevant redundancies and thematic, content-related, emotional, or process-related characteristics before an evaluative interpretation or an interpretative assessment and its examination takes place in the dialog with the coaching partner.

From my point of view, it seems to make sense to follow up a rather neutral diagnostic initial phase with an in-depth clarification phase on the coaching partner's ideas regarding the job she is seeking, i.e., to specify the requirements profile of the new desired job in order to be able to come to a realistic comparison of her ideas later on. For this phase, too, a critical discussion of her ideas and assessments, i.e., also a self-critical consideration of a possible fit seems, to me, to be too early. In my view, describing and analyzing the requirements profile as objectively as possible would be an important building block for a self-esteem-supporting acceptance of her view of the situation and her ideas about the fit. In this phase, it would also be important for me to clarify her motives for changing and her target needs. What is actually behind her desire to change?

This is also where my critical examination of her ideas, motives, and the extent to which her desire can be assessed as achievable would begin step by step—but not without a prior value-neutral summary of the expressed wishes and assessments. This would be an essential part of the appreciation to be expressed by me—before any explicitly positive reinforcement of her self-assessment or a critical examination of her ideas and motives regarding the possible fit for the new job.

At this point of a possible weighing or even critical examination of her view and way of experiencing, it seems important to me to work out a multi-perspective view of her situation by different actual or possible observers of the scene, before my personal view and evaluation could or should flow into the dialog. My goal: Not only to carry out a critical examination of her point of view but also to examine all other possible considerations and possibly to put them into perspective. In the sense of building or maintaining trust between the coaching partner and myself as a coach, my point of view would also have to be examined and weighed up by her. If it were to turn out that there were significant differences in assessment between her and me, then it might still be possible for me to make my idea and recommendation clearer.

Heidi Möller

That can happen, someone comes to me for coaching and would like to become Chancellor. My assessment may be: She is really not suited for it at all! Coachees have self-perceptions that sometimes do not match my perception of others. From my point of view, coachees underestimate or overestimate themselves. Now both perspectives can be distorted. So,

[1] If important impressions or even interpretations of this kind emerge, they could become part of a second protocol column to which the coach can explicitly return in a later process phase.

what can I do? If someone overestimates himself, it is my duty of care to prevent him from putting his foot in it. If someone underestimates himself, the self-view must be corrected upwards in order to expand the possibility space for the coachee. The same discrepancy experience can exist in goal setting. I may consider the goals my coaching client is aiming for to be attainable or unrealistic.

All coaches develop images from the first moment of meeting a coachee. Images about the person-job-fit, images about future scenarios, images about a successful working life of our clients. These can be developmental impulses for the coaching process. It seems important to me that a triangulation of perception can also be done with the help of diagnostic instruments (see Böning & Kegel, 2013). Reliable and valid instruments in job-related personality diagnostics and for different topics and occasions of the coachees are available as diagnostic help.

6.4 Practical Example 24

Case Description

Independently of each other, two members of the same work team requested individual supervision from me. In both individual supervision sessions, they reported that their supervisor was, in their view, incompetent and unable to provide professional guidance. Two weeks later, I was asked by this same supervisor to do team supervision. At first, I was worried whether I would be able to carry out the team supervision in an unbiased way with the previous information.

How Did the Supervisor Proceed?

After prior reflection with my supervisor, I conducted the team supervision. It was a very open and constructive session because the conflict could be discussed openly. The supervisor herself addressed the fact that she could not provide professional guidance, and the employees were also able to bring in their concerns constructively. In retrospect, it turned out that it was even beneficial that I had already spoken with two employees in the individual supervision sessions.

Joachim Sauer

What is striking about this unusual request situation is that there is no information at all about a respective clarification of the task, which makes the complexity of the problem and the content-related determination of the conflicts clear. Rather, the supervisor's concern is whether he can offer team supervision "in an unbiased way" based on his previous experience in individual supervision.

The independent inquiries of the two employees reduce the conflict, which has probably already escalated, to a dichotomy of bipolar thinking (see Tietel, 2012, p. 141) in the sense of capable employees and an incapable supervisor. This may be a hidden mandate to the supervisor to confirm the incompetence of the supervisor. What would be required would be the triadic competence of the supervisor (see Tietel, 2012; Busse & Tietel, 2018, pp. 57ff.) to reach a triangular contract (see Pühl, 2009; Gotthardt-Lorenz, 1994, 2009) via the basic triangulation of supervision or to reach a triangular contract via a thorough probing of the consultation request (see Rappe-Giesecke, 2012) to find a possible contract in which the supervisor actively shapes the assignment in the role of the institutional agent (see Gotthardt-Lorenz, 1994, 2009).

In my opinion, it can be assumed in the present case that the two individual supervision sessions that had already begun triggered a dynamic in the team that ultimately led to the supervisor's request for team supervision.

An important point for me in the supervisory procedure with the first inquiring employee would be a clarification of the assignment in the sense of a triadic structure, in which the supervisor does not simply take over the assigned and still unclear assignment, but keeps the triadic space[2] open in a professional analysis of demand. In this way, the third party who is not present is granted a quasi-virtual position, represented, for example, by empty chairs. The question to be balanced would be how to deal with the knowledge already gained without the supervision being abused to become an open season on the incompetent supervisor.

The situation is further aggravated by the colleague who inquires independently, whereby the problem of impartiality already arises here and not only when the supervisor inquires. The supervisor should not become the system's secret keeper. Overall, individual supervision is about the attempted exclusion of a relevant third party who is only present in the form of attributions and projections in a subjective, distorted form.

In my opinion, the aim should be, as supervisor, to clarify the situation with the proxy presence of the excluded third parties in supervision in the respective next session with the staff members—what Busse and Tietel (2018, p. 82) call triadic rehabilitation and includes the supervisor in a largely impartial role—in order to end this form of individual supervision and continue it in possible team supervision. Transparency by all parties (supervisor and supervisees) must be part of exploratory discussions for a possible assignment and triangular contract for team supervision, should this be able to be agreed upon by all parties. If not, there will be no joint contract: The course is set at the beginning (Rappe-Giesecke, 2012, p. 65)!

Eugen Würz

From my point of view, the supervisor's brief description of the problem allows for different interpretations of the process by which the problem arose in the situation. What the interpretations that make sense to me have in common is the question of the clarification of the task that took place in the run-up to the supervision processes. How did it come about that the supervisor accepted two individual supervisions within a team? How was the assignment triangle—supervisee, team leader, organization—sufficiently clarified at the

[2] Clients/supervisors/organization and their primary role.

time of assignment? No matter which part of the triangle of tasks is addressed, there are a number of uncertainties that make the start of individual supervision seem questionable to me. In the foreground, for me, are clarifications that have apparently not been made with the team leadership—and subsequently possibly also with the organization. Central questions here would be, for example: What was the intention of the supervisees to go to one and the same supervisor for individual supervision? How was the order for individual supervision examined in terms of clarification of the order and the attitude of the team management and organization? Was there sufficient clarification of the readiness and information transparency for individual supervision of the two colleagues?

From the aspects left open in the case study, the picture arises for me that the acceptance of the two supervision assignments can be questioned due to the lack of clarifications by the supervisor. It should be noted that lack of clarification can be corrected in a processual manner through appropriate interventions. However, the effort and the commitment required for this by the supervisor represent costs. In the case described, it seems to me that these opposites can hardly be reconciled and cannot be resolved.

As a result, the phenomenon of devaluing other people in their absence, which in my experience occurs quite frequently in supervision, arose. As an explanatory model, a "game of errors" can be used: The devaluation of other people in order to compensate for one's own experience of inferiority. However, what seems to me more significant here is the mutual, independent, collective construction of reality by the two supervisees. At the same time, it only corresponds to the real construction of two persons. For me, there is the urgent question of whether the mandate for joint team supervision is compatible here. The obvious dynamics in this team include thematic guidelines. These topics could already be addressed in the possible commissioning discussion for team supervision. The impartiality of the supervisor seems to be massively limited from the outset. A clear "contracting" could hardly be feasible from the point of view of the confidentiality agreement already made with the individual supervisees.

It seems to me to make sense here, as a supervisor, to make the incompatibility of the cooperation agreement transparent and to communicate it. The dilemma of the consultant's predicament could be brought to the attention of the respective supervisees in a corresponding clarification, which would make further cooperation possible through an adapted, new "contracting." Accepting the team supervision assignment does not seem to me to make sense and is not feasible in this sense. This process could usefully be rejected even before the upcoming cooperation agreement.

For the supervisor, it could be useful to reflect in detail on his or her seduction into accepting the complex assignment situation. For example, with the question: To what extent did a transference and countertransference phenomenon possibly occur here through one's evaluation dynamics in dealing with profession and claim?

Isabell Braumandl

Looking at the case description, my recommendation would be to focus in this supervision not on the concerns, but on the resources that are evident here. All participants have already become active through the various requests for supervision. I interpret this as a resource because a solution to a difficult situation is being sought—so this could be a common, unifying goal. It may just be that the ways and ideas to achieve this are different. This is what the supervisor has to clarify.

From my point of view, it would also be interesting to inquire about the concrete reason that led to the activity (request for supervision) of the individual persons at *this* point in time. What changes or discrepancies in the actual target status, if any, were there in the team and its environment? The experience of discrepancies could have been perceived as threatening and led to negative affect (e.g., devaluations). For me, this results in a central question for the case: What do the participants need to independently solve the difficult situation and to deal with each other in an appreciative manner?

In order to obtain a more comprehensive picture of the participants and the situation for the derivation of more precise working hypotheses and interventions, the following questions, among others, still need to be clarified in my view: What has been done so far by each stakeholder to address the current issue? What was the outcome, so what could be built upon and what is still open and unresolved? What is the goal of each of the parties involved? What are the underlying needs? What do the participants themselves have an influence on and what is beyond their sphere of influence?

I would conduct individual coaching with the supervisor to support her in strengthening her self-confidence in her ability to solve problems as a leader through decisions and actions. If we manage in the process to psychologically empower the manager to solve the problems in the team independently, an intervention with the employees is no longer of primary interest—and dispensing with it is also efficient.

My goal in this coaching would be to activate all the resources that led her to this position as a leader. I would trust that she can fully assume her responsibilities as a leader, otherwise, she would not be in this position. So, how can I support and enable her to be capable of action in terms of resolving the issue? I could imagine the following reflection contents for example:

- Goals and psychological needs of the participants for the respective intervention request with their respective commonalities and differences.
- Questioning verbal or non-verbal devaluations due to unsatisfied and violated own needs, e.g., through the method of perspective change.
- Identification of personal strengths, competencies, and resources as well as areas of development in order to be able to exert influence oneself.
- Roles in the team and the fit to the personal competences.

Sandra J. Schiemann

In my opinion, it is important in such team supervision to create a good basis of trust between all participants. Especially in the case described this seems important to me because two team members already confide in the supervisor before the team supervision begins and develop a certain trust towards him. For me, this means that there is a supervisor and other team members who do not yet have an advantage of trust and should be brought on board. In my opinion, a basis of trust should be established, in particular, with the supervisor as the client—for example in a one-on-one meeting, in order to ascertain her mission and her perspective in addition to building trust.

According to Schoorman et al. (2007), this trust can be established through benevolence, competence, and integrity—i.e., through benevolent and appreciative cooperation (benevolence), in which the supervisor appears as an authentic (integrity), competent and fair process-designer (competence). Each team member should be able to honestly (integrity) and yet appreciatively (benevolence) represent their own opinions as well as respect the opinions of others (benevolence). The competencies of the team members and especially of the supervisors should be clearly elaborated (see Diller et al., 2021; Schiemann et al., 2019). These fine points show that during such a one-on-one meeting and in team supervision it is important to show a lot of sensitivity and (self-)reflection for the needs and viewpoints of all in order to create an atmosphere of trust.

Eva Jonas

My view of the situation described is shaped by social psychology. Social psychology deals with the experience and behavior of persons in social situations and, according to the probably best-known definition of social psychology by Gordon Allport (see 1954, p. 5; emphasis in original), seeks "*to understand and explain how the thought, feeling, and behavior of individuals are influenced by the actual, imagined, or implied presence of other human beings*." This definition makes it clear that social context is quite essential to human information processing and emotional experience. Accordingly, persons influence our experience and behavior not only when they are directly physically present, but also when they are only indirectly present. Accordingly, it would be interesting to know to what extent the boss who was absent in the individual supervision sessions was nevertheless implicitly in the room. Perhaps it was even explicitly worked with the idea that she was sitting on an empty chair, or there was a role play in which her role was taken over—we know too little about this from the case description.

However, the difference between actual, imagined, or implied presence seems to me to be quite essential for this case. If persons are really present or not, this has an influence on the level of analysis. While in individual supervision it is rather the intrapersonal level of experience that is considered, in team supervision interpersonal and intra-group processes become more visible. It becomes clear that the cooperation between the employees and the supervisor raises questions from the perspective of all three persons. All three supervisees became active, i.e., there seems to be a desire for change in all of them. In this respect, team supervision, in which the three can meet on the work-related level of their cooperation in the team, seems to make sense in my opinion.

As a supervisor, however, the question arises for me whether I can be unbiased when I have previously worked intensively with the two staff members alone in each case. In the case description, we lack further information about the individual supervisions. Did the employees approach the supervisor individually or with the involvement of their organization? Have the individual supervisions already been completed or are they still ongoing? Depending on this, one could consider working with the supervisor individually first and suggesting individual coaching to her.

In a more direct way, however, I would carry out team supervision. Since reality is always constructed, all participants (including the supervisor) only see parts of an overall situation. If people want to work well together, they have to put together the sections they each see. In this respect, I would consider it important that the employees talk to their boss and compare their views. As a supervisor, I too would be curious and open to expanding my previous perspectives. Even though people rarely see themselves as blank slates in interactions whose perception and information processing are always influenced by their previous experiences and by previous activations in their cognitive network, this does not mean that they are defenselessly at the mercy of these processes and automatically transfer previous knowledge. According to the two-process theories (see Kahneman, 2014; Sherman et al., 2014) of social information processing, if we are highly motivated and capable, we can certainly reflect and influence these processes. In this respect, the question for me as a supervisor is: What rules do I give myself? For example, do I work with two people from one organization in parallel? In which setting can I work well in order to be able to absorb information as impartially as possible?

In terms of content, I find the devaluation of the superiors expressed by both employees in the case study interesting. As a social psychologist, I ask whether this devaluation is a defensive strategy of the employees in the sense of motivated cognition or whether an actual state of deficiency is being referred to here. In the case of motivated cognition, cognition has a function—presumably that of protecting oneself—but from what? I would use various contextual factors to try to ascertain whether there have been processes of change in the organization, in the team, or in the economic-social context that may have led to employee insecurity. It is possible that the employees themselves feel overwhelmed, experience anxiety that they have not yet been able to express or feel unappreciated and limited in their autonomy. There may also be a direct discrepancy situation regarding the supervisor's behavior that leads to the conflict. In this case, as in a facilitated conflict conversation or mediation, I would try to get the perspectives of the different parties and make sure that I have understood the position of each party. This is central so that I am not influenced by my prior experience to understand the two employees better than the boss. Often this translation work already has a good effect—so that the three can get back into the conversation and also hear what is important to the other person and not only what they expect to hear.

Heidi Möller

A classic: "My boss, that stupid cow, she can't do anything." This form of "bossing" can be described psychodynamically as a psychosocial defense mechanism (see Möller et al., 2018) and is often found in clinical organizations and psychosocial service companies. "Instead of focusing—together with the leadership—on the developmental needs of the institution in the face of demands and possibilities of the environment, and thereby inevitably repeatedly experiencing unpleasant feelings of helplessness and hopelessness, a basic fight-flight assumption (Bion, 1961) often emerges among employees at the group level, even under the conditions of an open-minded and participative leadership" (Lohmer, 2019, p. 208; translated). Personal devaluation and relational wars are understood here as a dysfunctional defensive strategy to avoid facing the primary tasks of the organization. The external reality is blocked out and employees focus their attention on what is going on within the organization. Instead of external challenges, leadership is now experienced as the enemy who could provide employees with greater safety and security but is apparently too self-centered, power-obsessed, or incompetent to do so. If leadership is fought, then an illusion of control is created: If only we had another boss, all would be well! Continued fighting and wrangling with leadership lead to a high level of coherence in the team. The price, however, is high: Trust in and loyalty to the leadership are lost, replaced by mistrust and even paranoid expectations. Here the "containment" of the supervisor could help to understand this defensive function, to interpret the function, and to build up appropriate, constructive organizational behavior.

Supervisory work in the direction of expectation management could be helpful in the present case: What does the manager want from the employees, what do they want from the supervisor? This role negotiation helps to clarify unspoken expectations that are always directed at each other but rarely expressed. People can only fail at expectations that are not verbalized. This can be done in the form of a traffic light system:

- Green: Sure, agreed, I will do it!
- Yellow: I do not know yet and need to think about it.
- Red: I definitely will not do that. I look for alternatives with the team in order to adequately answer the underlying needs of the employees for all parties involved.

6.5 Practical Example 25

Case Description

This is a recently started individual coaching with a still very young manager without leadership experience. The manager seems to be very overwhelmed with her new role. She has problems with an older employee whom she does not seem to accept and with whom she cannot deal. The difficulty for me was that the coachee seemed very lost and helpless during the initial interview and I ended up giving too much substantive advice on how the coachee could proceed to improve her situation. Her helplessness (in the sense of a transference offer) tempted me to do this. In retrospect, this was not very helpful, as it would have been more important to strengthen the coachee's self-efficacy and competencies.

How Did the Coach Go About It?

I felt that I was developing savior tendencies and felt responsible for the coachee developing good solutions quickly. I was afraid for her that this overload could become even stronger. I could tell by her reaction after a while that my advice was not really useful for her self-worth and agency. I have resolved at the second appointment, which is in the future, to address my perception of the client's lostness and to ask how she experienced the first session. I will use my interventions in a more mindful way and especially focus on the solution-focused approach.

Eva Jonas

If a young manager without previous management experience has to grow into her role, the first question for me is what kind of support she needs for this and which consulting format is suitable for her. Coaching is only one option among several. Other possibilities would be, for example, mentoring by an experienced, preferably female manager or training and exchange of experience with other young managers. As a coach, I would first discuss this with her. If coaching is chosen as a method, I would try to support her in a very resource-oriented way to find her path as a leader in the context of her organization and work activities. To do this, I would work on connecting and integrating her current experiences with existing experiences and lessons learned and support her confidence in her power. But what do I do if there is no existing network of experience in the central problem area? In this case, I find it useful to act as a model, to report on my own experiences, or to pass on knowledge. I would make this change of role clear and then I would support the coachee in establishing a connection to her person.

However, since social interactions are always a consequence of action and reaction, as a coach I should critically reflect on *what* I am reacting to with my potential advice. My client's experience of being helpless and lost could also be the result of my pattern. In this case, my behavior would rather serve my own needs and not be very attuned to the needs of my client.

My client is also in social interactions with her co-workers, in which action and reaction follow one another. The difficult interaction with the older employee should be considered separately in the coaching in order to better understand which emotion results from the current situation and which role possible previous experiences of the client play here.

Joachim Sauer

What happened in the countertransference and the counseling offered by the coach to the seemingly helpless coachee? What resonances—especially self-resonances—were triggered in the coach in the sense of Bauer (2016) and Schmid (2008)?

A brief digression: If resonance arises in a person, this person reacts to other people, his environment, and his inner experience in the form of self-resonance, empathic (concordant or complementary) and personal or dialogical resonance (see Schmid, 2008). Bauer (2016), derived from the work of mirror neurons, speaks here of concordant and complementary mirroring. An echo of one's feelings, fears, desires, etc. triggered in counselors is called self-resonance. In the context of counseling, one should be more or less aware of this self-resonance in order not to impose these emotions on the counselee without reflecting on them.

From the countertransference concept in counseling processes (see Schreyögg, 2018), it would be necessary for the coach to clarify why she has assumed the role of know-it-all so strongly in order to feed the helpless coachee with tips as quickly as possible.

It would also be exciting to analyze mirror phenomena according to Kutter (2012, p. 81ff.) in order to make the initially unconscious dimension of the relationship in the here-and-now between coach and coachee more conscious and to understand it as a reflection of the real encounter in the there-and-then between the young manager and the experienced employee against the background of the respective work assignment.

Another diagnostic approach to better understand the coaching situation, which goes beyond the (un)conscious dichotomization of *helpless, overwhelmed young executive* and *experienced, tip-giving coach,* would be to introduce the complexity of triadic thinking in addressing the work-world and life-world triads on the part of the coach on the one hand and the coachee on the other (see Busse & Tietel, 2018, pp. 80ff.)

The coach would have to become aware of her entanglements in the working relationship with the coachee in her self-reflection—with or without supervisory support. According to the case description, this is happening at least to some extent. The case description itself could already be a reflection of the working relationship between the young manager and the older employee. This could bring the third party, which has been somewhat lost sight of, back into the counseling focus of becoming aware again and again of the dual triadic function of the coach. "In this double function of being at the same time a third party as well as a representative of the third party, supervisors cannot at all be constantly on the level of triadic thinking or triadic competence. At best, we can strive [...] to struggle again and again for this double stance and for triangular spaces" (Tietel, 2012, p. 147; translated).

Against the background of the coach's self-reflection and the discomfort that has arisen, the next session would be about a differentiated clarification of the assignment, the goals and mutual expectations as well as the working relationship between coach and coachee.

In terms of self-input, the coach could start with her affective reactions and reflections on them after the initial interview in order to open the space also for the coachee's self-exploration, ultimately to strengthen her self-efficacy and her resources. In doing so, the coach's model of addressing difficult inner processes and her inner work—as it were, according to Busse and Tietel (2018, p. 90f.), providing a glimpse into the coach's inner triangle of reflection, empathy, and resonance—could be helpful for the coachee to see and understand her own behavior in the work process in a more complex way.

In the further course of the coaching process, the focus could then be on the joint development of her still-new leadership role and her working relationships with employees. The latter must always be related to the primary tasks, which are sometimes lost sight of in the work context (see Tietel, 2012).

Eugen Würz

For me, a self-assessment of the coach becomes visible here, what she could have done "better." For me, the described difficulty lies first of all in the dissatisfaction with the preliminary result of the coaching. In addition, there is dissatisfaction with the chosen intervention: Administering strongly content-based tips. This seduction of action can certainly also be perceived as a helpful element.

The possible transference phenomenon may be more far-reaching than the coach currently considers. What does it have to do with her being seduced into knowing what is helpful to the executive? How does she know the exact experience and behavior in the organization that she only knows from the coachee's account? To what extent does this transfer a theme from the coach to the coachee?

Based on a reflective transference option, the coach could take an approach that actively incorporates these perceptions into further coaching. Making transparent, offering one's seducibility, possibly triggered a change of perspective in the coachee.

Offering advice or tips does not necessarily constitute an inappropriate intervention (see Radatz, 2009). The question is: To what extent does offering solutions and tips coincide with the coachee's willingness to also accept advice? Exploiting systemic questioning techniques (see Patrzek, 2017) to stimulate the coachee's own ability to change could be useful here: "How would your colleague X notice that you have used behavior Y?"

Strengthening self-competence and self-efficacy can be a new objective in what is obviously still a young coaching process. Goals may well change in the coaching process and it makes sense to revise them if necessary. The image of what appears to be a somewhat hasty assessment of the coaching situation and the described short duration of the coaching process to date makes a reflection on the coach's impatience with the process to date palatable: *Deceleration* as an intervention possibly allows for a solution at other levels. For example, on the issue level that the coachee, as a *still very young* manager, probably has a different pace compared to an *older* employee. This difference in speed and perception could also cause difficulties between the coachee and her employee.

Isabell Braumandl

The coach herself reflects—which I see as a resource with her—that "much substantive advice" is not very helpful in coaching. In a counseling format that, according to my conception, should support the autonomy of the client. In my understanding, other intervention techniques would have made more sense here, e.g., questions that lead to the coachee's self-reflection and solution-finding.

If this coach were to seek my advice, I would work with her on how to support her in moving forward successfully with her coachee. The coach seems to be more concerned with herself than with the client. Therefore, the coach should look at her attitude, her tasks, and her roles in coaching.

In my view, the professional setting for this would be, for example, (individual or group) supervision. In my experience, the case study is a typical topic that is always part of the group supervision that takes place in the context of coach training. The following questions (among others) could be helpful for the coach to derive actions:

- What is the role, attitude, and self-image as a coach?
- What is conducive to ensuring target focus for the young leader in coaching?
- What resources does the young leader bring to the table?
- What specifically is unsettling the coach? Which of the coach's patterns might be activated that lead the focus away from the client to the coach's issues?

Relapse prophylaxis with the coach also makes sense to me. In this way, the coach would have a plan and a course of action if such challenges should arise again. The following questions, among others, can be guiding for this: What specific things can she do in the future before, during, and after a coaching session? What is helpful in order not to transfer one's triggered issues to one's clients?

If this young executive were my client, I would first work on what resources and strengths the coachee brings with her. As I understand it, everyone has these within themselves, but they often lose sight of them in moments that seem threatening. This leads to a loss of confidence in oneself to master challenges. My goal would therefore be to relativize the threatening nature of the situation and the people involved by strengthening the self-efficacy conviction.

A change of perspective, i.e., putting oneself in the shoes of the older employee, could help to analyze the situation from a meta-perspective in order to understand the older employee and her behavior and to derive possible solutions from this.

Sandra J. Schiemann

In my opinion, the main thing here is that the coach is very willing to help—i.e., quickly experiences the client as seeking or needing help and sees in herself the need or duty to want or be expected to help. I think this is where it is important for the coach to see how she can best help. This is because as a coach it is important to support the client in her autonomy and not to restrict her in this (see Imel et al., 2011; Schiemann et al., 2018). Autonomy-restricting behavior, such as giving advice, can happen quickly but is detrimental to success: Researchers found that coaches and consultants can often be autonomy-restricting, for example by giving advice (see Imel et al., 2011). Therefore, in my opinion, it is important to realize that the client has been able to live well before and will continue to do so after the coaching. If we look at the client described: Despite her young age, she is already an executive and has thus already been able to achieve great professional successes entirely without a coach. As a coach, I should therefore be aware of my role, that the client can achieve her own goals independently and self-determined—and therefore is definitely not helpless.

It is, therefore, more about giving the client the opportunity to determine and try out her ways—i.e., to meet her with autonomy-supporting techniques (e.g., showing empathy). Here the coach can offer support to work out resources (e.g., abilities, strengths, and successes) and make possible ways for solutions available with thought games by well-posed questions. Small phrases can make all the difference here: Our recent research shows that "imagine-other" (I understand how you are doing in your situation) can be autonomy-supportive and "imagine-self" (I understand how you are doing through my experience) can be autonomy-limiting (Schiemann et al., 2019). Further autonomy-supportive strategies can be found in research on Motivational Interviewing (see Cramer & Sauer, 2014).

Heidi Möller

Process consulting and expert consulting flow into each other in modern consulting concepts and result in new, hybrid or complementary offers (see Königswieser et al., 2012). Schein (1990) had still neatly separated these types of guidance and it is still important for guidance practitioners to know what they are doing. Which format they offer situationally should be professionally decided by coaches and not simply happen. Everyday counseling, however, often means an agile back-and-forth of procedural and instructional elements. Especially as the distinctions are of little interest to clients, nor helpful to them. At this point, I am interested in another aspect: Normative events in educational contexts. The impression of having done something really bad can be the result of training discourses that overly rigidly describe the process as the silver bullet of coaching. Explaining something to coachees once is not a mortal sin. For the coach in the case study, the strictly normative discourse led to a negative self-evaluation of her approach. If my coachee has no idea about project management, I can already tell him what milestones are. The same is true when banning closed-ended questions as set out in textbooks. As our study of instructional videos of famous coaches shows, they constantly ask closed questions and claim otherwise in a written interview (see Deplazes et al., 2016).

The coach's impression of having given too much technical advice may be due to transference.

The client is described as helpless. An important question for coaches' professional self-awareness might be, "What happens to me when I experience someone as helpless? What feelings do I then get in touch with?" Powerlessness and helplessness are undoubtedly the most unpopular emotional states. In order to be able to *contain* these without having to do anything—in other words, psychodynamically speaking, to avoid acting—it takes many phases of self-reflection in further training as a coach.

References

Allport, G. W. (1954). The historical background of modern psychology. In G. Lindzey (Ed.), *Handbook of social psychology I* (pp. 3–56). Addison-Wesley.

Bauer, J. (2016). *Warum ich fühle, was du fühlst: intuitive Kommunikation und das Geheimnis der Spiegelneurone*. Wilhelm Heyne.

Beumer, U., & Sievers, B. (2000). Einzelsupervision als Rollenberatung – Die Organisation als inneres Objekt. *Supervision, 3*, 10–17.

Bion, W. R. (1961). *Erfahrungen in Gruppen und andere Schriften*. Klett-Cotta.

Böning, U., & Kegel, C. (2013). Psychometrische Persönlichkeitsdiagnostik. In H. Möller & S. Kotte (Eds.), *Diagnostik im Coaching. Grundlagen, Analyseebenen, Praxisbeispiele* (pp. 81–99). Springer.

Busse, S., & Tietel, E. (2018). *Mit dem Dritten sieht man besser: Triaden und Triangulierung in der Beratung*. Vandenhoeck & Ruprecht.

Cramer, M., & Sauer, A. (2014). Motivational interviewing im coaching. *Organisationsberatung, Supervision, Coaching, 21*(1), 83–97.

Deplazes, S., Schwyter, S., & Möller, H. (2016). Ein Blick auf Coachingprozesse – Die Interventionen des Coachs, dargestellt und analysiert mittels des KaSyCo-C. *Coaching | Theorie & Praxis, 2*, 9–19. https://doi.org/10.1365/s40896-016-0010-4

Diller, S. J., Mühlberger, C., Loehlau, N., & Jonas, E. (2021). How to show empathy as a coach: The effects of coaches' imagineself versus imagine-other empathy on the client's self-change and coaching outcome. *Current Psychology*. https://doi.org/10.1007/s12144-021-02430-y

Giernalczyk, T., & Möller, H. (2018). *Entwicklungsraum. Psychodynamische Beratung in Organisationen*. Vandenhoeck & Ruprecht.

Giernalczyk, T., Lazar, R. A., & Albrecht, C. (2012). Die Rolle der Führungskraft und des Beraters als Container. In T. Giernalczyk & M. Lohmer (Eds.), *Das Unbewusste im Unternehmen. Psychodynamik von Führung, Beratung und Change Management* (pp. 25–38). Schäffer-Poeschel.

Gotthardt-Lorenz, A. (1994). Organisationssupervision, Rollen und Interventionsfelder. In H. Pühl (Ed.), *Handbuch der Supervision 2* (pp. 365–379). Marhold.

Gotthardt-Lorenz, A. (2009). Organisationssupervision – Raum für wachsende Anforderungen. In H. Pühl (Hrsg.), *Handbuch Supervision und Organisationsentwicklung* (S. 147–160). VS.

Imel, Z. E., Baer, J. S., Martino, S., Ball, S. A., & Carroll, K. M. (2011). Mutual influence in therapist competence and adherence to motivational enhancement therapy. *Drug and Alcohol Dependence, 115*(3), 229–236. https://doi.org/10.1016/j.drugalcdep.2010.11.010

Kahneman, D. (2014). *Schnelles Denken, langsames Denken*. Pantheon.

Klein, A. (2009). *Leadership im Kulturbetrieb*. Springer.

Königswieser, U., Burmeister, L., & Keil, M. (2012). *Komplementärberatung in der Praxis: Schnelle Optimierung bei nachhaltiger Entwicklung*. Schäffer-Poeschel.

Kutter, P. (2012). Spiegelphänomene in der Supervision. In H. Pühl (Ed.), *Handbuch der Supervision 3* (pp. 81–95). Ulrich Leutner.

Lawrence, G. W. (1998). Selbstmanagement-in-Rollen. Ein aktuelles Konzept. *Freie Assoziation, 1*, 37–57.

Lohmer, M. (2019). Der Berater zwischen den Fronten: Die Dynamik von Vertrauen, Misstrauen und Containment in Organisationen. In M. Lohmer, & H. Möller (Eds.), *Psychoanalyse in Organisationen. Eine Einführung in psychodynamische Organisationsberatung* (S. 201–225). Kohlhammer.

Lohmer, M., & Möller, H. (2014). *Psychoanalyse in Organisationen. Einführung in die psychodynamische Organisationsberatung*. Kohlhammer.

Menzies-Lyth, I. E. P. (1974). Die Angstabwehr-Funktion sozialer Systeme. *Ein Fallbericht. Gruppendynamik, 5*, 183–216.

Möller, M. L. (1996). Gegenübertragung in der Gruppenanalyse. In Förderverein Gruppentherapie e.V. Münster (Hrsg.), *Arbeitshefte Gruppenanalyse: Gegenübertragung in der Gruppenanalyse 2/96* (S. 40–73). Votum.

Möller, H., Giernalczyk, T., & Hinn, D. (2018). Individuelle und kollektive Abwehrmechanismen im Coaching. In S. Greif, H. Möller, & W. Scholl (Eds.), *Handbuch Schlüsselkonzepte im Coaching* (pp. 255–264). Springer.

Patrzek, A. (2017). *Systemisches Fragen – Professionelle Fragetechniken für Führungskräfte, Berater und Coaches*. Springer Gabler.

Pühl, H. (2009). Teamsupervision und Teamarbeit. In H. Pühl (Hrsg.), *Handbuch Supervision und Organisationsentwicklung* (S. 161–193). VS.

Racker, H. (1978). *Übertragung und Gegenübertragung*. Reinhardt.

Radatz, S. (2009). *Beratung ohne Ratschlag*. Literatur-Vsm.

Rappe-Giesecke, K. (2012). Sondierung – von der Beratungsanfrage zum Kontrakt. In H. Pühl (Ed.), *Handbuch der Supervision 3* (pp. 64–80). Ulrich Leutner.

Schein, E. H. (1990). A general philosophy of helping: Process consultation. *Sloan Management Review, 31*(3), 57–64.

Schein, E. H. (2003). *Organisationskultur*. EHP.

Schiemann, S. J., Mühlberger, C., & Jonas, E. (2018). Striving for autonomy: The importance of the autonomy need and its support within coaching. *International Journal of Evidence Based Coaching and Mentoring, 12*, 98–110. https://doi.org/10.24384/000543

Schiemann, S. J., Mühlberger, C., Schoorman, F. D., & Jonas, E. (2019). Trust me, I am a caring coach: The benefits of establishing trustworthiness during coaching by communicating benevolence. *Journal of Trust Research, 9*(2), 164–184.

Schmid, P. F. (2008). Resonanz – Konfrontation – Austausch. Personzentrierte Psychotherapie als kokreativer Prozess des Miteinander und Einander-Gegenüber. Person. *Internationale Zeitschrift für Personzentrierte und Experienzielle Psychotherapie und Beratung, 12*(1), 22–34.

Schoorman, F. M., Mayer, R. C., & Davis, J. H. (2007). An integrative model of organizational trust: Past, present, and future. *Academy of Management Review, 32*(2), 344–354.

Schreyögg, A. (2018). Übertragung und Gegenübertragung in ihrer Bedeutung fürs Coaching. In S. Greif, H. Möller, & W. Scholl (Eds.), *Handbuch für Schlüsselkonzepte im Coaching* (pp. 613–620). Springer.

Sherman, J. W., Gawronski, B., & Trope, Y. (Eds.). (2014). *Dual-process theories of the social mind*. The Guilford Press.

Tietel, E. (2012). Wenn der/das Dritte aus dem Blick gerät – Die Fallstricke beruflicher Dreiecksverhältnisse im Fokus der Supervision. In H. Pühl (Ed.), *Handbuch der Supervision 3* (pp. 141–147). Ulrich Leutner.

7 Influence of and from the Commissioning Organization

7.1 Practical Example 26

Case Description

The assignment was coaching for a new manager, paid by the employer. I was to support this executive in her new role. During the second coaching session, it became clear that the coachee was not loyal to her employer. Due to her influence, the motivation and loyalty of other employees could potentially be severely affected. As this was a commissioned coaching session with clear objectives agreed with the line manager, it was difficult for me as a coach to keep the agreed objectives in mind and at the same time respond to the coachee's negative and negating comments.

What Was the Coach's Approach?

In the situation, I first listened calmly and took note of the coachee's descriptions and perceptions without judgment. Then I asked the coachee how she would like to use our cooperation or what ideas she had about how this coaching could bring her forward in the agreed goals. The coachee did not give a clear answer to this. The coaching session was concluded with the coachee saying that she wanted to think about it. Thereafter, there was no contact between us for 8 months; upon inquiry, I also communicated this to the HR department without further explanation. After the said 8 months, I was invited to a final coaching meeting. The appointment was also attended by her manager and the personnel development (PD) manager. Prior to the appointment, I had 2–3 hours to work alone with the coachee. During this appointment, the coachee referred exclusively to the pre-agreed goals and indicated that the coaching had prompted her to reflect. In terms of her body language and attitude, however, the coachee gave me a completely different impression. What exactly had happened in the meantime, i.e., the past 8 months, I still do not know. She was praised by her supervisor and the PD management for her leadership in difficult times.

H. Möller, J. Zimmermann, *Difficult Situations in Business Coaching*,
https://doi.org/10.1007/978-3-658-35087-1_7

Sandrina Lellinger

In the situation presented, there is a classic triangular contract in which the client and the principal are not identical. This situation always arises when organizations commission coaches to work with employees. In the course of a job clarification meeting, the coach has clarified the goals of the coaching with the client and now, in contact with the client, discovers that she apparently has other interests. Instead of swearing the client to the employer's goals, it is important to work out her wishes and goals for the coaching. Any deviations or incompatibilities with the employer's goals must first be reported back to the client and then, if necessary, to the principal. In order to prevent such situations, an order clarification meeting can take place involving all parties involved—in this case: The client, principal, and coach.

The coach seems to be strongly identified with the client's goals and acts as if he were part of the organization. For example, he worries that the client's attitude towards her employer, which he perceives as disloyal, could negatively influence other employees. How does this concern come about? Does the coach see it as his responsibility to make his client an exemplary employee from the client's point of view? Thus, the coach becomes an instrument of the principal. Coaching then becomes an application that wants to develop clients solely in the sense of the client, instead of taking them seriously as individuals with their concerns.

It is unclear what happened in the time between the second coaching session and the final interview. The share of coaching in the development of the client and her leadership work, which was praised by the client, is to be assessed as low. It is possible that the coaching here fulfils the function of an alibi for the supervisor to have done everything for the successful induction of his employee. With her actions, the client maintains this impression, and she plays the game without really getting involved.

Sebastian Kunert

My view here is that the investigator is addressing a typical case in triangular contracting: The resource provider is not the coachee but a third party. This raises the question: Who is the client, to whom am I loyal? In a good triangular contract, one gives the money so that the other can develop. In the present case, the giver of the money has pain, and the client is supposed to relieve it. This is not an intervention in collaboration with the system but outside the system. The coaching, thus, becomes a service to the client and replaces the client's leadership activity. In a sense, the wrong person is attending the sessions. Instead of the leader, the client should be getting support in how to recognize and reciprocate waning commitment.

My methodical approach would be, in the first step, to escape the dilemma, to establish transparency: "Dear client, this is my mandate through your manager, did you know that and does it coincide with your ideas?" In case the latter is answered in the negative, one can consult with the funder whether one should continue working despite the change in the topic, or one can give back one's mandate.

However, the greatest danger in such constellations is to damage the relationship of trust with the client (in the case of psychologists, theologians, doctors, lawyers, and social pedagogues, this is even a criminal offence under Germany's §203 StGB). The crucial limit, in any case, is that the contents of the coaching sessions are confidential and—if at all—may only be passed on to third parties, e.g., the client, by agreement. An elegant solution, in my view, is to encourage the client and the manager to enter into conversation with each other, to formulate a joint brief and, if necessary, to agree on feedback. On the part of the coach, it should be clearly communicated to the client that no content or progress about the coaching process will be made public, nor will any assessments about the client be disclosed.

Thomas Bachmann

From my point of view, the case history is a classic constellation for coaching in an organizational context: The order triad of principal, client, coach. As a coach, you are now in a dilemma because there are differences in the objectives of what the coaching should achieve. What sticks out a bit for me here is that the coach reporting here seems to be strongly identified with the client and less so with the client, who should really own our unconditional positive attention. The loyalty is not balanced. As a coach, you should look both ways and say: "OK, the client is having difficulties here and cannot accept the coaching goals that have been agreed upon. At the same time, I have an obligation to the client and must now address the dilemma that has arisen in a professional manner." It is precisely this two-sided loyalty or all-partiality that is not clearly expressed in the case history. I am sure that the client sensed this.

For the further procedure, this would mean to clearly renegotiate the assignment with the client and to talk about the deviation from the coaching goals. For the coach, the question might be: Can I deal with this triad? Or is the difference in their respective intentions so strong that the coaching cannot go on, and we cannot work together? To me, the case sounds like an order clarification issue that particularly affects the coach's professional actions. Let me clarify this as follows: In the order clarification meeting, ideally, the goals are mutually agreed upon between principal, client, and coach. Then, in the first sessions, the gap between the principal's and the client's ideas appears, which is so large that we are no longer able to work together. As a coach, I am then in a typical loyalty dilemma and have to address this. The question should be: Why cannot the client engage in coaching, and what can I do to make it possible for her? One approach would be to achieve this common goal through transparency and the best possible preliminary clarification. If I work as a coach for a company, I can make it clear that my work is open-ended, that it can also happen that someone quits their job in the course of the coaching or does not support a certain company decision. Coaching is a person-centered consultation and not a fitness, education, or adjustment program for employees.

After sifting through the approach, I remembered a very similar assignment. At that time, I was asked to bill even though I had never coached the client. That is, the client acted as if he was coaching and as if he had engaged in a deep work process.

The client, in this case history, has shown a strong adjustment response to her company, and everyone ends up happy. The only question is whether you should play games like this. Probably not!

Beate Fietze

Here we have a nice template for the question of professional ethics and the question of the profession in general. Due to the conflicting orientations of the commissioning manager and his client, the coach finds himself in a conflict of loyalties which, according to my interpretation, he answers in favor of the client: He is concerned about the negative effect of his coachee on her employees. This sounds a bit like the coach himself being an employee of the company.

However, the coach should be independent in principle and be able to meet the individual client from the position of so-called client autonomy—both economically and mentally. In the case discussed here, the coach would have to clarify this if he recognizes a contradiction between the expectations of the client and the professional, ethical requirements of the coach.

One can very well agree to work on specified topics within the framework of a triangular contract without violating one's loyalty to the client. From the perspective of a profession, however, one should be allowed to assume that the commissioned coach decides for himself, within the scope of his professional discretion, how he will work on the coaching topics.

After looking at the approach to the solution and from the end of the case, the coaching seems to have been instrumentalized by both sides, by the manager as well as by the client. This example shows how important it is for coaching to become an independent profession that defines the rules of its professional practice itself, also and especially in relation to the commissioning organizations.

Heidi Möller

This case study raises the central professional ethics question: Who is the client in coaching? According to current research (see Middendorf, 2019, 2020), approximately two-thirds of all coaching in Germany is commissioned and paid for by the company. Here we can watch the difficulty with the universally proclaimed impartiality. Does the power lie with who pays (i.e., the company)? Do coaches really succeed in maintaining the unequal triangle between company, coach, and coachee?

Initially, the coaching client is well-advised not to let his non-loyalty to his company become apparent in an order clarification situation in a triangular or quadrangular contract discussion. We coaches can assume that this dynamic only becomes clear in the dyadic situation. Is my goal then to establish loyalty? Even if I vehemently deny it, who pays the commission (and onward) probably plays a preconscious role. Sovereignty in all-partiality is a high good; however self-critical questions about abstinence in the sense of being free of one's drive desires are always important.

7.2 Practical Example 27

Case Description

In this one-to-one coaching for middle management in the logistics sector, everything seemed clearly communicated. First, the HR manager contacted me, and then there was a meeting with the site manager and the client (division manager) of the globally operating logistics group. I was told upfront that the client (in his early 30s) had been with the group since apprenticeship and with a short break at this location. Since then, he has qualified from apprentice to division manager. Whereby—and here I come to the reason for the coaching—he now seems to be overwhelmed; no longer able to assert himself (with an employee, team colleague or superior). The client confirmed this. In the coaching itself, it turned out in the first three sessions that he does not want to lead at all, that he does not enjoy the job and that he is considering changing companies. In addition, it becomes an issue that he has just become a father and feels overwhelmed here. He seems personally unstable to me. After the fourth session, he canceled the next session by text message. After that, he stopped coming to the sessions. My efforts to initiate a closing session were unsuccessful. Contact with the group also broke off.

What Was the Coach's Approach?

In the coaching, I tried to work out strategies with the client on how he could lead the department. At the point where his desire to hand over the management and later leave the company became clear, I tried to encourage the client to talk to his superiors and to see together what possibilities there were as an alternative to the management task. We both knew that the company wanted to keep him because of the many years of cooperation, his reliability and the acute shortage of skilled workers.

Klaus Obermeyer

It seems exciting to me to ask whether the coachee's performance crisis described in the case is internally connected to his new role as a family father. Christophe Dejours (2012), a psychoanalytically inspired French occupational physician, has argued that a drop in performance cannot usually be explained by simply too much work. According to Dejours (2012), the situation becomes critical when the mental functional logic and coping mechanisms of working life can no longer be easily reconciled with those of private life. In his new role as a father, the coachee is confronted with completely different challenges than in his previous professional role in the company, in which he was previously promoted in a quasi-fatherly manner and was able to assume the role of the good son. As a newly appointed manager, he is now also faced with the new requirement to approach his employees in enabling and limiting attitudes. In relation to his former professional sponsors, demarcation, and negotiation at eye level would be required. In private, the role of the young father is obviously linked to qualities of caring, devotion, and responsibility. Suddenly the private space no longer fits the workspace, and the breakdown in either sphere at least takes the tension of incompatibility out of this dilemma. The failure of the optimization attempt is painful on the one hand and speaks clearly on the other. It takes the pressure out of the cauldron of seemingly incompatible mutual expectations.

It is easier said than done to intervene meaningfully here. The case once again sheds light on the necessity and difficulty of working out differentiated triangular contracts. It happens to us all too quickly that clients in coaching are virtually handed over to us by their company for repair. If we take triangular contracts seriously, clients are consistently involved in coaching processes, even if they are not consistently present in the conversations. As coaches, we depend on the willingness of our clients to adapt their assignments in the course of the process, to question themselves in their actions and, if necessary, to draw concrete consequences from the results of a coaching process. In this understanding, coaching actually always has more than one client. If we accept this program, it is obvious that there are usually no neat solutions that satisfy all parties equally. We are by no means all in the same boat.

Some additional mission clarification discussions with the coachee and his site manager might have provided an opportunity to keep the option of the coachee rejecting the leadership task as a possible outcome on the official radar screen. This would have limited the risk of excommunicating the possibility of failure at the leadership task alone to the inner life of the coachee, who was already under pressure.

When coach and client diverge—as in this case—I have had good experiences with investigating the question of what possibly connects the two without having admitted this to each other so far.

A final thought: The failure of the happy ending is probably associated with the coach's experience with fear of failure, anxiety, and sadness about the loss of previous recognition, perhaps also with shame. A tableau of effects that might not be too far removed from the client's experience. It might have opened a space to continue the joint work if the coach and client had shared these emotional states with each other, thus taking the risk of connectedness (see Jaenicke, 2014). Under certain circumstances, motifs such as variations on failure in both senses of the word, or the art of failing better, would have moved to the center of the coaching.

Magret Lüdemann

The coach has tried to implement the assignment by the organization conscientiously but may have missed what the actual conflict, the inner situation of the coachee was.

I suspect that the contract here was too narrow and the content corridor insufficiently described. The outcome of the coaching would fit this. The focus on the person should awaken in the coach what is hidden: All questions about what the organization and the relevant actors (site managers, team members) might have to do with the initial problem. It can be useful to include the following in the negotiation room: "From experience, things come up in the meetings that we have not yet considered. Possibly also such things that made your inclusion favorable. How do we want to proceed?"

Initially, in the confidential setting of the coaching, it should be found out once again what the goal of the coaching is from the coachee's point of view. In this way, the early determination that the person has the problem could be broadened.

As a coach, I would once again delve deeper into procedural diagnostics. The coachee is, it seems, doubly challenged as a leader: In the workplace and toward his child. He seems almost trapped. These are two offers of identity and role which the coachee cannot seem to answer in an ego-syntonic way, with the consequence of a psychic labilization, i.e., a crisis which has seized the person as a whole. In accordance with operationalized psychodynamic diagnostics (see Benecke & Möller, 2019), the hypothesis would be to test whether an attachment/autonomy conflict is virulent here.

According to the image of the clamp, as a coach, I would recreate the situation as it is experienced. Both the situation at work and the private situation would get a representation in the room. This would allow the coachee to work with the coach to find out the level of distress and impairment. After this step, it would be possible to introduce the third—perhaps represented by a chair. Only with the third position, space is opened, and what Moreno calls "surplus reality," as a projection of the coachee's inner world, can become visible (see Ameln, 2013). A rehearsal stage is created, which can lead away from an either/or logic towards a both/and logic.

Heidi Möller

If I first focus on the coachee as an individual, then the question of the diagnostic approach arises here (see Möller & Kotte, 2016). Is the client experiencing a neurotic conflict that prevents him from fulfilling the leadership role? Is it possibly negative experiences with power and influence that inhibit him biographically? If there were many negative experiences with powerful people in the life history, these old scenes must first be processed in order to become free to exercise power in a constructive and community-serving way (see Krug & Kuhl, 2006). Another diagnostic approach would be an analysis of the coachee's skills, abilities, and competencies (see Heppelter & Möller, 2013). Is there a person-job fit in this task constellation? Personality diagnostic approaches are also valuable (see Böning & Kegel, 2013). Talent analyses, as described by Rappe-Giesecke (2017), make sense at this point:

- What comes easily to the coachee?
- What is he naturally good at?
- What does he really like to do?

The assignment has its specific challenge in that in most organizations hierarchical advancement is the highest form of social recognition (see Möller & Volkmer, 2005). In this case, the problem is exacerbated because logic is broken from the company's point of view. Supervisors and personnel development are probably quite proud that the apprentice became a division manager. The common principle of higher-faster-further, which understands career as an incessant movement upwards, does not work here. What is often forgotten in this dynamic is that career growth also has its downsides. Promotions mean a change of milieu, and this entails parting with the familiar. Developmental tempos can also be too high. In developmental psychology, this is referred to as accelerated development: The soul cannot grow along with the increased responsibility and creative scope. The societal valuation of hierarchical advancement as highly desirable creates collective defense mechanisms (see Möller et al., 2018) and thus blind spots in the perspective of HR professionals and managers. This makes autonomous acts in a company difficult, such as saying, "Nah. I'm not doing the coaching. I don't want that career." There is little resolute resonance in the case study.

As a final aspect, I would not entirely rule out the possibility of derailment (see Möller & Müller, 2017). Well-functioning managers are suddenly thrown off track when their coping strategies are overloaded, or the context changes.

7.3 Practical Example 28

Case Description

During team coaching, the participants reported that they were very dissatisfied with the management (the owner) in many areas. They reported that salaries were not paid according to the contract, travel expenses were closely controlled and partly canceled. Attempts to talk to the boss had failed so far because he would then react personally offended. The dissatisfaction was very great. After consulting with the team, I, therefore, suggested inviting the boss to team coaching and addressing the conflict under my moderation. Unfortunately, this was rejected by the management, saying that my job was to motivate the team. In the next meeting, the employees informed me that they now intended to form a works council.

How Did the Coach Go About It?

The task of motivating the team could not be fulfilled, because an important basis, the fidelity to the contract, was not given. Unfortunately, the attempt to adapt the setting accordingly failed because the management could not share my point of view and was not willing to talk. I then advised the members of the team in a final meeting on the subject of setting up a works council. Here I remained in a neutral position. The question was: What are the possibilities to solve the conflict? What could be the best idea? How can this idea be implemented? I advised the employees well and helped them to make a conscious decisions. I lost the assignment. The boss was angry because he thought I had instigated the employees.

Klaus Obermeyer

In the case described, the discussion between management and staff about these unevennesses seems to have sunk into hopelessness and to have given way to mutual isolation. Much is reminiscent of the variant described by Bion (2001), in which management and employees are primarily focused on the basic assumption of their inescapable mutual dependence. Management and staff seem convinced that they are each mutually the cause of their misery. In such choreographies, which are usually also emotionally overheated, it is extremely difficult for counselors to protect their independence. More quickly than they would like, they are drawn into alliances—in this case, with the employees. In the case described, the coach apparently senses this risk and tries to include the boss in the counseling setting with her invitation.

In this context, the manager formulates, for the first or repeated time, an assignment for the coach: She should motivate the employees. Thus, the coach finds herself in the dilemma of idealizing the expectations of the boss and the employees.

Motivational assignments seem to me to be fundamentally problematic. I am inclined to the view (Sprenger, 2014) according to which motivation is not to be provided from the outside but unfolds autonomously in the individual as long as the framework conditions are right. Accordingly, any motivation has something infantilizing in the sense of guided feeling and ultimately undermines what it purports to promote.

The team coaching results in a vital impulse to establish a works council. From the perspective of the client, this is probably an undesirable side effect of the team coaching; for the employees, the coaching has led to a decision. Does this mean it has failed? Can consulting fail at all if we take into account that the participants actually always relate to the course and result of the consulting and do something with it (see Lackner, 2015)?

I find it difficult to say whether constructive intervention would have been possible here. Presumably, the managing director should have been much more involved in clarifying the assignment and the respective roles of the consultant and the managing director. At the latest, at the moment when the coach advised the formation of the works council, the legitimacy of the client is questionable. It is often helpful to explore with the participants at the beginning of team coaching sessions who bears and can bear responsibility for what is in the team's work process. Kaldenkerken (2014, p. 242 f.) has suggested doing this along the cascade of the *individual person in the team*, the *team as a collective*, *team leadership*, *organization or institution*, and *society*. This can make transparent which contributions are necessary and feasible at which level or which may be futile.

Nevertheless: The coach finds, in this case, a fighting formation from the beginning. Working teams also prepare themselves for bitter disappointments when working together (see Scanlon, 2019), which snub expectations and need to be metabolized. When this fails, long-lasting resentment can limit the team's ability to work. The common work task often no longer develops a unifying force under such frustration. So the question remains: What common, unifying the third party can management and employees still refer to here?

In order to clarify this crucial question and to develop the team, both the management and the employees must be present in the consultation room. The establishment of the works council at least opens up the possibility of making a given labor law framework a common point of reference again. At best, however, this stabilizes the structural framework. In order for management and employees to be able to meet without war paint, contexts of recognition are probably needed (see Benjamin, 2019).

Magret Lüdemann

In this case, highly dissatisfied employees are described, triggered by the behavior of the boss. My hypothesis is: In the organization described, a pattern of communication and interaction prevails that can be summarized with the conflict-constituting roles of persecutor (perpetrator), victim, rescuer of the drama triangle (see Karpman, 1968) of transactional analysis. While the managing director and the team alternately see themselves as persecutors or victims, the external person providing advice is automatically assigned the role of rescuer—an invitation that requires a high degree of self-reflexivity (see Zimmer-Leinfelder, 2003). In narratives that are as unanimous as in this case description in placing the blame on the superior, the counselor needs a high level of triadic competence, i.e., the ability to deal with the paradoxes, contradictions, and ambivalences present in the organization in a balancing way (see Heltzel, 2001).

The manager justifies his refusal to participate in the team coaching in order to bring both sides into the same room by telling the coach to motivate the team. Motivate for what? The question of whether coaching can motivate must be asked doubtfully. However, the consulting format can accompany those seeking advice in finding out their motives.

Is it possible to work with outraged teams who are led by affect?

Basically, yes. The hypothesis that the prevailing mood was a collective regression in the sense of Kampfflucht's basic assumption group (see the concept of basic assumption groups, Bion, 2001) would have to be tested. It led to an attempt to accompany the team, to return to the constitution of a working group. The indignation is to be stated first. It would need the translation of the coach. It would have to be sounded out what the basic needs of sufficient security, relationship, and autonomy were in this place of work. Only when reassurance was achieved could question such as: What keeps you (motives) in the company? What is the value of this activity, of these tasks? even gain resonance.

The end does not surprise me. The impossible order would have been needed in my opinion, in the contracting attempt to come to a connecting question with the managing director and the team with the organization order. At the latest, after the first meeting, in which the team was outraged by the owner and massively critical of his way of running the business, it would have needed a (re)negotiation.

Assignments of this kind put our triadic competence to the test. It threatens to break off contact to one side. "Holding the angle" is what Bauriedl (2004) calls the attempt to preserve the triangle threatened by collapse.

7.4 Practical Example 29

Case Description

A coachee explains during contracting that he perceives himself as a chatterbox and would like to work with creative methods in coaching: "I talk so much, I don't want to just monolog in coaching." The coachee comes back to his job after a cancer illness and wants to decide whether he should leave the job because of the high stress or whether he can develop strategies to deal with the stress. At the third session, there is a session on body awareness and body reminders while at work. The coachee leaves the coaching session inspired and in a good mood. In the next session, he opened the conversation by saying that he was not feeling well after the coaching. At his workplace, he talked to his colleagues about the coaching. They were all of the opinions that he would feel better if he ended the coaching and switched to talk therapy because it would make it easier for him to talk. The contract is terminated as requested.

What Was the Coach's Approach?

My emotional experience: Surprise, disappointment, anger, and helplessness. I thank the coachee for dissolving the contract in person, not by email or on the phone. The proposal to debrief the previous sessions revealed: The coachee's confidence is so affected by the consultation with his colleagues that he does not want to engage in evaluation work. We discussed what did and did not do him good. The decision to end coaching is, in my opinion, easier than leaving the workplace. The courage to end the coaching and to clarify in the conversation that the human level is not burdened, i.e., there is no grievance, is a successfully applied strategy. Perhaps it is also a good preliminary exercise for his further career path.

Klaus Obermeyer

The coachee's interaction with his coach seems to move primarily in psychodynamic fields of tension between self-sufficiency and provision, perhaps also between control and surrender (see Benecke & Möller, 2019). The client probably learned about his cancer not too long ago. At the very beginning of the coaching session, the client asks his coach to work with creative methods to control his—as he thinks—the often rampant flow of speech. This request to the coach seems to me to express a paradoxical longing: On the one hand, care and control are to be left in the hands of the coach; on the other hand, precisely self-care and control do not have to be given up entirely, since the use of methods is, after all, at the explicit request of the client. The coach may have been caught in a similar contradiction here. On the one hand, he is relinquishing a measure of direction and competence into the hands of his client when he follows his client's methodological suggestion. At the same time, he may be choosing a potentially regression-enhancing, body-oriented method that cares for the client but demands some loss of control. At first, this seems to fit together like a lock and key. The client leaves the session seemingly elated, only to experience involuntary, irritating after-effects shortly thereafter. He reveals himself to his colleagues and seems to have triggered caring impulses in them. These culminate in the concerned advice not to continue coaching and to seek therapeutic help instead. In an interactional perspective—which assumes that client and coach create and share a common reality (see Mittelsten-Scheid, 2012)—it can be surmised that client and coach jointly seek control over the mode of their cooperation, only to jointly lose it in the end and end the cooperation. What was designed to be caring and supportive seems to quickly turn into a rather overwhelming relationship quality.

The still-young working alliance between client and coach quickly becomes the victim of its first crisis. This may also have been a painfully frustrating experience for both. Perhaps both client and coach were surprised by the possible intensity of effects, longings for care and the need to endure them, which could have led to regressive overloading of the coaching context. Instead, he opts for conversational psychotherapy.

Against this background, it seems plausible that the client did not see any scope to understand this crisis together with the coach and to use it for an improvement of the working alliance. The decision to withdraw from the more work-related and performance-enhancing coaching towards the psychotherapeutic option can certainly be understood as a progressive self-care movement.

The ambivalence that emerges at this fork in the road sheds light on a complication of the case described, which seems to balance a boundary between work-related counseling and medical rehabilitation. Here, different functional logics of these two strands also overlap. Coaching focuses on optimizing and exploiting available personal and organizational resources. Medical rehabilitation focuses on overcoming the limitations imposed by the illness. It, thus, also keeps in mind that the question of the ability to work cannot be solved solely by the efforts and performance of those affected but is also subject to fate-mediated limitations. The question of coaching and/or psychotherapy is therefore not so easy to weigh up.

The case sketch illustrates the speed with which conditions in coaching can shift from cheerful to cloudy. However, such crises also hold the opportunity to deepen working alliances about the successful management of the crisis and to understand the dilemma of the respective client better. It can be helpful to talk to clients about the value of such crises already in initial conversations and to promote addressing emerging irritations in order to be able to work on them.

A final thought: We can trust that the problems clients struggle with in everyday life are also enacted in the counseling room. Such enactments can be understood as a language of action, a dialogue of action, in which dimensions of meaning are expressed for which we sometimes lack words. Alfred Lorenzer (1973) has described the decoding of this interweaving of language, action, body, mind, and unconscious as scenic understanding. It would have been nice if the client and coach in our case could have reflected together on what they had done together in the short phase of their collaboration and what this tells us about the client's coaching concerns.

Magret Lüdemann

In the description of the case, it is noticeable that the coachee initially refers to himself as a chatterbox, which is why he wants to work with creative media.

As a coach, I would translate this as, "I talk a lot and not very deeply. Outsmart me with non-verbal methods, otherwise, this won't work."

The talkativeness could be interpreted as a way of regulating closeness-distance and as a wall of words surrounding the person. My response to this would be the feeling of constriction, a kind of domination by the coachee: "I'll tell you how you should be!"

The request, “Shut my mouth through other methods!” would be tantamount to the coach giving permission for a kind of empowerment. Ostensibly, control is relinquished and one entrusts oneself to the guidance of the coach. At the same time, control is exercised over the knowledge of what is right to do here.

According to my resonance, I would work with this initial figure, the desire to exercise control and give it away, on the relational level: “Good that you know what you need! Please allow me to get a picture of it as well. To do this, I would like to ask you some questions. From this, my ideas of how I would work with you on your question will emerge. You could then see if this is a good fit for you.”

Before choosing any method, I would need an answer to the question of how much time the coachee gives us to find his answer. What is the significance of the pillars of work and performance and physicality for his identity (see also the model of the five pillars of identity in Petzold, 1993) and how are the other three pillars affected?

“You would want to learn strategies here to deal with the stress at work. I would like to know-how you are currently doing. Coping with cancer is a challenge. It is not without reason that those who have recovered are able to obtain” degrees of disability “which can be seen as compensation for disadvantages in relation to being fully capable and able to work under pressure. How is that for you?”

Whether the career anchors (see Schein, 1996) are determined diagnostically, resilience is strengthened with the Zurich Resource Model (see Storch et al., 2018), or self-management models are applied, I cannot say at this point. In my view, the central issue in this coaching is whether a sustainable working relationship develops.

From the perception of the successful third session, it is only too understandable that the coach is surprised by the termination of the coaching. The annoyance that colleagues from outside the profession know better what the coachee needs is also understandable. In the end, the beginning repeats itself. The coachee does not want to get involved in any evaluation work and takes over the direction of the last lesson. Whether the personal quitting of the coaching is the preliminary exercise to quitting the job or a substitute action can be weighted as an exculpatory interpretation of the counseling guild when we are in touch with feelings of failure.

Heidi Möller

The case description leads us to a central coaching topic: How do I deal with the clients’ world of wishes? I would probably react with astonishment or even annoyance if my methodological approach were prescribed to me. The issue of shaping the working relationship picks up steam right away in this description: Who follows and who leads in this process? I do not consider it professionally justifiable to serve the wishes of the clients one-to-one. Without a clear diagnosis of the differential indication, I cannot yet say which methodology will be appropriate and effective. As a coach, I claim to be an expert in the methodological procedure. Certainly, the physical dimension is neglected in coaching, but due to its effectiveness, it requires quite a lot of care and body-therapeutic competence.

I would also be irritated that the client thinks that he could succeed in monologuing in coaching. Monologuing means not being in contact with the coach. Soon enough, I would make contact design an issue and in no way let it happen. There may be a longing coming from the coachee to lift the loneliness that probably surrounds him when he has had the experience of being the determiner all too often.

It may be that the coach's perception that the client left the coaching "inspired and in a good mood" is not true. But it can also be that the perception is just right, and then on the preconscious level of the coachee, a completely different question arose: Cannot I catch a break? Can good things happen to me? There is a coach who is able to trigger so many beneficial emotional states in me that brings dangerous closeness with it. When I am feeling good, I lose my secondary illness gain. Maybe the client has an inner happiness ban. He walks out of coaching inspired and in a good mood, only to be startled: This cannot be happening! A negative therapeutic reaction is what this experience is called in psychotherapy. The psyche resists progress in coaching. The surprising turn may be an indication of this. Freud (1923) blames an unconscious need for punishment for this phenomenon. Interpreted more superficially, this would be loosely based on Tucholsky: Better the long-known suffering than the unknown happiness. The consideration of a negative coaching reaction is important to me because it shows the dangers of pure solution orientation. Systemic interventions, which naively assume that people want to progress and to overcome their problems, are quite far from this idea.

The outcome of the coaching would leave me offended. The trapper's reaction feels a bit like whistling in the woods—preparation for quitting: I do not want to feel any pain over a failed coaching session, nor do I want to rue and brood with myself.

But how do we coaches want to develop if we have to gloss over everything?

Optimally, the feelings of anger, disappointment, surprise, and helplessness would have been experienced in pairs, each of which would have been a starting point, a viable avenue for further process.

7.5 Practical Example 30

Case Description

The coaching assignment came from the internal institute for coaching a large Christian authority. A coachee in a high management position was sent for coaching by her new employer. The employer found the coachee to be uncooperative, brittle, inflexible, and unwilling to learn. He felt she was out of place, but now that she was part of the close management staff, he had to work with her. In coaching, she was to change. To this end, he had formulated three tasks that the coachee was to learn in coaching. The coachee agreed to work with me. She was of the opinion: Now the task is set, now let us see what we make of it. At the same time, she explained that she also considered her new employer to be incapable and was already considering changing institutions herself. I did a potential analysis with her, the language of which she could do little within the evaluation. She found the language wooden, insensitive, and outdated. I could disagree with her very little. She knew the Enneagram, which appealed to her more.

What Was the Coach's Approach?

Nevertheless, we went through the potential analysis with the focus on the three questions of the employer. There may have been clues about her personality in this regard that could be worked with further. Otherwise, she agreed to work with the questions asked. She showed herself to be very hurt by the mandatory coaching. We dealt with this hurt at length as well. In my opinion, she did the best she could even though her workload was full, and she had another additional coaching during another leadership training for senior female employees. After 6 hours of coaching, answers to her questions were presented in a joint discussion with the principal. The principal offered another 6 hours of coaching for the executive. Both the executive and I declined this until she completed her further executive training. Only then did we want to continue. In the meantime, the principal has changed jobs.

Kornelia Steinhardt

If you look at the organization, you can see that there is a strongly hierarchical culture. Here coaching becomes an enforcement body of management guidelines. The obviously conflict-ridden relationship between the superior and the coachee cannot be reflected upon or worked on within the framework of coaching because the superior can avoid it. In this organization, internal coaching ultimately does not represent a socio-emotional place for reflecting on and (re)shaping working relationships.

It is essential to include the triad of supervisor, coachee, and coach in the contract at the beginning of the process. The coaching assignment stands and falls with this triadic clarification of the assignment. This is because in this joint contract phase it must be clarified to what extent the supervisor's concern can become a joint mandate that is supported by all three participants. The process of contracting should not be reduced to the supervisor giving instructions on what is to be worked on in coaching. In the triadic clarification of the mandate, it can be checked whether coaching is the right format at all or whether the concerns require the framework of another training measure. In addition, it could be clarified whether a management task not taken over by the superior is being shifted to coaching. Here the temptation for a coach is always great to unconsciously take over the leadership task that has been assigned to him and not to reflect on his role. It could also be clarified that coaching is not a measure of personality change but serves to deal with work-related concerns.

In the context of triadic contracting, it would then also be brought up that the potential coachee is undergoing management training in which there is already accompanying coaching. It could then be questioned to what extent two parallel coaching processes make sense. With such a careful clarification in the contract phase, the (potential) coachee could be empowered to stand up for her interests. It could be considered whether coaching with the supervisor and (potential) coachee is indicated or whether individual coaching with the supervisor would be the means of choice—although this can hardly be addressed in the three-way conversation.

Wolfgang Knopf

A tense picture of an organization, a Christian ministry, is painted here: Among the tight management staff, employees are designated by the leader, the ministry leader, as unfit for the position. But the leadership does not have the authority to reject or remove this person. There is an unnamed higher authority above the principal who decides, who has the power. Orders are to be accepted and are then modified in the concrete as one wishes: Now, let us see what we make of it. There is an internal institute for coaching, so strangers should not see the problems. And the "we" is important: Commonality and demarcation from the outside are paramount. Conflicts are shifted to other levels like training courses and rumors. Procedures and processes that one personally does not stand behind in terms of content are nevertheless carried out (see potential analysis). Twice the attributes *brittle* (wooden), *inflexible*, *uncooperative* (insensitive) and *unwillingness to learn* (outdated) are used in the description of person and methodology. Attributes also seem to apply to the organization.

In this organization, an internal coach takes on an assignment that is a continuing education or training assignment. Rather, it is about changing a person and the coachee's behaviors. Neither coach nor coachee resists this assignment. On the contrary, they team up and see what they can make of it. There is something unproductively subversive about this interpretation of the assignment!

In my opinion, it becomes quite bizarre when the enneagram becomes involved. The enneagram is used in esotericism for the development of the personality.

The described procedure of the coach fits in with the organizational culture mentioned at the beginning: Not showing any offensive resistance; delegating conflicts, as here in the further training disguised as coaching; adapting, if necessary pseudo-moderately, and waiting; carrying out procedures after all despite skepticism and criticism. The case description also shows a problem of internal coaches: How much can they distance themselves, critically distance themselves from their organization? Do they recognize the dynamics of the organization in miniature? If there is an internal instance for supervision, there will certainly be one for internal training in that organization. As a coach, I would direct the request of the employer there!

Ursula Hermann

If a supervisor wants to make an issue of the effect a female employee has on him, there is a wealth of possibilities for giving feedback and setting interventions. In the case described, a coach is hired by the internal coaching institute, not to support the supervisor in his leadership of the employee, but to outsource the leadership and to turn a supposedly brittle, inflexible, uncooperative, and unwilling-to-learn employee into the exact opposite through coaching. In contracting, the expectations of the supervisor became—it seems—unquestioningly (by the internal institute for coaching and by the coach himself) the mandate. The strong focus on methods in the implementation of the assignment suggests an understanding of coaching that thinks of consulting more in terms of the methods to be used and subordinates the subject of the consulting to the method (see Weigand, 2009).

This case describes the attempt to delegate leadership tasks to a consultancy with the help of coaching. As a coach, I would not start my intervention in the course of the coaching process, but already in the phase of contracting. I would have met the manager's concern that the employee should change in her appearance, motivation, and attitude as a result of the coaching, and in fact in the way he envisages, by asking whether a discussion with the manager was possible in order to clarify the assignment. The role of the internal institute for coaching acts like an extended arm of the superior, therefore, it seems to me that a concrete clarification of the assignment with the superior and subsequently also with the coachee is crucial. It is important to get clarity about the background of the previous cooperation and about the superior's ideas about coaching. It is possible that the discussion of these two points could have resulted in a coaching assignment, perhaps for the superior himself, but not an assignment as described above.

Heidi Möller

The amazing thing for me is: The coachee accepts the prescribed coaching without resistance. She is told by her boss, "Become another," and she says, "Of course. Let's do that now!" Thinking of coaching as a brief intervention for personality change is questionable enough. After all, the very notion of personality is characterized by the enduring, the recognizable, the stable. The approach in coaching via an analysis of potential, however, designed, comes across as a message from the coach: "I'm now going to do some archaeological work and see what undiscovered treasures I can unearth to please the supreme master."

First, however, the coach seems to take on the personality analysis of the boss: Brittle, inflexible, not very cooperative or willing to learn. This perspective adoption would make me feel like a fellow aggressor. The fact that the coachee adopts this perspective and goes on her way has almost masochistic features for me.

I also see an overestimation of the coaching format. Someone is supposed to be trimmed from brittle to supple, from inflexible to flexible, from uncooperative to cooperative and then still be able to learn. But it does not seem to be an issue for the coach that these goals are not achievable at all. Perhaps the characteristics described above are even useful for the coachee's function!? Pseudo-adjustment and wait-and-see were the right choice, at least in this case, the boss is gone.

The coachee's compliance can be read both as a subversive gesture and as an act of submission. To refuse the boss at this point would have consequences—in this respect, the question of voluntariness in coaching in organizations must always be asked.

7.6 Practical Example 31

Case Description

Area management of a geriatric care provider asked me for coaching of house management. There were communication problems between the management and the team. After an exploratory discussion between the division management, the house management and me, I received the order for a coaching session in which the communication competence of the house management was to be promoted. Already in the first coaching session, I had to evaluate the assessment of the problem by the division management as not appropriate. From then on, I continued the contract development with the house management. The topic of the coaching was now the question of how the house management could bind its neglected team to rules and how the team could stop fighting management for the right to determine working methods and forms of cooperation. The team had previously been without leadership for several years and had developed its ways of working, which often did not conform to the rules. My conflict tension: Have I allied myself too much with the house management?—In my opinion, this working alliance was the basis for trusting cooperation and for the positive development of the work of the house.

What Was the Coach's Approach?

At the end of the contractually agreed ten sessions, I propose a final discussion with the divisional management to evaluate the process and its results.

Andreas Knierim

In many points, the description of the client, in this case, the departmental management, corresponds little or not at all with that of the coachee, in this case, the house management. Since the contract was agreed with the division management, changes should be discussed with them so that the results can be used later, e.g., in a joint review meeting. Here it looks like a unilateral reinterpretation of the contract.

Here I would start right at the beginning of the process and structure the exploratory meeting differently: As is usual with the triangular contract, the coachee, the manager, the coach and possibly someone else from PD sit at the table for the initial meeting. What I find helpful—and always design very formally—is proceeding with concrete questions in this three-way conversation.

In the first part—this is where both the house and division managers would be sitting at the table together—as a coach, I ask the question that can be asked of the supervisor or boss: What is different after coaching with house leadership? In this way, as a coach, I get concrete answers, document them and will refer to them in the later review meeting.

In the second part, the conversation continues only with the coachee—the client is no longer present—and I ask the question again: So then, between us in confidence—this all stays in the room—what is your gain at the end of the coaching? I suspect that in this exchange, the divergence between the goals of the division management and the coachee becomes apparent even before the actual coaching—we can react to this and, for example, conclude a modified contract with the division management.

On the question of the setting, I would like to say: In my experience, it is possible to coach the management and the team separately with a fellow coach. It is agreed with the client that both coaches can talk alone during the coaching process. Both positions (team and leadership) can come up in these conversations, and both coaches could bring interpretations and working hypotheses and go back to their respective coaching processes with these suggestions. In this evaluation, an intervision, we see our blind spots, which can be the starting point for subsequent supervision.

In one-on-one coaching, I always partner with my client to stabilize the trust situation. We would explore together what exactly constitutes neglect in the first place, why the coachee is strongly evaluating and perhaps projecting here. I would address and reflect on allying as a trust-building measure after a few sessions in the coaching process: What happens when we ally? Where does the alliance perhaps take place in the team of which we are currently a mirror?

A step into the meta-position supports the leaving of roles: Both for the coachee, who can see his work team and himself, and for the coach, who can also perceive in his supervision what he has overlooked in the work process with the coachee. Systemic constellation has proven to be a good format in my supervision: In the case discussed, the client system and the role of the coach would be quickly visible. In a constellation, I have a proxy and often see after a few minutes where the problem lies, where I was too involved as a coach, where I was too much of an ally.

Regina Gibhardt

The description of the case leads to the assumption that in the discussion between the head of the department and the head of the house, too little was asked about the causes of the current situation and that these were not sufficiently illuminated. A classic background for requests for advice is often that a culprit is sought and also quickly found when something is not going well. Of course, the complete system context is left out. If it had become clear in the first conversation that this was primarily a system dynamic and secondarily a communication issue, a more meaningful coaching assignment would have resulted. Division and house management would have a common understanding of the actual coaching goal.

The statement that this is a "neglected team" makes it clear that a somewhat longer process is probably needed here. This needs to be discussed with the two managers, establishing the milestones to be achieved and what will make it clear that they have been achieved. Of course, this also includes coaching from time to time together with the divisional and house management in order to check whether everyone involved is on a sensible development path.

In the actual coaching process, I would keep the following guiding questions in mind: Who needs what from whom? Where is there a lack of transparency and good communication? Which self-organization methods can be helpful? Which new rules would be good for the team? What external influences on the team are hindering it? What additional leadership and communication know-how does the house management need?

It would certainly also be useful to ask why it was not clear to the division management that the team was in a state of neglect. What was done in the past to change this state, or what was not done for it?

In principle, I agree in the joint conversation between client and customer that I will work for the person who comes to the coaching, and always against the background of the question of what the organization needs. I make it clear that issues can arise during the coaching process that requires a renewed coordination or correction of the assignment. And I point out that through coaching, it can also become visible that the common paths might part.

Apart from the insufficient clarification of the assignment, I asked myself in this case description whether the coach might be bringing his parentification issue into the assignment. If a coach has his unresolved systemic issues or blind spots with the topic of joining forces, this can also lead to such a constellation of assignments. Parentification is the reversal of the parent–child relationship: Children take on the parental role or are drawn into uneasy conflicts of loyalty. Classic parentification dynamics include: The mother discusses things with the child that she should be discussing with the father but does not because of conflict aversion. The son becomes an emotional substitute because the father is only physically present in the family due to his traumas, but not emotionally.

If a coach has his or her unresolved systemic issues or blind spots with the topic of connecting, this can lead to such an entangled constellation of assignments.

At the beginning of a coaching process and in exploratory conversations with third parties, I basically clarify my attitude as a coach: I do not see my task as behaving in such a way that I please clients and customers. My attitude as a coach is rather to contribute to awareness, development, and know-how growth in the coaching context. This also means that I address unpleasant issues and put my finger in the wound. If this approach is considered as essential for the participants as it is for me, a good basis for work exists. Furthermore, I point out at the beginning that I am happy to hand over the process to other hands if I get the impression that I can no longer be helpful with my competence. Getting to this point in my self-image as a coach was, of course, also a personal development process in which I was allowed to throw old patterns of entanglement and beliefs overboard.

Jannik Zimmermann

In work-related coaching, the organization for which a coachee works influences the coaching process in many ways. This sometimes creates challenges (see Louis & Fatien Diochon, 2014), which can be encountered at various points in the coaching process. This is also evident in the case described: After a short time, the assignment given by the divisional management turns out not to be purposeful. In the further course, the coach is confronted with different interests, demands, and opinions; the question arises for him how he should position himself. He decides to deviate from the original assignment but is concerned about allying himself too much with the management.

In the case described, there is a difference between the mandate originally given by the organization, and the coaching objectives worked out and desired between coach and coachee. Also, it seems that the interests of the three parties involved, coach, house management and division management, are not balanced. Furthermore, there is uncertainty on the part of the coach as to whether he has maintained his impartiality as a coach.

Dealing with such a situation as a coach is possible in different ways. At this point, I would like to discuss three different approaches briefly.

I see the first starting point in the (self-)reflection of the coach. Possible questions that can be used for this are: To whom do I feel a commitment in coaching? At what point do I feel allied with a party? How do I deal with the individual parties when these very parties have different interests? In addition to self-reflection, collegial exchange or supervision can be used for this reflection. In the context of such a reflection, it is possible to work on one's attitude in order to deal with such situations more confidently in the future. If necessary, new impulses can be conveyed in the form of thought-provoking impulses and new solutions.

I see a second starting point in diagnostics in coaching (see Möller & Kotte, 2013). Especially if the original mandate of the organization and the developed goals in coaching do not match, it is helpful to additionally secure one's working hypotheses. This primarily also refers to assumptions about existing problems and existing goals. This enables the coach to represent his working hypotheses more confidently in front of the commissioning party and to gain additional clarity for his further procedure.

I see the third starting point in the design of the contract and the involvement of the organization. When drafting the contract, it is important to take into account the interests of the parties involved in as balanced a way as possible. If the contract and the assignment turn out to be too rigid and not goal-oriented, it makes sense to talk to all three parties at an early stage. If a contract does not give a person in the role of coach any leeway to react to changes in the coaching process, it can be negotiated in such an interim meeting that the contract is structured differently.

Peter Döring

Initially, the consultant uncritically adopts the problem definition of the head of the department. The house management, whose communication competence is addressed here as a problem, is also present in this conversation and implicitly agrees to the problem definition through their presence.

Subsequently, however, the consultant *continues the contract development together with the house management* without involving the division management in this change. He now takes over the problem definition of house management.

Finally, the consultant asks himself whether he has allied himself too much with the house management. Even if trusting cooperation with the house management has developed, which has led to a positive development of the work of the house, I would answer this question with a yes.

Due to the alliance with the house management, the difference in the problem definition between the division management and the house management remains unresolved. Nor does the submissive attitude of the house management become an issue; in the joint discussion, it initially agrees with the problem definition of the divisional management, but contradicts the consultant so clearly in the first discussion that the latter agrees with the house management. If the team is indeed neglected because it has developed its working methods for several years without leadership, it would have to be clarified who is responsible for this. The fact that a clarification of responsibility remains open here means that the opportunity is missed to work out a common understanding of problems and tasks between the division management and the house management. Finally, one risk of the consultant's approach is that he must fear a conflict with the division management if the latter realizes that he is not working in the sense of the mandate agreed with it.

When it became clear in the first conversation that the house management had a completely different definition of the problem, as a coach I would have first discussed this with her and said, for example, "That's interesting, it seems completely different to me now than in the conversation with your manager," in order to encourage her to first say something about it herself. It would be important for me to initiate another joint discussion with both parties in order to clarify the assignment anew. The goal here would be to make the different points of view the subject of discussion and to adjust the assignment accordingly.

For the clarification of the assignment, I would prefer a different procedure: In the case of assignments with a problematic case, I quickly become alert and suggest conducting interviews with the various parties involved in the first step of the assignment (in this case, divisional management, house management and team members). I would conduct the interviews with the team members in two or three small groups. From the contents, I would create an analysis and make a proposal for further action—e.g., a workshop to clarify tasks and responsibilities between the team and house management.

To me, such an approach is closer to lifting the different perspectives of the parties involved, which otherwise remain under the carpet. At the same time, my goal would be that all parties (here at least three) trust me to be committed to an overriding interest in clarification.

With my approach, this could lead to me not getting the order because it is too complicated and time-consuming. For me, however, it has proved worthwhile to accept this in order not to be restrained by interests that I do not sufficiently understand.

Claudia Bredt

It seems as if the coach is surrounded by two opposing tendencies in feeling and acting and thus enters into an intrapersonal conflict: On the one hand, the coach feels obligated to the division management's mandate to improve the communication competence of the house management, on the other hand, he feels obligated to the house management's actual concern: How do I lead the team? He solves the conflict superficially by the conviction that the working alliance is the basis for trusting cooperation and for the positive development of the work of the house.

But the conflict remains, "Have I allied myself too much [. . .]?"

The coach allowed himself to be drawn into a process of delegation of blame, which possibly made clear contracting in the exploratory discussion difficult from the beginning. A possible hypothesis is: The division management allowed the position of house manager to remain vacant for more or less a long time. She may have had little knowledge of the team's functioning. She, thus, seems to avoid the duty of care for her area of responsibility. The associated blame is transferred to the house management and also to the coach who is supposed to fix it: The house management lacks communication competence. In this way, the division management also delegates part of its responsibility to the coach. The house management delegates the blame to the team, describing them as "neglected." The coach takes over this blame through the idea of an alliance.

At first, the coach seems to take over the problem definition of the head of the department, but in the first session, he judges the view of the head of the department as not appropriate and agrees with the interpretation of the head of the house. He places himself next to the house management in order to enforce the rule specifications in the team. The coach seems to have only the possibility to be loyal to one or the other. A third position is not apparent.

One direction of intervention would be to explore the different perspectives already in the contract discussion: The view of the team, the view of the division management and the view of the house management. The organizational conditions for the development of the situation should also be explicitly taken into account. Then the issue of guilt would not narrow the view in the counseling process.

Heidi Möller

The assessment of a team as "neglected" hovers in the room. This shows a distancing of the house management from this team: I would rather not have anything to do with them. Or: I find a staff here that does not correspond to my ideas about good work. An educational aspect resonates, that this team has to be educated or cleaned up, or whatever one does with neglected people. This perspective may be taken as a reference to the organizational culture of elder care. After all, to work in this field is to feel constantly in deficit: Too little time, too few staff, etc. A chronic feeling of guilt accompanies geriatric assistants; they cannot replace the closeness of relatives who are often absent, they have limited resources, e.g., to feed dementia patients, and yet they do their best. The organizational dynamics of this sector are reflected in the souls of the employees: The constant presence of death, the powerlessness in the face of the aging processes.

The danger of the alliance between house leader and supervisor could be described with the defense mechanism of pair formation, according to Bion (see Lohmer & Möller, 2019; Möller et al., 2018). Seeking stability in pair formation serves as a defense against anxiety, thus threatening a front: Two against the team. The case study vividly illustrates how difficult it often is to realize the professional superego of all-partiality, neutrality, or abstinence. Partiality can be examined according to preconscious psychodynamic mechanisms and at the same time subjected to a reality check. Do I manage to triangulate well even though the power relations are different and it is clear who bears the costs?

References

Ameln, F. v. (2013). Surplus Reality – der vergessene Kern des Psychodramas. *Zeitschrift für Psychodrama und Soziometrie, 12*(1), 5–19.

Bauriedl, T. (2004). *Auch ohne Couch. Psychoanalyse als Beziehungstheorie und ihre Anwendungen*. Klett-Cotta.

Benecke, C., & Möller, H. (2019). OPD-basierte Diagnostik im Coaching. In A. Ryba & G. Roth (Eds.), *Coaching und Beratung in der Praxis. Ein neurowissenschaftlich fundiertes Integrationsmodell* (pp. 127–147). Klett-Cotta.

Benjamin, J. (2019). *Anerkennung, Zeugenschaft und Moral: Soziale Traumata in psychoanalytischer Perspektive*. Psychosozial.

Bion, W. R. (2001). *Erfahrungen in Gruppen und andere Schriften*. Klett-Cotta.

Böning, U., & Kegel, C. (2013). Psychometrische Persönlichkeitsdiagnostik. In H. Möller & S. Kotte (Eds.), *Diagnostik im Coaching* (pp. 81–100). Springer.

Dejours, C. (Ed.). (2012). *Psychopathologien der Arbeit: klinische Fallstudien*. Brandes & Apsel.

Freud, S. (1923). *Das Ich und das Es*. Internationaler Psychoanalytischer Verlag.

Heltzel, R. (2001). Was heißt Leitung heute? *Gruppenanalyse, 11*(2), 131–154.

Heppelter, N., & Möller, H. (2013). Wie ich wurde was ich bin. Kompetenzorientierte Diagnostik im Coaching. In H. Möller & S. Kotte (Eds.), *Diagnostik im Coaching* (pp. 133–150). Springer.

Jaenicke, C. (2014). *Die Suche nach Bezogenheit*. Brandes & Apsel.

Karpman, S. B. (1968). Fairy tales and script drama analysis. *Transactional Analysis Bulletin, 7*(26), 39–43.

Krug, J. S., & Kuhl, U. (2006). *Macht, Leistung, Freundschaft*. Kohlhammer.

Lackner, K. (2015). Beratung scheitert nicht! *Supervision, 3*, 41–50.

Lohmer, M., & Möller, H. (2019). *Psychoanalyse in Organisationen*. Kohlhammer.

Lorenzer, A. (1973). *Sprachzerstörung und Rekonstruktion*. Suhrkamp.

Louis, D., & Fatien Diochon, P. (2014). Educating coaches to power dynamics: Managing multiple agendas within the triangular relationship. *Journal of Psychological Issues in Organisational Culture, 5*(2), 31–47.

Middendorf, J. (2019). *17. Coaching-Umfrage Deutschland*. https://coachingumfrage.wordpress.com/startseite/umfragen/. Zugegriffen am 02.06.2020.

Middendorf, J. (2020). *[18.] Coaching-Umfrage Deutschland*. https://coachingumfrage.wordpress.com/startseite/umfragen/. Zugegriffen am 02.06.2020.

Mittelsten-Scheid, B. (2012). Die Bedeutung der intersubjektiven Wende der Psychoanalyse für eine gruppenanalytische Supervision. In W. Dinger (Ed.), *Gruppenanalytisch denken – supervisorisch handeln. Gruppenkompetenz in Supervision und Arbeitswelt* (pp. 161–184). Kassel University Press.

Möller, H., & Kotte, S. (Eds.). (2013). *Diagnostik im Coaching. Grundlagen, Analyseebenen, Praxisbeispiele*. Springer.

Möller, H., & Kotte, S. (2016). *Essentials: Diagnostik im Coaching*. Springer.

Möller, H., & Müller, A. (2017). Manager-Derailment. *Gruppe, Interaktion, Organisation, 48*(4), 351–354.

Möller, H., & Volkmer, U. (2005). Das Karriereplateau. Herausforderungen für Unternehmen, Mitarbeiter/innen und Berater/innen. *Organisationsberatung, Supervision, Coaching, 12*(1), 5–20.

Möller, H., Giernalczyk, T., & Hinn, D. (2018). Individuelle und kollektive Abwehrmechanismen im Coaching. In S. Greif, H. Möller, & W. Scholl (Eds.), *Handbuch Schlüsselkonzepte im Coaching* (pp. 255–264). Springer.

Petzold, H. (1993). *Integrative Therapie*. Junfermann.

Rappe-Giesecke, K. (2017). Triadische Karriereberatung. *Organisationsberatung, Supervision, Coaching, 24*(4), 379–396.

Scanlon, C. (2019). 'Practising disappointment'. From reflection to action in organizations and communities. In C. Thornton (Ed.), *The art and science of working together* (pp. 76–83). Routledge.

Schein, E. H. (1996). Career anchor revisited: Implications for career development in the 21st century. *Academy of Management Perspectives, 10*(4), 80–88.

Sprenger, R. K. (2014). *Mythos motivation. Wege aus einer Sackgasse*. Campus.

Storch, M., Tschacher, W., & Weber, J. (2018). Embodiment in coaching und training. *Supervision, 36*(3), 19–24.

v Kaldenkerken, C. (2014). *Wissen was wirkt. Modelle und Praxis pragmatisch-systemischer Supervision*. Tredition.

Weigand, W. (2009). Methodenfetischismus und Angstabwehr. In H. Pühl (Ed.), *Handbuch der Supervision 3. Grundlagen – Praxis – Perspektiven* (pp. 261–277). Leutner.

Zimmer-Leinfelder, I. (2003). Ich sei, erlaubt mir die Bitte, in Eurem Bunde die Dritte. Gedanken zum Dreieckskontrakt in der Supervision. *Forum Supervision, 21*, 43–53.

8 Concluding Remarks

Expressed in Gestalt language, it can be assumed that the situations described in the online survey, which served as a template for the 31 examples of practice discussed, are not closed Gestalts. As a coach, I am asked in a questionnaire to describe difficult situations in my counseling practice. We can assume that as a respondent, I can think of stories that are not yet sufficiently understood or digested. Something is missing to file them away in memory or possibly forget them simply. The background can be manifold: It may be about slights, my professional self-worth may have been wounded in the situation, or a diffuse job-related dissatisfaction lingers until the time of the interview. So participation in such a survey can also be read as a preconscious attempt at problem-solving. Perhaps there is a desire behind participation in the research to find a solution to an unpleasant situation.

In the best-case scenario, the colleagues recognize themselves, read the comments of the participants in the group discussions and learn constructive tips that help them to understand the situation better. One or the other perspective may be taken into account in future professional practice. In this way, the Gestalt could be closed.

The descriptions of the situations are certainly subject to subsequent editing. We all want to feel competent, skilled, and confident. Our memory gives difficult professional situations a soft focus. From this perspective, it is not surprising that some of the scenes described do not feel like difficult situations, but like heroic stories, as the resolution of the case describes the skillful handling of the challenges.

Filling out a questionnaire mostly presupposes an imaginary interlocutor. I tell my story to an invisible other: In this case, the research team of the University of Kassel, Department of Theory and Methodology of Counseling. The professional superego may like to look good. Hinn et al.'s (2015) research shows that *not wanting to look worse than one's often only fantasized better colleagues* is an often-cited barrier to engaging in coaching research. The research comes into the role of a censor, separating the wheat from the chaff. Despite

H. Möller, J. Zimmermann, *Difficult Situations in Business Coaching*,
https://doi.org/10.1007/978-3-658-35087-1_8

complete anonymization, research partners seem to compare themselves with equally invisible others, and it seems important to do well in this imaginary competition.

Coaching is a lonely profession. The doors are closed; we are alone with the client. Only in supervision or intervision groups or, if there is a community of practice, in conversation with colleagues, are questions asked, mistakes admitted, and irritations acknowledged. I am alone with the question: How good am I as a coach? In less solitary professions, I have the opportunity to measure myself daily and develop a secure professional identity as a result. As a car salesperson, I know how many cars I have traded compared to my peers. As a coach, I do not know and am at the mercy of my inner evaluation patterns, and they are not always attuned in a kindly way. Competence doubts are the result.

To coach is to take one's offer of labor to market. The collective mental model of the community seems to be: Only perfect coaches carry out their business! In acquisition situations, you need "impression management!" We do not believe this, because sales can also be successful through authenticity. Having the courage to show that I cannot do everything also helps clients who may themselves be subject to a dysfunctional perfectionism doctrine. The book wants to make a contribution here, and we hope that you all felt comfortable in a community of imperfect coaches!

If we follow Schröder and Davis (2004), the following classification offers itself for the background of difficult situations—at least in psychotherapy, where comparatively much research on this area is already available: Difficult situations can be explained by

- Difficult framework conditions (crises in the organization, setting structure, Covid-19 pandemic, etc.).
- Competence doubts or deficits of the consulting party (lack of knowledge, lack of methodological expertise, etc.).
- Characteristics of the consulting party (interpersonal difficulties with specific people, personal vulnerabilities, own unprocessed issues, etc.).

In his 1997 publication, Schröder also identifies the category of a difficult patient as a mode of explanation. In our context, coachees are experienced as difficult if they block, we find them unsympathetic, we are opposed to their values and views, and much more.

In the online survey, the difficult situations described repeatedly had unifying aspects in terms of content. The following are worth mentioning here

- Coachee behaviors (unreliability, high need to talk, etc.).
- Challenges with psychological problems of the coachees (differentiation of coaching from psychotherapy, referral of the coachee, etc.).
- Expectations of the coaches, starting from the coachees (according to high solidarity, fulfillment of other services, etc.).
- Challenging working or living conditions on the part of the coachee (life crises, bullying, etc.).
- (Low inner) demarcation of the coaches (being in love, reservations, etc.);
- Coaches' behaviors (overreaching, acting inappropriately, etc.).

- Influence (from) the commissioning organization (forced coaching, misunderstandings in the clarification of the assignment, etc.).

Interestingly, most of the case studies can be assigned to these classifications. The problem is often located with the client, often attributed to the coachee. Much less is reported about the own feelings of being overwhelmed. Rarely did we read about feelings of helplessness, anger towards the coachee, persistent brooding, anxiety, or even somatic reactions, as they are often described in psychotherapy research as a response to difficult clients (see Odyniec et al., 2016). Sure, our clientele is different, but the few reports of coaches' doubts about competence or feelings of being overwhelmed may also have to do with the coaching community's "impression management." This is a shame because psychotherapy research shows that frequent therapist competence doubts correlate with better relationship quality and better therapy outcomes (see Nissen-Lie et al., 2010, 2015). Self-doubt is thus quite beneficial; it increases the quality of work and promotes self-reflection. However, the prerequisite for self-doubt to result in an improvement of the coaching offer is that the self-questioning is done from an appreciative attitude towards oneself. Only under this condition can the questioning of one's professional actions contribute to an improvement in quality. Eidenschink describes it in the group discussion as follows: "I say to our training participants: 'You can be as self-critical as you want. Just not while you're working.' Otherwise, I resent myself and whenever I resent myself, it becomes harder, the threshold to get in touch with it or be kind with me becomes higher."

Our clients come to us with their difficult situations, so it is almost logical that we coaches are also irritated and unsettled from time to time, have the impression of being stuck and not really getting anywhere. Not all coaches will experience the same situation as difficult. Some readers may ask themselves, what is difficult about the case descriptions? If we take the stress model of Lazarus (see Lazarus & Folkman, 1987; Section 1.2) to explain difficult situations, then it is always evaluated internal or external demands that are challenging. A situation is evaluated as difficult when the available strategies for action and/or professional and personal resources are seen as insufficient. The professional coping strategies reach a limit; the demands of the respective coaching process cannot simply be answered with the acquired routines. Then a feeling of disturbance occurs, which our research partners expressed in their answers.

The psychodynamically oriented coaches (Eidenschink, Lohmer, Giernalczyk) from the Munich group discussion took stock at the end. What they observed across the cases dealt with is that crises in coaching often occur when the ability to shift to the meta-level is lost. We are all familiar with *entanglement* and *complication* (see Lohmer, 2019)—these are characterized by the fact that acting and counteracting dominate and the jump into the meta-level is no longer possible. Here the coach either needs supervising help, or she can activate her *self-supervising attitude:* What is happening to me right now? What is happening to us right now? Strange, why am I so strict right now? Strange, why am I so indignant? Why does the client want to jump up right now?

A "first-order solution" (Watzlawick et al., 1979) out of the entanglement would therefore be *self-questioning* or *countertransference analysis*: Strange, what is going on here right now? Strange, I am behaving differently than normal.—A thinking and speaking with oneself. This can then also turn into thinking and speaking aloud with the client: "I just noticed, I can't make sense of it yet." Humor can also help there, "I feel like I almost want to put you up against the wall, I don't know anything like that about myself. What's going on?"

A second-order solution would then lie in the supervisory work after the involvement has occurred with the help of others. I describe the case in a supervisory session; thereby group members and supervisor come to identify with me and the client, illuminate blind spots and strengthen the coach's ability to go into the meta-level. In the supervision of coaching processes, the central question might be: How can I create such a *triangulation* in my inner dialog that I can observe myself from an eccentric position—from the outside?

In coaching, a lot of work is done on error tolerance in the company. However, this must go hand in hand with the question: How can I, as a coach, deal with myself in an error-tolerant way and give weight to errors as an important indication. In Kernberg's transference-focused method (see Yeomans et al., 2017), as Lohmer describes it, the way would be, "Interesting that I am reacting in this way right now and that we now have a tension between us. How are you doing with that?" So I first allow myself to be startled, upset, and ashamed of myself, I do not trivialize it—then move on and use those sensations for the cognition process. Giernalczyk describes the process this way, "So I realize I'm tangled. That I've done something that I'm unhappy with and I can address it. I might say, 'Oh, now I said something stupid,' or 'I think that offended you,' or 'Now you want to run away. What happened?' Naming the potential mistake, the disagreement, the implication right away, without having already understood the phenomenon of entanglement in all its fullness." Central to this is not engaging in more of the same unfavorable behavior, i.e., *not* continuing to act that way and not letting on, rather than saying stop.

Of course, this does not release us from the obligation, if we have indeed made a mistake, not to conceal it, but to admit it openly, to regret it, and subsequently to examine it psychodynamically.

References

Hinn, D. E., Kotte, S., & Möller, H. (2015, Mai). *Why do coaches (not) participate in coaching research?* Unveröffentlichte Posterpräsentation auf dem 17. Kongress der European Association of Work and Organizational Psychology, Oslo, Norwegen.

Lazarus, R. S., & Folkman, S. (1987). Transactional theory and research on emotions and coping. *European Journal of Personality, 1*(3), 141–169. https://doi.org/10.1002/per.2410010304

Lohmer, M. (2019). Der Umgang mit Verwicklungen und Verstrickungen – Abstinenz, Containment und Verantwortung im Beratungsprozess. In M. Lohmer & H. Möller (Eds.), *Psychoanalyse in Organisationen* (pp. 226–236). Kohlhammer.

Nissen-Lie, H. A., Monsen, J. T., & Rønnestad, M. H. (2010). Therapist predictors of early patient-rated working alliance: A multilevel approach. *Psychotherapy Research, 20*(6), 627–646.

Nissen-Lie, H. A., Rønnestad, M. H., Høglend, P. A., Havik, O. E., Solbakken, O. A., Stiles, T. C., & Monson, J. T. (2015). Love yourself as a person, doubt yourself as a therapist? *Clinical Psychology & Psychotherapy, 24*(1), 48–60. https://doi.org/10.1002/cpp.1977

Odyniec, P., Victor, P. P., Berner, A., & Willutzki, U. (2016). Schwierigkeiten in der psychotherapeutischen Arbeit. *Psychotherapeut, 61*(3), 216–221. https://doi.org/10.1007/s00278-016-0105-4

Schröder, T. (1997). Was lange währt, wird auch nicht leichter – Schwierigkeiten und Bewältigungsstrategien in der psychotherapeutischen Arbeit. In P. L. Janssen, M. Cierpka, & P. Buchheim (Eds.), *Psychotherapie als Beruf* (pp. 223–239). Vandenhoeck & Ruprecht.

Schröder, T. A., & Davis, J. D. (2004). Therapists' experience of difficulty in practice. *Psychotherapy Research, 14*(3), 328–345. https://doi.org/10.1093/ptr/kph028

Watzlawick, P., Weakland, J. H., & Fisch, R. (1979). *Lösungen. Zur Theorie und Praxis menschlichen Wandels*. Hans Huber.

Yeomans, F. E., Clarkin, J. F., & Kernberg, O. F. (2017). *Übertragungsfokussierte Psychotherapie für Borderline-Patienten. Das TFP-Praxismanual*. Schattauer.

Further Reading

Greif, S., Möller, H., Scholl, W., Passmore, J., & Müller, F., (Eds.). (2021). *International handbook of evidence-based coaching. Theory, research and practice.* Springer.

Hinn, D., & Kotte, S. (2021). Participating in coaching research?! Attitudes of coaches toward coaching research and their impact upon research participation. *Consulting Psychology Journal: Practice and Research, 73*(3), 229–250. https://doi.org/10.1037/cpb0000200

Korotov, K., & Bernhardt, A. (Eds.). (2018). *Cases in executive coaching: From the annals of the ESMT coaching colloquia.* ESMT Center for Leadership Development Research.

Korotov, K., Florent-Treacy, E., Kets de Vries, M. F. R., & Bernhardt, A. (Eds.). (2012). *Tricky coaching: Difficult cases in leadership coaching*. Palgrave Macmillan.

Louis, D., & Diochon, P. F. (2019). *Complex situations in coaching. A critical case-based approach.* Routledge.

Möller, H., Oellerich, K., Hinn, D., & Kotte, S. (2017). Research on consulting – With, for or against practice? In B. Geiβler-Piltz, É. Nemes, & S. de Roos (Eds.), *Inspire and be inspired – A sample of research on supervision and coaching in Europe* (pp. 43–62). L'Harmattan.

Müller, A. A., Kotte, S., & Möller, H. (2020). Coach and no regrets about it: On the life satisfaction, work-related mental strain, and use of supervision of workplace coaches. *Coaching: An International Journal of Theory, Research and Practice, 13*(1), 16–29. https://doi.org/10.1080/17521882.2019.1636841

H. Möller, J. Zimmermann, *Difficult Situations in Business Coaching*,
https://doi.org/10.1007/978-3-658-35087-1

The manufacturer's authorised representative in the EU is Springer Nature Customer Service Centre GmbH, Europaplatz 3, 69115 Heidelberg, Germany. If you have any concerns regarding our products, please contact ProductSafety@springernature.com

Printed and bound by CPI Group (UK) Ltd, Croydon, CR0 4YY
22/09/2026
02220982-0020